Expanding the Pie

Expanding the Pie

Fostering Effective Non-Profit and Corporate Partnerships

Susan Rae Ross

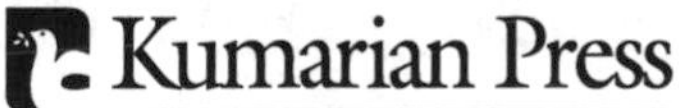

A Division of Lynne Rienner Publishers, Inc. • Boulder & London

Published in the United States of America in 2013 by
Kumarian Press
A division of Lynne Rienner Publishers, Inc.
1800 30th Street, Boulder, Colorado 80301
www.kpbooks.com
www.rienner.com

and in the United Kingdom by
Kumarian Press
A division of Lynne Rienner Publishers, Inc.
3 Henrietta Street, Covent Garden, London WC2E 8LU

First published in 2012 by Kumarian Press.
Reprinted here from the original edition.

Library of Congress Cataloging-in-Publication Data
Expanding the pie : fostering effective non-profit and corporate partnerships /
Susan Rae Ross. — 1st ed.
p. cm.
Includes bibliographical references and index.
ISBN 978-1-56549-465-7 (cloth : alk. paper)
ISBN 978-1-56549-466-4 (pbk. : alk. paper)
1. Nonprofit organizations—Management. 2. Non-governmental organizations—Management. 3. Industrial management. I. Title.
HD62.6.R679 2012
658;'.046—dc23

2011040325

British Cataloguing in Publication Data
A Cataloguing in Publication record for this book
is available from the British Library.

Printed and bound in the United States of America

∞ The paper used in this publication meets the requirements of the American National Standard for Permanence of Paper for Printed Library Materials Z39.48-1992.

5 4 3 2

Contents

List of Tables vii
List of Figures ix
Acronyms xi
Acknowledgments xv
Introduction 1

1 Setting the Stage 5
Background 5
Key Institutional Definitions 10
Key Engagement Definitions 15
Long-Arnold Framework on Successful Partnership Factors 18
Partnership Decision-Making Framework 19

2 Global Trends 23
Overview 23
Globalization 23
Advances in Information, Communication, and Technology 30
Widening Income Gap Between Rich and Poor 32
Complex Problems Requiring Multi-Sector Response 34
Changing Roles of Government, Business, and NGOs 35
Alternative Organizational Models 37
Changes in Philanthropy Trends 40
Shifts in Development Assistance 46
Summary of Global Trends 48

3 NGO Trends 55
Overview 55
NGO Trends 58
Summary of NGO Trends 69

4 Business Trends 75
Overview of the Business Sector 75
Business Trends 75
Corporate Social Responsibility 80
Greater Corporate Accountability 91
Summary of Business Trends 92

5 Partnership Options 99
Should NGOs and Businesses Partner? 99
Stakeholder Engagement Framework 114

6 Bilateral NGO-Corporate Partnerships 133
What Are Bilateral NGO-Corporate Partnerships? 133
How Do NGO-Corporate Partnerships Work? 133
Summary 160

7 Tri-Party Partnerships 165
What Are Tri-Party Partnerships? 165
How Do Tri-Party Partnerships Work? 168
Summary 188

8 Multi-Stakeholder Initiatives 193
What Are Multi-Stakeholder Initiatives? 193
How Do MSIs Work? 194
Summary 219

9 Partnership Decision-Making Framework 225
Overview 225
Partnership Decision-Making Framework 226

Bibliography 255
Appendix 265
Index 267

List of Tables

Table 1.1	Timeline of Sustainable Development Key Events	11
Table 1.2	Stakeholder Engagement Continuum	17
Table 1.3	Long-Arnold Framework on Partnership Success Factors	19
Table 2.1	Summary of Key Globalization Events and Institutions	26
Table 2.2	Results of Globalization	28
Table 2.3	Number of Private Foundations by Assets Level, 2006	41
Table 3.1	NGO Function by Type of NGO Structure	59
Table 4.1	Differences Between CSR and Shared-Value Approaches	82
Table 4.2	Illustrative Corporate Social Responsibility Activities and Business Units	90
Table 5.1	Benefits of Cross-Sectoral Partnerships	102
Table 5.2	Stakeholder Engagement Continuum	116
Table 5.3	Potential CSR Activities by Business Unit	122
Table 5.4	Examples of Corporate Support of Social Causes	127
Table 5.5	Types of Partnerships	130
Table 6.1	Examples of Bilateral Partnerships	134
Table 6.2	Long-Arnold Framework on Partnership Success Factors	144
Table 7.1	Examples of Tri-Party Partnerships	170
Table 7.2	Tri-Party Partnerships and Financial Agreements by Type of Organization	176
Table 8.1	MSIs Adopting General Principles and Codes	195
Table 8.2	MSIs Addressing Industry-Specific Issues	197

Table 8.3	MSIs: Creating New Value and Addressing Development Issues	199
Table 8.4	MSI Member Requirements	203
Table 8.5	MSI Organizational and Governance Structures	207
Table 8.6	Summary of MSI Results	217
Table 9.1	Steps in the Partnership Decision-Making Framework	227
Table 9.2	Types of NGO-Corporate Engagement	230
Table 9.3	Partnership Portfolio Map	233
Table 9.4	Involvement of Business Units in Key Engagement Efforts	237
Table 9.5	Due Diligence Matrix	243
Table 9.6	Elements of Partnership Agreement	248

List of Figures

Figure 2.1	Trends influencing NGO-business partnerships	24
Figure 7.1	Traditional market segmentation	166
Figure 7.2	Overlapping market segmentation	167
Figure 9.1	Partnership decision-making framework	228

Acronyms

AED	Academy of Educational Development
AIDS	acquired immune deficiency syndrome
AGM	Aqua Gold Mississippi
AMA	American Medical Association
ASHA	Association for Social and Health Advancement
BAT	British American Tobacco
BP	British Petroleum
BPD	Business Partners for Development
CEO	chief executive officer
CoC	code of conduct
CRM	cause-related marketing
CSR	corporate social responsibility
DFID	Department for International Development
DML	Dana Mitra Lingkungan
EDF	Environmental Defense Fund
ESG	environmental, social, and governance
EHS	environmental, health, and safety
ETI	Ethical Trading Initiative
FSC	Forest Stewardship Council
FUNEDESIN	Foundation for Integrated Education and Development
GAIN	Global Alliance on Improved Nutrition
GATT	General Agreement on Tariffs and Trade
GB	Grameen Bank
GDA	Global Development Alliance

GDP	gross domestic product
GEP	Guangdong Environmental Partnership
GiG	Gambia is Good
GP	Grameen Phone
GRI	Global Reporting Initiative
GRSP	Global Road Safety Partnership
HIV	human immunodeficiency virus
ICCR	Interfaith Center on Corporate Responsibility
ICML	Integrated Coal Mining Limited
ICT	information, communication, and technology
IFRC	International Federation of Red Cross and Red Crescent Societies
ILO	International Labour Organization
IMF	International Monetary Fund
ISC	Institute of Sustainable Communities
ITN	insecticide-treated bednets
IYF	International Youth Foundation
KPCS	Kimberly Process Certification Scheme
L3C	low-profit limited-liability corporations
LOHAS	lifestyles of health and sustainability
M&A	mergers and acquisitions
M&E	monitoring and evaluation
MBO	membership-based organizations
MDGs	Millennium Development Goals
MNC	multi-national corporation
MOU	memorandum of understanding
MSC	Marine Stewardship Council
MSI	multi-stakeholder initiatives
NGO	non-governmental organization
NPO	non-profit organization
OECD	Organisation for Economic Co-operation and Development
PDA	Population and Community Development Association
PET	polyethylene terephthalate

RSP	Rural Sales Program
SdE	Senegalese des Eaux
SIDA	Swiss International Development Agency
SMEs	small and medium enterprises
SOS	Share our Strength
SRI	socially responsible investing
SSI	Sakhalin Salmon Initiative
TBL	triple bottom line
TNC	The Nature Conservancy
UN	United Nations
UNDP	United Nations Development Program
UBTI	unrelated business taxable income
USAID	United States Agency for International Development
USAID/GDA	United States Agency for International Development/ Global Development Alliance
WBCSD	World Business Council on Sustainable Development
WHO	World Health Organization
WTO	World Trade Organization
WWF	World Wildlife Fund

Acknowledgments

I would like to thank all the managers from various organizations who have given generously of their time, which is scarce and precious, and provided valuable insights and inspired me by their work.

A special thanks goes to Tanis Cordes for supporting me in the writing process.

There are many friends and colleagues who provided me with enthusiastic support and spurred me forward, including Lucille Pilling, Virginia Vaughn, and Kate Jones.

Introduction

I have been involved in partnerships since the beginning of my career. As an intensive care nurse, I developed partnerships with physicians, nurses, other hospital staff, and families to provide the best care for my patients. As I moved to designing programs, I participated in partnerships with non-governmental organizations (NGOs), governments, foundations, academia and research institutes, businesses, local leaders, and communities in over 30 countries in Africa, Asia, and Latin America. Aiming to enhance the effectiveness of programs and relationships with the private sector, I pursued a master's degree in business administration that provided me with a framework to combine my international development experience and my business skills.

When I began doing research for this book I found it interesting that a Google search for "NGO-corporate partnerships" yielded results that were mostly under the heading of "business-NGO partnerships." This made me wonder if there is a difference in these terms. After many interviews with NGO and business managers, I have reached the conclusion that these terms are different, which is a matter of perspective rather than who leads the partnership. Business-NGO partnerships relate to how businesses select and develop relationships with NGOs. On the other hand, NGO-corporate partnerships encompass an NGO's strategies for working with corporations. Thus, the focus of this book is on assisting managers—in the NGO, business, and government sectors—to develop effective partnerships.

We live in a rapidly changing world with an interdependent global economic system combined with dramatic technological, communication, and scientific advances. Expansion of global trade has improved economic opportunities and living standards for millions, but it has left many behind as well. It is clear that the "status quo" interventions are not working. The world is now at a critical "tipping point" to develop effective and sustainable solutions. If actions are not undertaken soon, the effects of key issues, such as climate change, may be irreversible or severely jeopardize our children's future. New paradigms are needed to find effective solutions that maximize the strengths of all the sectors to overcome these challenges. As a result, partnerships have become all the rage. Although partnerships have many benefits, they are hard, time-consuming, messy, and often do not produce the desired results. With that said, when partnerships do work, as demonstrated by the 46 case studies presented in this book, they can produce groundbreaking approaches that result in benefits for companies, NGOs, governments, and the society at large—thus *Expanding the Pie* for everyone.

The purpose of this book is to provide a user-friendly reference that provides guidance to managers on how to know when to engage in an NGO-corporate partnership and how to create effective partnerships that add value—or *Expand the Pie*—for all parties involved. There are different terms and frameworks that relate to these partnerships that are defined in Chapter 1. Many factors in the external environment, such as globalization, advances in technology, and widening income inequalities, are changing the roles of the public, NGO, and private sectors, blurring the boundaries among the sectors (Chapter 2). In addition, there are key trends within the NGO sector (Chapter 3), such as changes in revenue streams, and the business sector (Chapter 4), such as shifts in consumer and investor priorities, that have influenced how NGOs and businesses relate to and partner with each other.

NGOs and businesses engage with each other through a variety of mechanisms, ranging from confrontational approaches to collaborative relationships. Over the last decade, the types of NGO-corporate partnership have expanded and the relationships have become more substantial, not just philanthropic efforts. Chapter 5 presents a framework that encompasses how NGOs and businesses can engage both with and without an exchange of resources.

In order to understand the factors that make a partnership successful, I used the Long-Arnold framework to analyze 46 NGO-corporate partnerships. Three types of partnerships are reviewed: (1) 25 bilateral partnerships between an NGO and corporation (Chapter 6); (2) 10 tri-party partnerships including an NGO, business, and government agency (Chapter 7); and (3) 11 multi-stakeholder initiatives (Chapter 8).

Managers need tools to assist them in making decisions about partnerships. Chapter 9 presents a comprehensive eight-step decision-making framework to systematically and strategically approach initiating, implementing, and evaluating partnerships. It also provides several tools to help managers manage their existing partnership portfolio, assess if current partnerships are still creating value, design effective partnership agreements, and create indicators to evaluate the partnership's added value.

1

Setting the Stage

Background

In 1983, the United Nations (UN) established an independent commission, the World Commission on Environment and Development—better known as the "Bruntland Commission"—to address global environmental protection, particularly as there was a growing recognition that environmental problems affected the poor much more than the rich. In 1987, the Bruntland Commission final report, *Our Common Future,* presented the concept of sustainable development as a solution to global environment degradation and widespread poverty. The Commission cited the source of environmental and social problems as the conflict between an open (infinite) economic system versus a closed (finite) ecological system.[1] "Sustainable development" was defined as "development that meets the needs of the present without compromising the ability for future generations to meet their own needs and it embodies two key concepts: (1) the essential needs of the world's poor should be given overriding priority and (2) the environment's ability to meet present and future needs is limited."[2]

It should be noted that although many corporate social responsibility (CSR; sometimes called "corporate sustainability") definitions embrace the main concept of sustainable development, until recently there has been very little focus on the specific needs of the poor. CSR is often described as encompassing a triple bottom line (TBL), which values a corporation's economic (profit), environmental (planet), and social (people) practices rather than just its financial returns such as maximization of shareholder value. Historically, the first area of focus for the TBL was economic, looking at how profits are made, followed by environmental practices. Although there has been movement in the social sector, it still lags behind the other two aspects. Thus I utilize the broad sustainable development framework to discuss cross-sectoral and multi-stakeholder initiatives (MSIs) throughout the book.

The environmental movement, led largely by non-profit organizations (NPOs) and non-governmental organizations (NGOs) in the 1960s, was the first group to embrace the concept of sustainable development. The establishment of the Bruntland Commission marked the first time that business leaders started to understand that economic development might be dependent on a healthy environment; recognition of the effect of business on social issues came many years later.

During the 1970s and 1980s, advocacy-oriented NGOs worked toward sustainable (environmental) development by (1) increasing awareness of harmful environmental practices, (2) promoting global policies to protect the environment, (3) lobbying for stronger environmental regulations such as the Clean Air and Clean Water Acts, and (4) campaigning against bad practices of both governments and business. Service-oriented (operational) NGOs focused on increasing the adoption of environmentally friendly practices such as conservation and recycling.

Earth Summit

The preparations for the Earth Summit began in 1990. The hope was that treaties on climate change and biological diversity, and a general Earth Charter would be ratified. Unfortunately, the United States refused to sign the treaties or promise to provide funding for less developed countries to implement environmental protection efforts. The United States said that the treaties were too restrictive for American businesses and might damage their economy, but finally signed the biodiversity treaty in 1993.[3]

The 1992 Rio Summit was a watershed event for sustainable development. Great strides were made during the Summit in connecting poverty to environmental destruction. Issues such as sustainable development and justice also had a prominent place on the negotiating table for the first time. Furthermore, this meeting provided a unique forum for discussing the disparity between the rich industrialized (northern) nations and the poorer underdeveloped (southern) nations. More than 9,000 NGOs sent delegates to Rio de Janeiro. Although the official Summit proceedings were important, the informal Global Forum of NGOs, or the "shadow assembly" whose participants were not delegates to the official Summit, allowed thousands of activists to debate, protest, trade information, and build informal networks. The shadow assembly turned out to be more productive than the official Summit.[4]

In contrast, the business sector was not very engaged in the sustainable development discussion and few attended the Summit. Yet on the eve of the Summit, Mr. Stephan Schmidheiny founded the World Business Council on Sustainable Development (WBCSD) as a way to involve business in sustainability issues. He believed that "business could act as a catalyst for change toward the achievement of sustainable development; and moreover that business needed a sustainable development approach in order to fulfill its potential."[5]

Although there has been some progress since Rio, many feel that more could have been achieved. In the NGO sector, the idea of sustainable development has grown beyond solely an environmental focus to include economic development, health, education, and other sectors. In addition, approaches matured and resulted in changes including (1) a greater focus on improving the capacity of local individuals and organizations in a sustainable manner and (2) more emphasis on system-wide approaches to create lasting institutional changes that are locally owned and sustained.

In the 1990s, NGOs pushed companies into the sustainable development arena because of those companies' negative business practices, such as Nike's management of working conditions in their contracted factories and Shell's handling of issues in the Niger Delta. Never before had stakeholders, many of whom companies thought were insignificant, been able to access information to hold businesses accountable for their actions as well as the actions of their partners. This negative stakeholder reaction to irresponsible business practices challenged companies to reexamine their roles and responsibilities in relation to their shareholders, customers, employees, suppliers, and society in general. Initially, most businesses focused on damage control and risk management as ways to minimize or prevent bad publicity from "happening to them." Companies focused on addressing issues such as child labor or environmental dumping that had legal implications.

World Summit

A second watershed event for sustainable development was the 2002 World Summit held in Johannesburg. To reverse some of the disappointing trends since Rio, the UN facilitated broad stakeholder participation prior to and during the conference. NGOs composed 30% of all conference delegates, and there was much greater business involvement with the participation of 40 chief executive officers (CEOs). This resulted in the broadest representation of stakeholder groups brought together to address key global challenges, as articulated in the Millennium Development Goals (MDGs). This was the first time that the business community made commitments to addressing key development issues.[6] Jeff Swartz, CEO of Timberland, has stated,

> Never before has the notion of sustainability been so prevalent—the idea that we must consider the consequences of our actions not on tomorrow, but on the world we leave behind for generations to come. And while making a conscious effort to reduce our negative impact on the environment and our communities is a good first step, doing "less bad" isn't enough. We've got to start doing more good—to try to repair some of the damage that has already been done and invest in positive, sustainable change.[7]

Johannesburg was known as the "Partnership Summit." It was built on the premise that (1) governments cannot achieve sustainability on their own, (2) businesses are part of the solution, and (3) NGOs have good ideas. The MDGs created a common language and agenda for business, NGOs, governments, and others to work together.

The presence of Greenpeace and Shell on the same platform at the Summit was in stark contrast to the classic notion of NGO protests against unethical business practices. For example, in 1995 Greenpeace activists occupied Shell's Brent Spar oil tanker to make a statement in opposition to ocean dumping. At the Summit, Greenpeace joined with the WBCSD, making a joint call for action on climate change. This partnership symbolized the changing perceptions on both sides that NGOs can often achieve more by working with businesses than by using confrontational tactics. Although many campaigners were suspicious, many partnerships have been developed out of relationships developed or strengthened during the Johannesburg Summit.[8]

UN Global Compact

The UN Global Compact was launched in 2000 to bring together businesses, UN agencies, labor, civil society organizations and NGOs, and governments to advance 10 universal principles encompassing human rights, labor, environment, and anticorruption. Through the power of collective action, the UN Global Compact seeks to mainstream the economic, environmental, and social principles into business operations around the world and to catalyze actions in support of broader UN goals.

Sustainable development is an evolving process, with a host of different stakeholders—business, government, NGOs, and civil society—and it appears that greater participation of stakeholder groups will continue to grow in the coming decades. As rising numbers of companies from around the world are embracing CSR as a management imperative, the mainstream capital markets, including major institutional investors, have begun groundbreaking efforts to retool their investment strategies and models to adjust to new global realities.

Before 2004, much of the activity in the investment community had focused on socially responsible investing in which investors and fund managers employed a negative-screen methodology, meaning they removed investments in companies deemed objectionable for ethical or moral reasons, such as production of weapons, tobacco, or gambling. In 2004, the UN Global Compact released a report titled *Who Cares Wins* to support the financial industry's efforts to integrate environmental, social, and governance (ESG) issues into mainstream investment decision-making and ownership practices.[9] "Global governance" is defined as the political interaction of transnational actors aimed at solving problems that affect more than one state or region when there is no power of enforcing compliance.[10] "Corporate governance" is the set of processes, policies, and institutions that affect the way a corporation operates, including its relationships with its many stakeholders.[11] At the heart of the initiative lay the conviction that increased consideration of ESG issues will ultimately lead to better investment decisions, create stronger and more resilient financial markets, and contribute to sustainable development. As a result, the UN Global Compact developed an additional principle in 2004 that dealt with anticorruption and governance issues.[12] Currently, the UN Global Compact has over 6,600 corporate participants and other stakeholders from over 130 countries, making it the largest voluntary CSR initiative in the world.[13]

Other Concepts

In 2003, Jeb Emerson introduced the concept of the "blended value proposition," which proposes that all organizations, whether for-profit or not, create a value that consists of a blend of economic, social, and environmental components and that investors simultaneously generate all three forms of value by providing capital to organizations. In the past, there has been a separation in the notions of value. Corporations have sought to maximize economic value, whereas NGOs have sought to maximize social or environmental value. However, a growing group of practitioners, investors, and philanthropists are advancing strategies that intentionally blend social, environmental, and economic value. These activities have resulted in an exciting wave of new practices across the for-profit and NGO sectors.[14]

Corporations are realizing that increasing the positive social and environmental effects of their work can increase (or at least not compromise) shareholder value while simultaneously addressing the concerns of wider stakeholder groups. Many NGOs are seeing that by incorporating business practices that create economic value into their management strategies, as well as by creating new ventures and partnerships, they can better deliver on their social and environmental missions. A growing number of philanthropic and traditional investors are backing these practices. Practitioners and investors involved in CSR, social enterprise, social investing, strategic philanthropy, and sustainable development all pursue strategies that:

1. Strive to blend social, environmental, and economic values.
2. Share the challenges of creating more efficient capital markets and developing common metrics.
3. Face leadership and organizational development concerns as well as policy and regulatory issues.[15]

There are many lessons that could be shared across the areas—economic, environmental, and social—to address these challenges, but in many cases these lessons remain within the relative vacuum of each area. Yet only by leveraging this knowledge and working *across* the various areas of activity can these challenges be most effectively met and the potential of blended value be fully realized.

In 2004, Michael Porter introduced the concept of "shared value" and with Mark Kramer further refined this concept in the 2011 *Harvard Business Review* article, "Creating Shared Value: How to Reinvent Capitalism and Unleash a Wave of Innovation and Growth." The authors argue that "shared value" involves creating economic value in a way that also creates value for society by addressing its needs and challenges. Shared value is not a redistribution approach; it is about expanding the total pool of economic and social value. Companies have overlooked opportunities to meet basic societal needs and they misunderstand how societal harms can weaken value chains. Lastly, Porter and Kramer argue that companies will make real strides on a specific issue, such as the environment, when they treat it as a productivity driver rather than a feel-good response to external pressures. This approach requires different thinking and development of new skills for companies as well as NGOs and government officials.[16] Table 1.1 provides a summary of key events that shaped the evolution of sustainable development.

Key Institutional Definitions

To foster meaningful discussion, it is important to have a clear definition of terms. For the purposes of this book, I use the terms as defined in this section.

Table 1.1
Timeline of Sustainable Development Key Events

Date	Event
1983	• UN establishes an independent commission to address environmental problems. • First cause-related marketing (CRM) effort in the United States launched by American Express, which raised $1.7 million for the restoration of the Statue of Liberty.
1986	• The Caux Roundtable establishes Principles for Business. • Uruguay Round trade talks: Developed countries agree to eliminate agriculture subsidies and less developed countries agree to open markets.
1987	• World Commission on Environment and Development Bruntland Commission present a concept paper on sustainable development. • River blindness prevention program established. • Fairtrade coffee starts in Dutch supermarkets. • SustainAbility established.
1989	• CERES establishes Valdez Principles.
1990	• KLD Research and Analytics created.
1991	• Rainforest Action Groups (RAGs) organized; directly targets U.K. retailers. • World Wildlife Fund (WWF) recruits 10 companies to sign on to their 1995 target for sustainable forestry. • International Chamber of Commerce: Business Charter for Sustainable Development written.
1992	• Earth Summit held in Rio de Janeiro. • World Business Council for Sustainable Development (WBCSD) established. • Investor's Circle: Venture Network established. • Business for Social Responsibility (BSR) established.
1993	• Forest Stewardship Council (FSC) established. • Brent Spar (Shell) Greenpeace protest. • Cafedirect (Oxfam, Tradecraft, Equal Exchange, and Twin Trading) fairtrade coffee established.

(*continues*)

Table 1.1 (*continued*)

Date	Event
1994	• Media covers child labor in producing soccer balls around the 1994 World Cup. • Caux Round Table Principles of Business. • McDonald's raised $9 million for the Ronald McDonald Houses.
1995	• WWF and Unilever begin discussion on long-term sustainability global fish stocks and the integrity of the marine ecosystem. • AccountAbility established. • Commonwealth Foundation *NGO Guidelines for Good Policy and Practice* developed. • FSC has 47 members, accounting for 25% of U.K. consumption of wood products, 1995 target not met, extended to 2000.
1996	• *Life* magazine runs a story about a 12-year-old boy making soccer balls around the time of the European Football Championships. • Report on Kathy Lee Gifford clothing line made in sweatshops, attacks on Nike and other footwear and apparel brands.
1997	• Social Accountability 8000 standard established. • Index of Corporate Environmental Engagement developed. • Siaklot Initiative to Eliminate Child Labor in the Soccer Ball Industry in Pakistan established. • Global Reporting Initiative (GRI) formed by CERES and Tellus Institute, with the support of the United Nations Environment Program.
1998	• Norms on the Responsibilities of Transnational Corporations and Other Business Enterprises with Regard to Human Rights written. • Nike begins to develop code of conduct for supplier factories. • WWF-Unilever established Marine Stewardship Council (MSC). • World Bank's Business Partners for Development (BPD). • Ethical Trading Initiative (ETI) launched with Department for International Development (DFID) support. • International Labour Organization (ILO) declaration on Fundamental Principles and Rights at Work developed.
1999	• Protests against the World Trade Organization (WTO) in Seattle. • First version of GRI Sustainability Reporting Guidelines developed. • Global Partnership for Road Safety (GPRS) established by the World Bank.

(*continues*)

Table 1.1 (*continued*)

Date	Event
2000	• UN Global Compact established. • Voluntary Principles on Security and Human Rights established to address the security needs of extractive companies and human rights of local communities. • USAID launches the Global Development Alliance. • FSC has 90 members and 200 million hectares of forest are certified.
2001	• African Institute of Corporate Citizenship established. • Equator Principles established. • Doha Trade Talks occur.
2001	• Business Alliance for Local Living Economies (BALLE) established.
2002	• Kimberley Process Certification Scheme (KPCS) initiated. • Johannesburg World Summit occurs. • Tony Blair announces the Extractive Industries Transparency Initiative (EITI).
2003	• International NGO Accountability Charter written.
2004	• WHO dedicates World Health Day to road safety. UN passes resolution. • Global Road Safety Initiative launched in six countries. • UN Global compact *Who Cares Wins* to support the financial industry's efforts to integrate environmental, social, and governance (ESG) issues. • UN Global compact adds principle on anticorruption.
2006	• UN Global Compact develops Principles of Responsible Investments.
2007	• UN Global Compact launches Principles for Responsible Management Education. • First Social Capital Conference occurs.
2009	• FSC has certified 5% of the world's productive forest.
2010	• Tenth anniversary of UN Global Compact; excludes 2,000 companies over the decade.

Non-Profit Organizations and Non-Governmental Organizations

In 2008, NGOs in the United States reported over $1.4 trillion in revenues; they constituted the eighth largest economy in the world and provided 5% of the nation's gross domestic product. They had $2.6 trillion in assets and employed about 10% of the nation's workforce, 12.9 million people.[17] However, this sector is not homogenous; it is extremely fragmented and diverse in terms of organizational size and structures. In addition, these entities have a wide array of missions, such as religious, social justice, health, education, housing, economic, and environmental protection, to name a few. Thus it is essential to understand the breadth, depth, and scope of the different entities that constitute this sector in order to effectively engage and partner with these organizations.

The term "non-governmental organization (NGO)" comes from the UN Charter Article 71, which defines these entities as not-for-profit, non-governmental bodies. Common terms used to describe NGOs include "voluntary organizations," "charities," and "non-profit organizations." The terms "charity" or "voluntary organization" are commonly used in Britain, whereas "non-profit" is more often used in the United States relating to organizational benefits, such as tax exemption. NPOs and NGOs can also be divided into (1) northern and southern geographic entities, (2) grassroots and community-based organizations, (3) faith-based organizations, (4) trade unions, and (5) people associations.

Because of the plethora of terms, missions, and modus operandi, it is difficult to develop a comprehensive definition that fully captures the NGO sector's diversity. These definitions raise two key issues. First, they define these organizations by what they are *not* (profit earning) rather than by what they do (e.g., create social capital, conduct research, undertake advocacy, and provide services). Second, this is a very broad definition, categorizing a large number and wide range of entities together when in reality they are structurally and functionally unrelated.

Business (For-Profit Corporations)

Businesses range in size from small and medium enterprises (SMEs) to large multi-national corporations operating globally. They can be privately held or publicly traded. The main aim of corporations is to maximize shareholder value, although there is a growing understanding of the importance of engaging with key stakeholders and the larger society.

Social Enterprises

Many social enterprises, such as Juma Ventures's youth development program, began as a way to provide additional revenue streams for NGOs while providing employment opportunities for the disadvantaged groups that the NGOs were working with. Over the past decade there has been an explosion of social enterprises in terms of the types of issues they address, organizational structures, and operating mechanisms. For example, Ben and Jerry's Ice Cream and The Body Shop are both considered successful for-profit social enterprises. Thus this approach can be implemented in any type of organizational structure, whether for-profit or non-profit.

"Social entrepreneurs" are leaders who see opportunities for change and innovation and devote themselves entirely to making that change happen. The term "entrepreneur" was originated by the French economist, Jean-Baptiste Say, who said, "[A]n entrepreneur shifts economic resources out of an area of lower productivity into an area of higher yield. . . . [T]hey create value that can be in economic, educational and/or social terms."[18]

Key Engagement Definitions

Stakeholder Engagement

One key term that needs to be defined is "stakeholder engagement." Partnerships and strategic alliances are a subset of stakeholder engagement, as defined here.

Every organization and individual exists within a larger society. Many factors (e.g., family, friends, laws, and religion) influence individual and organizational behaviors. Some of these factors are more important than others, depending on the timing and type of decisions or actions being considered, and some may be seen as more positive or negative in nature. The term "stakeholder" refers to individuals or groups who affect or are affected by an organization's activities. Stakeholder groups can include investors, shareholders, customers, employees, suppliers, NGOs, communities, and government agencies.[19]

"Stakeholder engagement" is a broad set of approaches that organizations can use to engage with key groups that affect their work. For example, politicians develop relationships with their constituents, NGOs create relationships with communities, and businesses address shareholders.

Until recently, many businesses have embraced Milton Freeman's philosophy that "the sole role of business is to maximize shareholder value."[20] Thus it is not surprising that "stakeholder management" grew out of the idea that corporations needed to protect themselves against stakeholders. As a result, corporate activities focused on risk management and minimizing negative reactions. Under this approach, corporate managers had the power to direct and control the interactions between corporations and stakeholders.

In the late 1990s, in response to greater consumer, investor, and stakeholder expectations, many businesses have adopted a broader engagement approach that views engaging with stakeholders as a reciprocal, mutually defined, and iterative process. They view these processes as a source of opportunity and competitive advantage rather than risk management. This does not mean that corporations agree to every stakeholder request, but it allows for greater understanding of the issues from many perspectives, whether they agree or not.[21] John Brown, CEO of British Petroleum, has stated,

> Previously, corporations approached building mutually beneficial stakeholder relations as an ad hoc activity and as a way to pass as much risk as you can to the other guy. Instead, we need to view these relationships as a way to create value in a way that no individual organization could do—it is something that makes the pie get bigger and is to both of our advantage.[22]

In the 1970s, many NGOs and some government agencies began to use participatory approaches to involve different stakeholders. These approaches have been refined over the last several decades. Stakeholder engagement encompasses a range of actions that vary in terms of (1) level of involvement of each party, (2) timeframe, (3) strategies utilized, and (4) expected outcomes. These relationships can range from minimal involvement and expectations to greater involvement of both parties. Stakeholder engagement can start with informal information sharing or communication forums. These small beginnings can develop to a level at which the stakeholder's expertise is tapped to drive business innovation. On the other hand, these relationships can be confrontational, such as campaigns or boycotts.

Stakeholder Engagement Framework

I have adapted several stakeholder engagement models to fully capture the breadth of interactions between NGOs and corporations, including those seen as somewhat more negative and those with positive, close relationships. This engagement framework is divided into two components, as outlined in Table 1.2.

> *Engagement without exchange of resources (influence):* These interactions require less involvement between the organizations and often have a short timeframe. Their main aim is to influence business practices, but there is no shared objective; thus they are *not* partnerships.
>
> *Engagement with exchange of resources between an NGO and a corporation (bilateral partnerships):* These are deliberate actions between

Table 1.2
Stakeholder Engagement Continuum

Level of Involvement	Engagement *Without* Exchange of Resources *(Influencing)*	Engagement *With* Exchange of Resources for Common Purpose *(Partnership)*
Minimal	• *Consulting and advising* may encompass NGOs providing technical expertise and representing voices of their clients and members to interested companies.	• *Resource exchange (philanthropy)* includes the exchange of financial resources (money), skills (people), and in-kind goods and services (things).
Moderate	• *Consumerism and procurement* practices allow NGOs to reward corporate practices by their buying practices.	• *Transactional (fee for service)* includes fee for a specific service with clearly articulated deliverable(s).
Medium	• *Shareholder resolutions* are petitions brought by the shareholders against corporations to change their practices.	• *Joint programming* builds on the strengths of each of the entities to create new value that benefits all parties such as cause-related marketing or licensing agreements.
Intensive	• *Campaigning* includes protests, media campaigns, and boycotts against bad corporate or government practices.	• *Integrated programming* occurs when organizational missions become interdependent.

Source. Adapted from James Austin, *The Collaboration Challenge: How Nonprofits and Business Succeed Through Strategic Alliances* (San Francisco: Jossey-Bass, 2000).

the parties to work on mutually identified common issues with the exchange of some form of resources, which may include funds, skills, technology, or access to networks. These are NGO-corporate partnerships.

Partnership Terms

The three key partnership terms used throughout the book are presented here. "Bilateral NGO-corporate partnerships" (see Chapter 6) are direct partnerships between an NGO and a corporation. Other organizations may have some involvement, but the primary relationship is between the NGO and the corporation.

"Tri-party partnerships" (see Chapter 7) are partnerships among an NGO, a corporation, and a government office, often a donor agency. Other organizations may also be involved, but the primary relationship is between the NGO, corporation, and the government office.

"Multi-stakeholder initiatives" (MSIs) (see Chapter 8) bring together the expertise of representatives of NGOs, businesses, government agencies, academia, trade unions, foundations, and other civil society groups in an effort to find joint solutions to complex problems and identify new subjects for the international policy agenda.[23] These groups may organize around a common theme such as the Ethical Trading Initiative, or around an industry-specific issue such as improving conditions for workers in footwear and apparel factories, as in the Fair Labor Association.

Two key terms are often misused and need to be clarified. "Public-private partnership" describes a government service or private business venture. This is usually funded through a government contract with one or more for-profit companies.[24] They do not involve NGOs. The project assumes substantial financial, technical, and operational risk that is shared by the partners.

"Strategic alliance" is probably one of the most overused partnership terms. Although these relationships are described as being "strategic" for both organizations, few have established measurable criteria that articulate the value added by the partnership approach. In addition, many organizations lack a formal plan or process to further the relationship. Although the desire to work with an organization for the long term may be useful, such a relationship is not automatically strategic or does not provide additional value for the organizations.[25]

Long-Arnold Framework on Successful Partnership Factors

There are many different partnership frameworks. In 1995, Frederick Long and Matthew Arnold developed a matrix that indicated nine key success factors of environmental partnerships between NGOs and corporations. The Long-Arnold framework is based on a Partnership Lifecycle, which starts with a seed phase that includes all the prepartnership activities, such as conducting an internal assessment, making the business case, selecting a partner, and negotiating the general principles of a partnership agreement.

There are three partnership phases: initiation, execution, and closure and renewal. In each phase, the Long-Arnold framework identifies three key factors that influence the success of the partnership, as presented in Table 1.3: people, goals, and capacity building.[26]

Although the Long-Arnold framework only looked at environmental partnerships, it provides a simple yet comprehensive approach to understanding a variety of types of NGO-corporate partnerships. Thus this framework is used to review the 25 bilateral cases in Chapter 6, the 10 tri-party partnerships in Chapter 7, and the 11 MSIs in Chapter 8.

Partnership Decision-Making Framework

There are many facets and decisions that create and influence a partnership's success. Capitalizing on the best of the literature and interviews with over 100 NGO and business managers, I have developed an eight-step decision-making framework to assist organizations in designing and implementing effective partnerships (see Chapter 9). Although the framework focuses on partnerships between an NGO and corporation, many of the steps can be used for partnerships with other types of organizations.

Table 1.3
Long-Arnold Framework on Partnership Success Factors

	Phases of the Partnerships		
Factors of Success	**Initiation**	**Execution**	**Closure/Renewal**
People	INCLUDE all critical stakeholders.	RESPECT each partner's needs and interests.	SHARE success and credit.
Goals	DEFINE a viable and inspirational shared vision.	STEWARD based on process leaning and new science and technology.	EVALUATE results against goals and alternatives.
Capacity building	INVEST in relationships needed for long-term success.	TRANSLATE knowledge into signs of progress.	SUSTAIN progress by institutionalizing partnership arrangements.

Source. Fredrick Long and Matthew Arnold, *The Power of Environmental Partnerships* (Washington, DC: The Dryden Press, Harcourt Brace College Publishers, 1995).

This partnership decision-making framework embraces a partnership lifecycle approach based on continuous value creation, meaning that if the partnership is not providing value, other mechanisms should be explored. Each step provides key questions for consideration and tools to assist managers in making partnership decisions. The eight steps in the decision-making framework are:

1. Conducting an internal assessment
2. Identifying, researching, and short-listing potential partners
3. Determining how to approach potential partners and making the business case
4. Selecting appropriate partners
5. Negotiating a partnership agreement with partnership structures and systems
6. Initiating the partnership
7. Executing and implementing the partnership
8. Evaluating and reassessing the partnership

If the partners want to continue the partnership based on the results of the evaluation and the partner's assessment of their relationship, then the process circles back to step 1.

Notes

1. World Commission on Economic Development, *Our Common Future* (Oxford, UK: World Commission on Economic Development, 1987).

2. Ibid.

3. Shelley Preston, "The 1992 Rio Summit and Beyond," *Swords and Ploughshares: A Chronicle of International Affairs*, 3, no. 2 (1994). http://www2.fiu.edu/~mizrachs/Nets-n-NGOs.html.

4. Ibid.

5. World Business Council for Sustainable Development. http://www.wbcsd.org/templates/TemplateWBCSD5/layout.asp?type=p&MenuId=MQ&doOpen=1&ClickMenu=LeftMenu.

6. Ibid.

7. Jane Nelson and Simon Zadek, *Partnership Alchemy: New Social Partnership in Europe* (Copenhagen, Norway: The Copenhagen Center, 2002).

8. World Business Council for Sustainable Development.

9. UN Global Compact, *Who Cares Wins: Connecting Financial Markets to Changing World,* (New York, NY: United Nations, 2004).

10. "Global Governance," *Wikipedia.* http://en.wikipedia.org/wiki/Global_governance.

11. "Corporate Governance," *Wikipedia.* http://en.wikipedia.org/wiki/Corporate_governance.

12. UN Global Compact, *Who Cares Wins.*

13. United Nations, "Overview of the UN Global Compact." http://www.unglobalcompact.org/AboutTheGC/index.html.

14. Jeb Emerson, "The Blended Value Proposition: Integrating Social and Financial Returns," *California Review Management,* 45, no. 4 (Summer 2003):35–51.

15. Ibid.

16. Ibid.

17. Urban Institute, *The Nonprofit Sector in Brief: Public Charities, Giving and Volunteering* (Washington, DC: Urban Institute, 2010).

18. J. Gregory Dees, "The Meaning of 'Social Entrepreneurship,'" (Durham, NC: Center for the Advancement of Social Entrepreneurship, Duke Fuqua School of Business, October 1998). www.caseatduke.org/documents/dees_sedef.pdf.

19. Ann Svenserson, *The Stakeholder Engagement Theory* (San Francisco, CA: Berrett-Koehler, 1998).

20. Milton Friedman, "The Social Responsibility of Business is to Increase its Profits," *The New York Times Magazine,* September 13, 1970.

21. Svenserson, *The Stakeholder Engagement Theory.*

22. Ibid.

23. "Multi-stakeholder Initiatives," CSR Welt-Weit, http://www.csr-weltweit.de/en/initiativen-prinzipien/multi-stakeholder-initiativen/index.nc.html.

24. "Public-Private Partnership," *Wikipedia.* http://en.wikipedia.org/wiki/Public-private_partnership.

25. Anna Claudia Pellicelli, "Strategic Alliance: Clusters and Global Value Chains in the North and Third World," Paper presented at EADI Workshop, Nova, Italy, October 30, 2003.

26. Fredrick Long and Matthew Arnold, *The Power of Environmental Partnerships* (Washington, DC: The Dryden Press, Harcourt Brace College Publishers, 1995).

2

Global Trends

Overview

Based on interviews with non-governmental organization (NGO) and business leaders, there are several trends that have shaped existing cross-sectoral partnerships and will continue to influence their evolution. At the global level, there are eight main trends, including:

1. Globalization
2. Advancements in science, technology, and communications
3. Increases in the gap between rich and poor countries and communities
4. Increases in the complexity of existing and emerging problems
5. Changes in the roles of government, business, and NGOs
6. Growth of alternative organizational structures
7. Changes in philanthropy
8. Shifts in development assistance

Figure 2.1 outlines the key global, NGO, and business trends that are influencing the evolution of NGO-business partnerships.

Globalization

What Is It?

For the purpose of this discussion, "globalization" is defined as "the global expansion of foreign trade, capital, and investment flows, and communication and information technology." The potential of globalization suggests that it can (1) expand economic freedoms, largely through free trade; (2) spur competition, resulting in higher quality products at lower prices; (3) increase

Figure 2.1 Trends influencing NGO-business partnerships.

productivity by improving economic efficiency; and (4) raise living standards for all. For developed countries such as the United States, Germany, and Japan, globalization means increasing access to markets for their goods and services, largely in less developed countries. For less developed countries, globalization holds the promise of access to foreign capital, export markets, and advanced technology.

Trade liberalization—the free flow of goods, capital, and services—is a key concept of globalization. Many free-market economists think that markets by themselves are efficient, and the best way to reduce poverty is to let them grow without regulation. For a quarter century after World War II, most of the less developed countries insulated their economies from the rest of the world. In the last two decades, many of these emerging economies, such as Brazil, India, and China, have been opened through free trade agreements and regional trading blocs. For example, between 1980 and 2000, China's trade of goods and services expanded from 23% to 46% of its gross domestic product (GDP) and India's trade grew from 19% to 30% of its GDP.[1]

Opening economies was thought to stimulate a larger pool of competitors, creating more jobs and expanding supply chains. Competition in a free market is believed to yield a higher quality of goods and services by increasing productivity and raising labor standards. Job creation and its resultant economic growth are believed to result in high living standards for all.

How Did It Happen?

It is important to understand the events that shaped the evolution of globalization as outlined in Table 2.1. After World War II, three key organizations were established to manage global markets: (1) The World Bank provides capital to less developed countries, (2) the International Monetary Fund (IMF) oversees macroeconomic policy, and (3) the General Agreement on Tariffs and Trade (GATT) regulates international trade.

GATT went through three phases. First, it focused on freezing existing tariff levels; later they aimed to lower tariffs. Second, in the 1970s and early 1980s, the combination of reduced tariffs and a series of economic recessions drove developed countries to devise other forms of protection to reduce competition, skewing the markets. High rates of unemployment and factory closures led developed, industrialized countries to seek bilateral market-sharing arrangements, undermining GATT's credibility and effectiveness. The third phase of GATT included the 1986 Uruguay Round in which the developed countries pushed for less developed countries in Africa and Asia to open their markets, in return for which the developed countries would eliminate agriculture and textile subsidies. The less developed countries agreed to open their markets and accepted reduced tariffs on intellectual property, but the developed countries never eliminated their agriculture subsidies.[2]

By the early 1990s, globalization was largely being led by services that were not covered by GATT and agriculture loopholes were heavily exploited by the developed countries. In 1995 the World Trade Organization (WTO) was created to include more countries and cover a wider array of products, goods, and services. Today there are 153 members of the WTO.

By 1999, many people began to question the benefits of globalization and protested against the WTO. As a result of these protests, there was an agreement that the next trade negotiations (held in Doha, Qatar, in 2001, and known as "Doha 2001") should focus on the needs of less developed countries. However, developed countries continued to refuse to live up to

Table 2.1
Summary of Key Globalization Events and Institutions

Dates	Institution/Event	Issues/Agreements
1944	• World Bank established	• Increased access to capital for less developed countries.
1947–1958	• First phase of GATT	• Focused on freezing existing tariff levels.
1959–1979	• Second phase of GATT • Tokyo Round (1973–1979)	• Focused on reducing tariffs.
1986–1994	• Third phase of GATT • Uruguay Round (1986)	• Developed countries promised to get rid of agriculture and textile subsidies. Less developed countries accepted reduced tariffs on intellectual properties.
1995	• World Trade Organization established	• Expanded trade agreements to reach other services not included in GATT.
1999	• World Trade Organization protests in Seattle	• U.S. factory workers lost jobs because of outsourcing. Farmers in less developed countries could not compete with highly subsidized agriculture products from industrialized developed countries.
2001	• Doha trade talks	• No meaningful agreement was signed because the developed countries refused to give up agricultural subsidies.

Source. Joseph Stiglitz, *Making Globalization Work* (New York: WW Norton and Company, 2006).

their 1986 promise of eliminating agriculture subsidies. So in the end, no meaningful agreement was signed. By 2003, the IMF stated that for many less developed countries market liberalization had led to more instability, not growth.[3]

What Are the Results of Globalization?

It is clear that we live in a time of an integrated global economy, as evidenced by the widespread and interdependent effects of the current financial and banking crisis. Although GDP may be a good measure of short-term growth, it is not an adequate indicator for long-term sustainable growth. It is estimated that 4 billion people, with a purchasing power of $5 trillion, are not yet part of the formal market system.[4] Countries can increase GDP while increasing pollution, raising the deficit, and depleting natural resources. Most economists now agree that markets by themselves do not lead to economic efficiency because there will always be too much of some things like environmental pollution and too little of other things like basic scientific research.

Although every country has benefited in some way from the effects of globalization, some countries and individuals have benefited much more than others, resulting in widening inequality gaps among and within countries. For example, 80% of people living in poverty reside in less developed countries. In addition, there are a growing number of countries with widening income gaps, which is further discussed in "Widening Income Gap Between Rich and Poor" later in this chapter.

Although globalization suggests that it was built on free trade, there are many asymmetries in the existing trade agreements that have benefitted some groups at the expense of others, as outlined in Table 2.2.

As a result of the Uruguay Round of trade talks, it is estimated that Africa has lost $1.2 billion a year in trade, whereas the developed countries gained $350 billion. In addition, these agreements have resulted in developed countries costing less developed countries three times more in trade than they provide in total foreign aid.[5]

A decade after the Uruguay Round, more than 66% of farm income in Norway and Switzerland, 50% in Japan, and 33% percent in Europe came from government subsidies.[6] By 2000, aid to U.S. farmers had reached more than $22 billion, three times the 1996 levels. In addition, developed countries have close to monopoly power in the market. For example, the United States is the world's largest exporter of cotton (25,000 farmers), supported by $3 billion of annual subsidies. Without these funds it would not be profitable for U.S. farmers to produce cotton. As a result, there is an oversupply of cotton, naturally depressing global prices, and hurting some 10 million farmers in Africa. The combined agricultural subsidies of the United States, the European Union, and Japan equaled 75% of a total annual income of sub-Saharan Africa.[7] For example, the average European cow gets a subsidy of $2 a day, whereas 2.6 billion people live on $2 a day.[8]

As a result, products from developed countries have flooded many less developed country markets at prices that local farmers cannot compete with, in many cases crippling the domestic agricultural markets, causing many to question the existence of a free market.

Table 2.2
Results of Globalization

	Developed Countries	Less Developed Countries
Trade agreement	• Promised to eliminate their agriculture subsidies that would level the playing field for farmers from less developed countries.	• Based on the promise of agricultural subsidy elimination, they opened markets to developed countries' products.
Tariffs and levies	• Levied tariffs on goods produced by less developed countries that were four times higher than those levied on other developed countries. • Used other creative approaches to replace tariffs. For example, they charged antidumping fees if products were below the cost of other developed country products.	• Reduced tariffs on developed countries' intellectual property and information, communication, and technology (ICT) products.
Markets and industries	• ICT companies, most based in developed countries, have near-monopoly power in these industries.	• Not allowed to protect their nascent industries, which helped the United States (1940s) and Japan (1960s) to become global leaders. • Have to compete with advanced industries that have already recovered their capital and infrastructure investment costs.
Ability to adopt new technology	• Easier because they have an educated population with good infrastructures and systems to bring their products to the global market.	• Harder because they lacked an educated workforce and an adequate infrastructure to move products within the country to the global market.
Employee protection	• Workers have more protection in terms of severance packages, job retraining. They usually are more educated so they have more options.	• Most people work in the informal market with little legal employee protection.

Source. Joseph Stiglitz, *Making Globalization Work* (New York: WW Norton and Company, 2006).

Although globalization claims to increase the base of competitors, industries have become more consolidated over the past several years among fewer companies. For example, 51 of the largest 100 economies in the world are multi-national corporations (MNCs). In addition, MNCs hold 90% of all the technology and product patents worldwide, and they are involved in 70% of world trade.[9] MNCs and their business associations claim that deregulated trade and investment will produce enough growth to end poverty and generate resources for environmental protection. The unrestricted free trade and investment-based growth, beloved by MNCs, however, is the same kind of development that has led to overexploitation of land and natural resources; air, water, and soil pollution; ozone depletion; global warming; toxic waste generation; and widening income gaps. Economists Herman Daly and Robert Goodland have argued, "The dream that growth will raise world wages to the current rich country level, and that all can consume resources at the U.S. per capita rate, is in total conflict with ecological limits that are already stressed beyond sustainability."[10]

Globalization, in the form of export-led growth, helped pull the east Asian countries—South Korea, Singapore, Malaysia, and Japan—out of poverty. It provided access to international markets and enabled increases in productivity. But it must be emphasized that these governments managed the globalization process. They made sure that the benefits went to many and not to just a few, with large sustained investments in social services, particularly education and health. Markets were measured and paced by government regulation. Planning and advancing technology was deliberate; these governments selected which sectors to develop rather than letting the market decide. More recently, China has benefitted by this growth and it has followed a similar model of slowly opening up its markets. In addition, these countries do not allow speculative monies in their market. This approach has allowed them to avoid the boom-bust cycle experienced by many other countries. Thus government regulation is required for effective markets. The debate is about how much and what types of regulation are required to create a level playing field and a truly free market.

Even when better jobs are created from globalization, less developed countries struggle to make the transition to the global market. The vast numbers of poor people, particularly women, in less developed countries (1) are uneducated and unskilled, (2) work in the informal sector or on their own small farms, (3) lack access to credit, and (4) lack secure land rights. The combination of weak governments, poor social systems, lopsided wealth distribution, and inept or corrupt politicians often hinder opportunities for the poor. For example, Bangalore has experienced significant growth caused by the information technology industry, raising the living standards for 250 million people. This is a major achievement, but 800 million people (76% of the population) still remain very poor, and are unable to tap into these benefits. Opening markets without relieving these domestic constraints forces people to compete with one hand tied behind their back, and it can result in deepening poverty.[11]

The current process of globalization is generating unbalanced outcomes, both between and within countries. Wealth is being created, but too many countries and people are not sharing in its benefits. They also have no voice in shaping the process. Seen through the eyes of the vast majority of women and girls, globalization has not met their simple and legitimate aspiration for decent jobs and a better future for their children. Many live in an informal economy without formal rights and in a swathe of poor countries that subsist precariously on the margins of the global economy.

In summary, although globalization has increased opportunities, jobs, and wealth for many, a significant portion of the population is not able to participate in and reap these rewards. The consolidation of industries has skewed many of the advantages toward large companies and highly educated workforces. Although there have been some advantages for small and medium entities and a growing recognition of the need to involve women and the poor, it has been much more challenging for these groups. Globally, the challenge is to develop fairer trading terms that do not doubly disadvantage less developed countries. For individual countries, the goal is to manage the globalization process to maximize its strengths, build capacity of its citizens to participate in the global process, and to safeguard their population against its negative implications.

Advances in Information, Communication, and Technology

In *The World Is Flat,* the celebrated *New York Times* commentator, Thomas Friedman, states that globalization and technology have flattened the world, creating a level playing field in which developed countries and less developed countries can compete on equal terms. He discussed the key information, communication, and technology (ICT) "flatteners."

1. The fall of the Berlin Wall and Communism tipped the global balance of power, which opened markets and resulted in a major change in global trade.

2. An Internet platform was created. Netscape went public, making the web truly interoperable. In addition, the community ensured that software protocols remained open and could be used by everyone. This strategy greatly expedited the use of new communication technologies throughout the world.
3. The dot-com boom and the Telecommunications Act coincided, launching a fiber-optic bubble that resulted in excessive cable infrastructure. As a result, several less developed countries, particularly India, benefited from this over-capacity, so they could use this technology for a greatly reduced price.
4. The dot-com bust resulted in a surplus of Indian engineers returning to India. The combination of skills and infrastructure fueled the growth of the Indian tech sector.
5. The development of new interoperable systems, such as the ability to share data and media files, dramatically changed workflow and revolutionized many industries. First, there was the personal computer. Then e-mail allowed sharing and manipulation of digital content. This has evolved into video conferencing, webinars, and other interactive online experiences.
6. The ability to share data resulted in people wanting to buy things on the Internet. E-commerce began with PayPal in 1998, which enabled the web to accept credit cards.
7. The availability of information via search engines like Yahoo and Google made the world smaller and fostered the development of collaborative relationships. This empowered individuals to select the information they wanted and determine how they wanted to use it. Information could come from a variety of sources, not just from the top.
8. The concept of "outsourcing," moving manufacturing jobs to lower-wage countries, provided many jobs in less developed countries that often had few existing industries.
9. The idea of "offshoring," moving all functions to another location, was utilized by many Japanese and Chinese companies that moved their total operations to other east-Asian countries.
10. The ability to get quicker information about consumers' buying habits allowed companies to develop "just-in-time" inventories that reduced inventory costs. This also meant that the supply chain needed to be closely aligned and streamlined.

11. The concept of "insourcing"—one company providing more services—allowed companies to expand their services through partners and acquisitions. For example, United Parcel Service not only ships Toshiba computers to be repaired, but they also perform the repairs in-house.[12]

Although Friedman is correct that the world is flatter than it has ever been, there are still inequalities. Countries that want to participate in the high-tech world need new technologies and infrastructure requiring upfront investments and access to affordable credit to participate in this economy. People who are illiterate or only functionally literate need significant education to utilize the new technology and effectively engage in the global economy.

Even with all these advances, Friedman states, "the world has grown flatter with dramatic technological advances yet looming social and environment issues have not fully benefited from these efforts . . . requiring society to marshal [the] knowledge, skills, [and] resources of all its sectors."[13]

Widening Income Gap Between Rich and Poor

As previously stated, every country has benefited in some way from the effects of globalization, but some countries and individuals—largely the poor, women, and other disadvantaged groups—have benefited much less than others, resulting in widening income inequalities. There are two aspects of income inequality: (1) the gap between developed and less developed countries, and (2) segments of the population within a given country, whether developed or less developed.

There is broad awareness about the vast income inequalities between developed countries and less developed countries for many of the reasons previously described in "Globalization" earlier in this chapter. One-third of the world's population (2.6 billion) lives on less than $2 a day and 42% (880 million) of these people live on less than $1 a day; a significant portion of these are women and children.[14]

Most of these people live in developing and emerging countries. More than 80% of the world's population lives in countries where income differentials are widening. The poorest 40% of the world's population account for 5% of global income. The richest 20% account for 75% of the world's income.[15]

There is often less recognition about the issues relating to income inequalities within countries, particularly within developed countries. A 2008

Organisation for Economic Co-operation and Development (OECD) report found that the income of the top 10% of Europeans is nearly 9 times that of the poorest citizens; in the United States the gap is 16 times greater.[16] Another study found that the top 300,000 Americans collectively enjoyed almost as much income as the bottom 150 million Americans.[17] It is interesting to note that the four richest people in the world—Bill Gates, Warren Buffet, Carlos Slim (of Mexico), and Larry Ellison—have combined assets totaling $135 billion, which is more than the GDP of many countries.[18]

Studies show that 63% of the wealth in Sierra Leone—the worst case—is owned by 20% of the population, whereas the lowest 20% of the population only own 1% of the wealth, a gap of 62%. In contrast, in Slovenia—the best case—31% of the wealth is owned by the top 20% and the lowest 20% own 12%, a gap of 20%. Interestingly, Egypt, Rwanda, and Pakistan all have lower income gaps (28%–31%) than the Netherlands (33%) and the United States (41%).[19]

Despite strong economic growth in many countries over the last decade, there is a widening income equity gap because rich households have done significantly better than middle-class and poor households. Changes in the population structure and the labor market over the past 20 years have contributed greatly to this rise in inequality. Wages improved for those already well paid and stagnated for those less well compensated, and unemployment increased among less educated people.[20]

Poverty among the elderly has fallen in OECD countries, but rates have increased among young adults and families with children. One out of every eight children in Europe lives in poverty.[21] In 2008, 19% of children or 14 million American children lived in poverty, a 21% increase from 2000. An additional 15.8 million children were considered low-income (two times the poverty level), meaning a total of 29 million children in 2008 lived in low-income families. More worrisome is the fact that children (0–18 years) represented a larger share of people living in poverty, 27% compared with 14% of the adult population (18–64 years).[22] Estimates are that 1.5 million American children were homeless in 2010.[23]

Another key factor in the widening income gap is the demographic shifts resulting from aging populations in developed and middle-income countries, such as Brazil, China, Thailand, and Egypt, who face looming pension and health care issues. In contrast, less developed countries are experiencing increasing youth population, because of high fertility rates. These countries are plagued by high unemployment rates. For example, a 2009 International Labour

Organization (ILO) survey estimated an unemployment rate of 13% for 15- to 24-year-olds, the highest number reported since 1991. There is a concern about a "lost generation" as young people drop out of the labor market and are discouraged from returning.[24]

These disparities existed before the current economic crisis and will only worsen under the present conditions. The ILO estimates that 20 million more people could be unemployed, bringing the total to 190 million people globally; 22 million more women will be unemployed, jeopardizing the gains made in the last few decades in women's empowerment; and the number of people working for less than $2 a day will rise by 100 million people.[25] Juan Somalia, director-general of the ILO, states,

> The 2010 global jobs picture is one of contrasts and uncertainty. While global growth is annually producing millions of new jobs, unemployment remains unacceptably high and may go to levels not seen before this year. Moreover, too many people, if not unemployed, remain among the ranks of the working poor, the vulnerable or the discouraged.[26]

These income inequities will continue both among and within countries. Serious multi-sectoral action is required to develop solutions that benefit society as a whole rather than just a privileged minority.

Complex Problems Requiring Multi-Sector Response

Globalization and the technology revolution have made the world smaller, but the nature of our problems has become more global in scope and complex in nature. For example, diseases such as acquired immune deficiency syndrome (AIDS) and swine flu easily transcend national borders, requiring cooperative surveillance and treatment. In addition, climate change and environmental pollution have multiple sources and effects, requiring wide-scale actions at many levels. There are no silver bullets. The more interconnected the world becomes, the broader the ripple effect individual actions have on the interdependent system. In addition, a more collaborative and collective action is required to develop innovative and sustainable solutions.

Issues have become too complex and interdependent and the financial and managerial resources required too scarce for any single sector to effectively respond to current challenges. New forms of partnerships are needed to address societal and environmental problems for which traditional single-sector approaches are proving inadequate.[27]

Changing Roles of Government, Business, and NGOs

Over the past 50 years the sphere of influence and roles of citizens, NGOs, governments, and business have dramatically changed and become increasingly blurred.

Role of Government

The main role of government is to protect and provide key services for its citizens through laws, regulations, and policies that create an enabling environment for all sectors and individuals to thrive. However, the ability of many governments to implement these responsibilities has stagnated or weakened for four main reasons.

1. Many countries have deregulated key industries, such as telecom and utilities, aimed at benefiting consumers. However, these actions have had mixed results, with some reduction of competition and higher prices for consumers of some industries.
2. Many countries have reduced the authority of regulatory bodies, hindering their credibility and ability to monitor and regulate corporate practices. They have privatized government functions or decentralized key services to local governments. This has some advantages in terms of being more responsive to local needs. However, it has also resulted in poorer areas continuing to struggle with fewer resources and capacities such as limited management skills. It also creates a leadership vacuum on systemic issues that cannot be solved solely by individual communities such as immigration and health care.
3. Many countries have faced challenges in effectively negotiating with large institutions that may have greater resources and influence. For example, if a government wants to enforce a living wage to benefit its citizens, which causes higher labor costs, a company might move to another location where it can have lower labor costs, regardless of the societal implications.
4. Many countries have experienced growing fiscal deficits that require them to limit social services provided to their citizens, either directly or indirectly, although needs are increasing.

Role of the NGO Sector

The role of the NGO sector is to (1) advocate for key social and environmental issues; (2) conduct key research; and (3) implement social and environmental programs, largely for disadvantaged and vulnerable groups.

There has been a tremendous growth in the NGO sector and a significant change in their approaches and operations. NGOs have moved from being "outsiders" challenging the system to being increasingly part of the system. Many have shifted from identifying market failures to creating new market solutions with greater inclusion of groups that were previously marginalized.[28] Many governments and multi-lateral agencies, such as the United Nations (UN) and World Bank, are increasingly recognizing the crucial role that NGOs play in implementing development programs, fostering peace and security, promoting respect of human rights, and mobilizing resources and stakeholder groups.

NGOs' modus operandi has significantly evolved, with greater attention paid to effective operating systems, such as financial and managerial practices. This has come about from the growing professionalism and technical expertise of NGO staff as well as support and pressure from donors and the general public. Many NGOs have moved away from directly providing services and toward developing local ownership, building social capacity, and fostering sustainable systems that are locally owned.

Role of Business

Business often defines its role as "maximizing shareholder value" or, in short, making a profit. Over the past several decades, there has been a growing discussion and recognition about expanding the role of business to include responsibility to the broader society.

There has been a tremendous growth in the wealth and influence of the private sector on society. The assets of many MNCs easily outstrip the economy of an average nation. For example, in 2005, Walmart had revenues of $285.2 billion, which was larger than the combined GDP for all sub-Saharan African countries.[29] This wealth shift has enhanced the business sector's ability to influence—and some would say dictate—political agendas that are in their best interest and may be in contrast with other sectors of society.

Thirty years ago, 70% of resources from the United States to the developing world came from official development assistance, primarily through the United States Agency for International Development (USAID), and 30% came from foreign direct investment, remittances, and private giving from individuals, religious groups, and foundations. Today, about 85% of resources from the United States to the developing world come from private transactions and only 15% are a result of foreign aid. This shift is a result of globalization created by the MNCs, migration flows, and technology adoption that is bringing the world closer together.[30]

Although the role of corporations has expanded, so have public demands. Never before have consumers had access to so much information about corporate practices and the ability to have their voices be heard. This was clearly evidenced by protests against Nike, Shell, and other corporations in the 1990s, which resulted in changes in business practices. Many businesses feel greater pressure to make investments in the environmental and social sector because of the government limitations, described previously, and greater consumer and stakeholder expectations.

The growth of corporate citizenship, driven by both the companies and civil society, has helped business understand that development is good for business and society. Over the last decade businesses have become more engaged in addressing environmental, social, and governance issues through mechanisms such as the UN Global Compact. Many companies are committed to contributing to key development challenges outlined by the Millennium Development Goals (MDGs), which is further discussed in "Shifts in Development Assistance" later in this chapter.

The MDGs provided a common framework that provided many opportunities for cross-sectoral discussions and partnerships with other sectors. Engaging with other sectors to address the MDGs enables companies to invest in creating a sound business environment, manage their costs and risks of doing business, and harness new business opportunities.[31]

Alternative Organizational Models

U.S. law does not allow any organization to simultaneously accept (tax-deductible) donation and invested capital—equity in which investors seek a financial return. As a result, some organizations have been created as a "hybrid model" that separates the non-profit (donation) and for-profit (investment capital) efforts, but they are linked through governance or legal agreements.

Many NGOs have for-profit businesses associated with them. Probably one of the best-known examples of an NGO with for-profit businesses is Goodwill Industries, which is over 100 years old. Goodwill is composed of 165 independent, community-based Goodwill organizations in the United States and Canada with over 2,500 retail stores and an online auction site. The local Goodwill organizations are flexible and sustainable social enterprises that fund job training, employment placement services, and other community programs by selling donated clothes and household items at Goodwill retail stores and online. Goodwill also generates revenue by contracting with businesses and government to provide a wide range of commercial services, including packaging and assembly, food service preparation, cleaning services, document imaging and shredding, and more. As a result of these efforts, in 2010 Goodwill Industries was able to generate $2.69 billion in retail sales and $632 million from industrial and service contract work. These revenues supported 20.1 million people who received workforce development services.[32] Five other examples of social enterprises are described here.

1. *Delancey Street* is the country's leading residential self-help organization for former substance abusers, ex-convicts, homeless, and others who have hit bottom. This NGO owns a for-profit restaurant, a moving company, and a corporate car service. They currently have contracts with The Gap, Inc., Williams-Sonoma, Pottery Barn, and several law firms. These businesses are used as employment opportunities for the Delancey Street program participants and the profits are used to support their housing, employment training, and substance abuse treatment activities for the program participants.[33]
2. *Juma Ventures* owns two ice cream franchises (formerly Ben and Jerry's franchises). These concession stands are located at AT&T Park, where the San Francisco Giants baseball team plays. These franchises provide job-training opportunities for underprivileged youth and the revenues from the ice cream sales support the NGO's other youth development activities.[34]
3. *Rubicon*'s social businesses, Rubicon Bakery (sold in 2009) and Rubicon Landscape, employ and train economically disadvantaged individuals. Revenues from these enterprises contribute to Rubicon's social programs and integrated services that help low-income and mentally challenged people find housing and jobs, handle their finances, obtain legal advice, and manage their mental illnesses.[35]
4. *The Foundation for Integrated Education and Development (FUNEDESIN)*, an Ecuadorian development NGO, created Yachana Gourmet, a for-profit fair-trade chocolate company. A portion of the profits from Yachana Gourmet supports the social activities of FUNEDESIN.[36]

5. *Grameen Telecom*, a Bangladeshi NGO, the sister organization of Grameen Bank, owns 35% shares in Grameen Phone, an international for-profit company. Thus Grameen Telecom receives dividends from Grameen Phone that support their development efforts to expand access to information among the rural poor in Bangladesh.[37]

Hybrid models are not new, but social enterprises have taken these models to a new level, crafting business structures into an effective single structure that can operate as a for-profit company with a socially responsible purpose.

Although NGOs created enterprises to create more revenues, some businesses want to incorporate more social and environmental missions into their business structures. This has resulted in new organizational structures that better balance financial aims of for-profits with the ability to integrate more effectively stakeholder concerns and include a mission focus. The three most common alternative business models are presented here. It should be noted that these models are not accepted in all states.[38]

1. B Corporations are a new kind of company that uses the power of business to solve social and environmental problems. B Corporations (1) meet comprehensive and transparent social and environmental performance standards, (2) legally expand the responsibilities of the corporation to include stakeholder interests, and (3) build collective voice through the power of the unifying B Corporation brand.[39]
2. Benefit corporations are a legally distinct type of business committed to accomplishing one or more social or public purposes and must have at least one "benefit" member on the board whose sole duty is to protect the mission rather than profits. The company must also be certified by an independent third party as complying with standards promulgated by the certifying agency. In return, the directors of the benefit corporation are protected from liability for decisions that further the social mission, even if they impair profitability.[40]
3. Low-profit limited liability corporations (L3Cs) are essentially limited liability companies with a purpose limited to "low-profit" activities that further a charitable purpose; the generation of income is not a significant purpose of the venture. The L3C was originally designed to be a special-purpose vehicle so

> that private foundations could more easily make program-related investments. The brand has caught on and many people now regard it as a way to signal their intent to place mission at a level that is equal to or greater than profit, while still enjoying the advantages of a business structure (the ability to accept private investment and enter into a broad range of business relationships).[41]

It is clear that this is a growing trend and there will be more experimentation in this field that both NGOs and companies will need to consider.

Changes in Philanthropy Trends

For purposes of this discussion, "philanthropy" includes the exchange of resources to support NGO efforts, which encompasses cash grants, in-kind contributions, and volunteerism. Some basic facts about philanthropy are described here.

Small individual donors provide the lion's share (82%) of funding, and foundations provide about 18% of all philanthropic funds. Even as Americans began feeling the pinch of the recent recession with soaring gas prices, falling stock portfolios, and a looming mortgage crisis, they donated $306 billion to charity in 2007, more than ever before. A 2007 American Express Survey found that the vast majority of donors give many small donations ($50–$100). Religious efforts receive the most funding, followed by education, human services, and health care.[42]

Individual Giving

There has been a growth of online contributions; 64% of individual donors gave online, largely because of its convenience.[43] For example, the launch of Causes.com, Facebook's sister company, has created the world's largest platform for activism and philanthropy by connecting individual donors, NGOs, and businesses, and granting access to causes that they can support through the Facebook platform.

In addition, increased individual wealth has spawned the growth of investment circles (groups of people who pool their money and decide what to fund). This approach often appeals to people who have not traditionally been involved in philanthropy, such as women, minorities, and young people. These donors gravitate toward alliances that help them learn, network, and give. According to a study by the Forum of Regional Associations of Grantmakers,

Table 2.3
Number of Private Foundations by Assets Level, 2006

Total Assets Level	Number of Foundations	Percentage
$0–<$1M	58,222	53%
>$1–$10M	47,236	43%
>$10–$25M	2,197	2%
>$25M	2,197	2%
	109,852	

Source. "Number of Private Foundations in the United States, 2010," *National Center for Charitable Statistics*, http://nccsdataweb.urban.org/PubApps/profileDrillDown.php?state=US&rpt=PF.

the number of giving circles more than doubled from 2004 to 2006 to at least 400, although some estimates are as high as 2,000 with assets ranging from $5,000–$100,000. These groups have raised an estimated $100 million to support a wide range of charitable causes.[44]

Institutional Giving

There are two types of foundations: public and private. There are two main types of private foundations. The first is the independent foundation, which includes family foundations and corporate foundations. Most foundations (53%) are small with $1million or less in assets, whereas less than 2% of foundations have assets greater than $25 million, as outlined in Table 2.3.[45] In 2008, private foundations contributed about $44.4 billion, up from $42 billion in 2005. Estimates for 2009 indicate that:

- Independent and family foundations, which represent close to 90% of all foundations, reduced their giving by 8.9% to $30.8 billion.[46,47]
- Corporate foundation giving decreased by 3.3% to $4.4 billion.[48]

Some new trends in philanthropy include venture philanthropy and Social Impact Bonds. "Venture philanthropy," also known as "philanthrocapitalism," takes concepts and techniques from venture capital finance and business management and applies them to achieving philanthropic goals. Venture philanthropy is characterized by:

- Willingness to experiment and try new approaches
- Focus on measurable results in terms of both financial and social returns
- Giving financial, intellectual, and human capital
- Funding on a multi-year basis
- Focus on capacity building instead of programs or general operating expenses
- High involvement by donors with their grantees (for example, some donors take positions on the boards of the non-profits they fund)

There are three models for engaging in venture philanthropy. First, foundations are practicing high-engagement grant making (e.g., the Rockefeller Foundation's Pro-V project). The second model is an organization funded by individuals, but in which all engagement is done by professional staff (e.g., the Robin Hood Foundation and Tipping Point Community). The third model is a partnership model in which partner investors both donate the financial capital and engage with the grantees (e.g., the Social Venture Fund, Acumen Fund, and Full Circle Fund).[49]

Social Impact Bonds, known as "impact investing," are innovative ways to attract new investments to improve social outcomes benefiting people and communities. President Obama's proposed 2012 budget proposes changes in legislation that would allow various government agencies to issue "Pay for Success" bonds. These bonds are bought by private investors to finance programs implemented by NGOs to address key social or environmental issues. Private investors are only paid or make a profit when results are achieved. The Social Impact Bond was first launched in the United Kingdom, where private funds were raised to support NGO programs to reduce the recidivism rate among certain criminals. If the recidivism rate falls far enough, investors will earn up to a 13.5% annual rate of return.[50]

Family Foundations

The term "family foundation" does not have any legal status, but the Council on Foundations defines a "family foundation" as one in which the founder, donor, or the donor's relatives play a significant role in governing or managing the foundation. Most family foundations are relatively small. Three-fifths reported less than $1 million in assets in 2006. There are about 40,000 grant-making independent foundations categorized as "family foundations." They represent over 50% of all independent foundations and account for a similar share of giving and assets. Giving by family foundations rose by 14% from 2007 to 2008.[51]

There is a new generation of large family foundations—for example, foundations created by Bill and Melinda Gates, Warren Buffet, Robert Branson, Pierre Omidyar, Jeffery Skoll, and Steven Case—dubbed "philanthrocapitalists" by Matthew Bishop and Michael Green.[52] This new breed of billionaire wants to harness the benefits of the marketplace as a force for doing good while making a profit. Pierre Omidyar wants to use investment capital as well as donations to expand the microfinance industry. Stephen Case is investing $250 million in companies to help consumers gain control of their health care. The philanthrocapitalists' approach reflects the culture of their (innovative) businesses that brought them their wealth. They believe that the marketplace can have the same "level-the-playing-field" effect while supplying the world's poor with basic needs like food, sanitation, shelter, education, and health care. They view money as an investment that can have both social and financial returns, not a donation.[53] Alan Abramson, director of the non-profit Aspen Institute, states,

> More and more people are asking who else is going to finance doing good if government isn't. These guys have firsthand knowledge of the market's power and they're asking themselves why they can't make money and tackle some of the problems once addressed primarily by government at the same time. It sounds simple, but the idea of such hybrid philanthropy is upsetting long-held conventions. These new philanthropists view the current foundation model, built on the fortunes of earlier industrial titans like Carnegie and Rockefeller, as ineffective. They have an urge to change the world, and argue that in some cases only the speed of capitalism is fast enough.[54]

Corporate Foundations

Corporations provide funding through three main sources: (1) direct cash from business units; (2) cash and grants from foundations; and (3) other groups, which include regional offices, manufacturing plants, marketing, research and development units, and human resources. This section only discusses efforts funded through corporate foundations. The other two components are discussed in Chapter 4.

In 2008, corporate foundations composed 10% of all private foundation giving. These foundations are created by existing for-profit companies and usually act as independent organizations, with separate boards. In 2008, there were about 2,500 grant-making corporate foundations. A 2008 study by the Committee for Encouraging Corporate Philanthropy found that 24% of corporate foundations are endowed; 38% are considered "pass-through," which means the corporation provides an annual budget; and 28% are a hybrid between an endowed and "pass-through" foundation.[55] Key information about corporate foundations are presented in the following list.

- Giving by corporate foundations represents 32% of all corporate contributions.
- About 9% of corporate contributions come from employee matching programs.
- Giving decreased by 3.3% between 2007 and 2008.[56]
- Giving dropped from $4.4 billion in 2008[57] to $3.9 billion in 2009.[58]
- Banking and financial corporation foundations provided 25% of all corporate funding for the past several years.[59]
- Corporate foundations prioritized giving for education, human services, public affairs, and societal benefit.
- Most (75%) corporate foundations indicated that for 2010 they anticipate continued decreases in giving.[60]

Twenty-five years ago, businesses allocated an average of 2% of their pre-tax profits for gifts and grants. Some have suggested a target of 5% of pre-tax income. A *Chronicle of Philanthropy* survey found that companies gave a median of 1.2% of the 2008 profits. Only 11 companies in the survey gave 5% of their pre-tax earnings during 2008. Convincing senior management to increase rather than cut back a company's philanthropy budget may seem a daunting, if not impossible, task, particularly at a time when the overall corporate profit picture has become so uncertain. But if executives understand that an effectively managed contribution program can deliver strong returns to a corporation, then it can be worth the investment.[61]

The largest corporate foundations include Bank of America ($204.5 million in 2008), Wells Fargo ($202.4 million in 2009), Sanofi-Aventis ($177.4 million in 2007), Walmart ($110.9 million in 2008), General Electric ($103.9 million 2009), and Citibank ($89.9 million in 2008).[62]

Community (Public) Foundations

The first community foundation was started in Cleveland, Ohio, in 1914. The number grew as a result of the 1969 Tax Reform Act that gave greater tax advantages for public foundations. The greatest growth of these foundations occurred between 1970 and 1973, when many private foundations were dissolved and their assets were transferred to community foundations. In the 1980s, large private foundations, such as the Ford Foundation, began to champion community foundations as a way to meet local community needs. In the 1990s, these foundations were promoted as donor-advised funds. By 2000, there were an estimated 664 community foundations in the United States, a 150% increase from 1990.[63] Several community foundations have been established to assist corporations in supporting local initiatives. For example, the Silicon Valley Community Foundation receives funds and manages programs for companies such as Cisco, Ebay, Palm, Hewlett Packard, and Yahoo. In 2009, giving by community foundations fell by 9.6% in 2009, and 2010 estimates project a continued decline in giving.[64]

There is a great deal of consolidation among these foundations. In 2000, the top 20% of community foundations controlled more than 88% of the sector's assets and the top 5% held 60% of assets, as presented in Table 2.3. Almost half of all U.S. community foundations are located in the midwest and California, and they received over 25% of all gifts.[65,66]

Community foundations, which may be established as NGOs, have also been established in other countries. For example, in 1995, President Suharto of Indonesia established three foundations to undertake community development efforts, asking companies to donate 2% of their net annual profit to one foundation.[67]

Community Service

Community service is another key component of philanthropy. It is estimated that about 61.8 million people, or 26% of the population, volunteered between September 2007 and September 2008.[68] Some key findings regarding community services include:

- Women volunteered more than men.
- People age 35 to 44 were most likely to volunteer (31%).
- Millennials have had greater participation (83% in 1999) in youth service programs than older cohorts (27% in 1984).
- Whites (28%) volunteered more than blacks (19%), Asians (19%), or Latinos (14%).
- Married people volunteered at a higher rate.
- Parents with children under age 18 were more likely to volunteer.
- Seniors are less likely to volunteer. However, if they do volunteer they devote many more hours than younger cohorts.[69]

In 2009, President Obama signed the Edward M. Kennedy Serve America Act to strengthen national community service efforts by boosting federal funding to triple the number of AmeriCorps volunteers and establishing a national day of service to commemorate 9/11.[70] President Obama stated, "Our government can help to rebuild our economy . . . [but] we need Americans willing to mentor our eager young children, or care for the sick, or ease the strains of deployment on our military families."[71]

Among employed persons, 29% volunteered. Part-time workers (34%) were more likely to volunteer than full-time workers (28%).[72] In contrast, 22% of unemployed persons volunteered.[73] Public companies are more likely to provide paid time off for employees to volunteer, which is further discussed in Chapter 4.

Although companies have reduced their cash donations, there is a growing trend (54% of companies) of encouraging employees to volunteer more and including families and retirees as volunteers. For example, Cisco Systems increased its total corporate-wide giving, including foundation money, from $65 million in 2005 to $129 million in 2009. Contributions from corporate products and people accounted for 44% of total giving in 2005, a share that jumped to 65% in 2009. Cisco has worked with governments, NGOs, and other companies in 168 countries to create online learning academies that have graduated over 3 million students, with another 800,000 currently enrolled.[74]

Shifts in Development Assistance

Over the last two decades, there have been significant changes in the strategies utilized to implement development assistance programs. In the 1960s through the 1980s, this was largely the purview of government and NGOs. There has been a complete reversal between development assistance and foreign direct investment. Thirty years ago, the majority, 70%, of U.S. assistance to developing countries primarily came from government assistance programs. Today, about 85% of U.S. resources come from private transactions and only 15% are a result of foreign aid. This has changed how governments, NGOs, and companies operate and relate to each other. There is a growing awareness that multiple sectors are required to address complex problems.[75] Kofi Annan, UN secretary general, argued in 2002, "One of the most important trends in international development over the past decade has been a growing awareness of the critical role that a productive and responsible private sector plays, not only in underpinning economic growth and wealth creation, but also in supporting the other key pillars of development."[76] In 2000, 189 heads of state ratified the Millennium Declaration that resulted in the MDGs. The Millennium Declaration focuses on reducing poverty, improving the quality of people's lives, ensuring environmental sustainability, and building partnerships to ensure that globalization becomes a more positive force for all the world's people.

The MDGs are eight time-bound targets to be achieved by 2015 that aim to:

1. Eradicate extreme poverty and hunger.
2. Achieve universal primary education.
3. Promote gender equality and empower women.
4. Reduce child mortality.
5. Improve maternal health.
6. Combat HIV and AIDS, malaria, and other diseases.
7. Ensure environmental sustainability.
8. Develop a global partnership for development.

The MDGs have provided a common framework for all sectors to work together toward common objectives. In the late 1990s, there was a growing interest among government and international donor agencies in leveraging the resources, skills, and technology of the private sector. The growth of corporate citizenship, driven by both the companies and civil society, has helped business understand that development is good for business and society. Businesses are uniquely positioned in terms of their skills and geographical reach to respond to these challenges. The MDGs therefore represent not just a responsibility but also a business opportunity. Engaging with other sectors to address the MDGs enables companies to invest in creating a sound business environment, manage their costs and risks of doing business, and harness new business opportunities.[77,78]

The 2009 *Partnering for Global Development* report identified 10 international development agencies that were developing programs to involve the private sector in development programs. For example, in 1995, Vice President Gore announced USAID's New Partnerships Initiative to further USAID's approach to partner with a variety of organizations.

In 2001, this grew into the USAID–Global Development Alliance to be "an innovative public-private alliance model for improving social and economic conditions in developing countries."[79] In 1998, the World Bank developed a three-year project called Business Partnerships for Development to explore tri-sector partnerships between NGOs, government, and business.

As a result of these strategies, more donors are requiring grantees to develop partnerships with private-sector entities. In addition, more donor procurements, such as requests for proposals, mandate a higher level of "matching" funds (5%–25% of the total amount of the budget), leading NGOs to seek more private-sector funding. Although there is a great deal of interest and support for developing tri-party partnerships, there is still a limited capacity among all parties to develop effective, mutually beneficial relationships.

Summary of Global Trends

- *Globalization and advances in ICT:* It is clear that the integration of the global economy and advances in ICT have created a world that is more interconnected than at any other time in history. Although globalization held the promise of benefiting all, its asymmetrical implementation has provided opportunities and wealth for many often at the expense of others, such as the less educated, poor, women, and other disadvantaged groups, as evidenced by widening income gaps. These practices were successful in the short term but have been shown to be financially, environmentally, and socially unsustainable. As a result, we have arrived at a place of unprecedented global economic, environmental, and social crisis.
- *Increases in income inequity:* Many global economies are stalled or growing slowly with modest predictions of future growth, which contributes to high unemployment rates. Even in economies that are rapidly growing, such as India and China, there are still high unemployment rates and vast numbers of people living in poverty. Over the past decade, countries have seen strong economic growth with widening income gaps because the growth was not designed to include less advantaged groups or train employees of dying industries in new skills for the twenty-first century, such as clean technology.
- *Increases in the complexity of existing and emerging problems:* Problems that exist are much more complex, with many factors contributing to the problem without clear-cut solutions. Thus it is essential for the different sectors—government, NGO, and private—to work together to develop effective solutions that can be locally owned and sustained.
- *Changes in the roles of government, business, and NGOs:* Over the past decade there has been a shift in the role and capacity of the public, private, and NGO sectors, with increased wealth and in-

fluence of the private sector globally, reduction in government financing and regulation capacity, and a growing demand for NGOs to provide more services to more people with less funding.

- The current environment has created widespread public distrust of all three sectors. The public is skeptical of corporations because of high executive pay during large layoffs of workers, lack of transparency, and poor practices that are seen as favoring the company at the expense of its customers and workers. Governments have lost much of their credibility because of their inability to prevent the recent financial crisis, the lack of effective regulation to protect consumers, and their inability to deal with long-term issues that will continue to jeopardize economies and national security if they are not addressed in the short-term. Lastly, NGOs are criticized for not effectively dealing with the growing needs of the population and ensuring transparency and accountability for their actions. It is highly likely that the role of these sectors will continue to change in response to these crises. But it is clear that new paradigms and strategies, utilizing collaborative approaches among many diverse stakeholders, will be required in order to survive the current situation and to ensure that future generations will thrive.
- *Growth of alternative organizational structures:* There is a growth of alternative organizational structures to better address social and environmental issues. On the NGO side, there are many NGOs that also have for-profit businesses, such as Goodwill. Revenue from these businesses, which include catering, restaurants, retail stores, cleaning, and car services to name a few, are used to support the NGO's programs such as employment training, substance abuse treatment, and youth development. On the for-profit side, new business models are being created to more effectively integrate stakeholder views and integrate environmental and social issues into the business, such as B Corporations, benefit corporations, and L3Cs. These models provide more opportunities for partnerships across sectors to address similar issues from multiple perspectives.
- *Changes in philanthropy:* Despite the growing economic constraints, individual Americans still provide the majority of philanthropic dollars. Technology, such as text messaging and social media, is providing more options for donors to make contributions.

In addition, many people have found it beneficial to participate in investor groups that have included people who have not traditionally been involved in philanthropy, such as women, minorities, and young people.

- There are two types of private, independent foundations. These are the family foundation and corporate foundation. Although there are a few large family foundations, such as the Gates and Buffet foundations, most (53%) are small, with $1 million or less. In addition, corporate foundations compose only 10% of all foundations, but their efforts supported directly through the business units, such as marketing, are not included in this figure. New approaches to philanthropy include venture philanthropy, also known as "philanthrocapitalism," and Social Impact Bonds. Both of these efforts aim to have both financial and social returns. These approaches provide ways for NGOs to tap investment capital, which they cannot usually access.
- *Shifts in development assistance:* There has been a growing recognition among development agencies of the complexity of the problems and the need to work with other sectors, particularly the private sector, to successfully address these issues. The MDGs have provided a common framework in which governments, NGOs, and the private sector can work together on these issues.

Notes

1. Joseph Stiglitz, *Making Globalization Work* (New York: WW Norton and Company, 2006).
2. Ibid.
3. Ibid.
4. International Finance Corporation and World Resources Institute, *The Next 4 Billion: Market Size and Business Strategy for Bottom of the Pyramid* (Washington, DC: International Finance Corporation and World Resources Institute).
5. Stiglitz, *Making Globalization Work.*
6. Ibid.
7. Ibid.
8. "Agricultural Subsidies," *Questia,* http://www.questia.com/library/encyclopedia/agri cultural_subsidies.jsp.
9. "Transnational Corporations," *Library of Halexandria,* http://www.halexandria.org/dward318.htm.

10. Norma Hertz, *The Silent Takeover: Global Capitalism and the Death of Democracy,* (London: Arrow Books, 2001).

11. Ibid.

12. Thomas L. Friedman, *The World is Flat* (New York: Farrar, Straus, Giroux, 2005).

13. Ibid.

14. United Nations, *Human Development Report 2007–2008* (New York: United Nations, 2008).

15. Ibid.

16. Organisation for Economic Co-operation and Development (OECD), *Growing Unequal? Income Distribution and Poverty in OECD Countries* (Paris: OECD, October 2008).

17. David Cay Johnston, "The Gap Between Rich and Poor Grows in the United States," *New York Times,* March 29, 2007.

18. Michael Edwards, *Small Change: Why Business Won't Change the World* (San Francisco: Berrett-Koehler, 2010).

19. "Gap Between Rich and Poor: World Income Inequality in 2002," *Infoplease,* http://www.infoplease.com/ipa/A0908770.html.

20. Terry J. Fitzgerald, "Where Has All the Income Gone? Middle American Incomes Rise Substantially Even While Inequality Increases," *The Federal Reserve Bank of Minneapolis,* September 2008, http://www.minneapolisfed.org/publications_papers/pub_display.cfm?id=4049.

21. OECD, *Growing Unequal?*

22. National Center for Children in Poverty, www.nccp.org.

23. Coalition for the Homeless, "How Many Children Are Homeless in America," *Hope for the Homeless,* http://cflhomeless.wordpress.com/2010/03/31/how-many-children-are-homeless-in-america/.

24. Christy Macy, *Workable: Tackling Youth Unemployment Crisis* (Baltimore: International Youth Foundation Spotlight, Spring 2009).

25. International Labour Organization, *The Financial and Economic Crisis: A Decent Work Response* (Washington, DC: International Labour Organization, 2009).

26. Ibid.

27. Jane Nelson and Simon Zadek, *Partnership Alchemy: New Social Partnership in Europe* (Copenhagen, Norway, The Copenhagen Center, March 2002).

28. Ben Schiller, *Business-NGO Partnerships* (London: Ethical Corporation, December 2005).

29. Stiglitz, *Making Globalization Work.*

30. The Corporate Citizen, *Interview with Daniel Runde: Outlook for Public-Private Global Development Initiatives.* Washington, DC, US Chamber of Commerce, March 2007.

31. Jane Nelson and David Prescott, *Partnering for Success: Business Perspectives on Multi Stakeholder Partnerships* (New York: World Economic Forum Global Corporate Citizen Initiative, January 2005).

32. Goodwill Industries International, http://www.goodwill.org.

33. Delancy Street Foundation, http://delanceystreetfoundation.org/.

34. Juma Ventures, http://www.jumaventures.org/.

35. Rubicon Programs, http://www.rubiconprograms.org/socialenterprise.html.

36. Cynthia Goytia, *FUNEDESIN, Case Study: Amazon Cacao Development Alliance, Partnering for Sustainable Agriculture and Rainforest Conservation* (London, UK: The Partnership Initiative, November 2005).

37. Shyamal Chowdhury, *Attaining Universal Access: Public-Private Partnership and Business-NGO Partnership,* ZEF Bonn (Bonn, Germany: Discussion Papers on Development Policy, July 2002).

38. Allen Bromberger, "A New Type of Hybrid," *Stanford Social Innovation Review* (Spring 2011):49–53.

39. Ibid.

40. Ibid.

41. Ibid.

42. Center on Philanthropy at Indiana University, *Giving USA 2009* (Bloomington, Ind: Giving USA Foundation, 2009).

43. Ibid.

44. "Giving Circle FAQs," *Forum of Regional Associations of Grantmakers,* http://www.givingforum.org/s_forum/doc.asp?CID=25&DID=5301.

45. "Number of Private Foundations in the United States, 2010," *National Center for Charitable Statistics,* http://www.nccsdataweb.urban.org/PubApps/profileDrillDown.php?state=US&rpt=PF.

46. Ibid.

47. *Key Facts About Family Foundations* (New York: Foundation Center, 2010).

48. Ibid.

49. "Venture Philanthropy," http://en.wikipedia.org/wiki/Venture_philanthropy.

50. "Performance Bonds: Who Succeeds and Gets Paid. Barack Obama Imports a Big Idea from Britain," *The Economist,* February 17, 2011.

51. *Key Facts About Family Foundations.*

52. Matthew Bishop and Michael Green, *Philanthrocapitalism: How the Rich Can Save the World* (New York, Bloomsbury Press, 2008).

53. Stephanie Strom, "The Philanthropreneurs," *New York Times,* November 13, 2006.

54. Ibid.

55. *Giving in Numbers* (Washington, DC: Committee Encouraging Corporate Philanthropy, 2008).

56. *Key Facts About Corporation Foundations.*

57. Ibid.

58. Noelle Barton and Caroline Preston, "America's Biggest Businesses Set Flat Giving Budgets," *Chronicle of Philanthropy* (August 7, 2010).

59. *Key Facts About Corporation Foundations.*

60. Ibid.

61. Barton and Preston, "America's Biggest Businesses Set Flat Giving Budgets."

62. Vanessa Wong, "America's Most Generous Corporate Foundations," *Bloomberg Business Week,* http://images.businessweek.com/ss/10/01/0114_most_generous_corporate_foundations/.

63. "A Brief History," *Community Foundations,* http://www.communityfoundations.net/page14094.html.

64. *Key Facts About Corporation Foundations.*

65. "A Brief History."

66. *Key Facts About Community Foundations.*

67. Manuel Contreras, ed., *Corporate Social Responsibility in the Promotion of Social Development* (Washington, DC: Inter-American Development Bank, 2004).

68. Corporation for National and Community Service, Office of Research and Policy Development, *Volunteering in America 2010: National, State, and City Information* (Washington, DC: Corporation for National and Community Service, June 2010).

69. Ibid.

70. Ibid.

71. Ibid.

72. Strom, "The Philanthropreneurs."

73. *Giving in Numbers.*

74. Points of Light Foundation, *Business Leadership Forum Monograph 2005: Senior Executives at Award-Winning Companies Share Keys for Successful Employee Volunteer Programs* (Washington, DC: Points of Light Foundation, 2005).

75. The Corporate Citizen, *Interview with Daniel Runde.*

76. Jane Nelson and David Prescott, *Business and the Millennium Development Goals: A Framework for Action* (New York: United Nations Development Program and International Business Leadership Forum, 2003).

77. Nelson and Prescott, *Partnering for Success.*

78. Nelson and Prescott, *Business and the Millennium Development Goals.*

79. "Global Partnerships," *USAID From the American People,* http://www.usaid.gov/our_work/global_partnerships/gda/.

3

NGO Trends

Overview

As previously mentioned it would be useful to have a typology of non-governmental organizations (NGOs) that captures the diversity of the NGO sector, but this is difficult because there are so many facets to examine. One challenge is that many NGOs have similar missions but very different operating approaches. For example, "saving the environment" is the mission for numerous NGOs, but an NGO such as Greenpeace may focus largely on advocacy efforts, whereas another such as the Audubon Society may focus more on preservation.

Where Do NGOs Belong?

There are at least three world views on where NGOs fit within society. NGOs can be seen (1) as a separate, independent sector; (2) as a subset of the private sector, both for-profit and non-profit; or (3) as a mixed sector. Although the details of these views are not discussed, it is important to understand their implications.

First, if NGOs are seen as a separate sector, it suggests that they embrace completely different practices than other public- or private-sector entities. This may inhibit partnerships among the sectors because NGOs could be perceived as having nothing in common with these institutions.[1]

Second, if NGOs are viewed as a subset of the private sector—for-profit and non-profit entities—then it implies that they utilize some common practices. Many for-profits and non-profits have similar ways of relating to their governance structures, accounting for resources, and interacting with stakeholders, even though they have different drivers—profits versus social or environmental outcomes.[2]

Third, if the NGO sector is seen as crossing sectors, with some NGOs operating more like for-profits and others functioning more like civil-society groups, this could mean that the NGO sector is much broader than traditional sectoral divisions and NGOs vary greatly in how they relate to different segments of society. It also suggests there may be more common areas among the sectors—public, private, and civil—leading to more partnership opportunities.[3]

NGO Organizational Structures

One key factor that is somewhat consistent across NGOs is the type of organizational structure that influences an NGO's mission, governance structure, decision-making processes, and *modus operandi*. There are two key types of organizational structures—membership-based organizations (MBOs) and constituency-based organizations (CBOs).

MBOs work to help their members directly by providing goods and services, or indirectly by promoting their members' concerns and values such as saving the environment. These entities are founded, at least in part, with member investments.[4] There are two types of members. Individual members are often part of religious organizations, professional associations such as the American Medical Association (AMA), or clubs like the Rotary. Institutional members represent their organizations and they commonly participate in affinity groups. For example, the American Council for Voluntary International Action (InterAction) consists largely of organizational members that are development NGOs, whereas Business for Social Responsibility (BSR) is composed of members that are socially responsible businesses.

Because the members are involved in establishing the NGO and are the main beneficiaries, these institutions are directly responsible and accountable to the membership.[5] MBOs work in a variety of sectors, for example (1) the environment (e.g., the Sierra Club), (2) health (e.g., the Christian Health Association of Nigeria), (3) protection of rights (e.g., the Children's Defense Fund), and (4) agriculture (e.g., farm cooperatives).

It is important to understand how decision-making processes are made or influenced by the members. Senior managers in these entities are equally accountable to the members and the board of directors. The board usually consists of elected members with some independent directors.[6] Thus members have significant voice and greatly influence decision-making in these NGOs.

"Constituency-based organizations" (CBOs) are started by investors or individuals. They exist to provide goods and services to third-party clients, so there is no membership body. Decision-making processes in CBOs require senior management to be primarily accountable to the board of directors, donors, and investors. Because the clients did not establish the CBOs, they have less ability to hold them fully accountable for their actions, unlike members in

MBOs.[7] That is not to say that these NGOs do not try to be accountable to their clients. Often other mechanisms, such as community advisory councils, are established, but these are not required to be accountable. CBOs also work in a variety of sectors, including (1) education (e.g., World Education), (2) microfinance (e.g., Freedom from Hunger), and (3) protection of rights (e.g., Planned Parenthood).

NGO Core Competencies

All organizations need key support systems to effectively operate, such as finance, human resources management, information management, fundraising, and monitoring and evaluation systems. However, this discussion focuses on the "core" business of NGOs. In general, NGO core businesses can be classified into three categories: (1) advocacy and policy change, (2) research and consulting, and (3) operations and service provision.

Advocacy and Policy Change

NGOs with advocacy and policy change as a core business often work to (1) identify negative practices and violations by governments and businesses (e.g., Nestlé's aggressive promotion of infant formula to hospitals in lieu of healthier breast milk); (2) raise both political and public awareness about these issues; and (3) work to ensure that changes in laws, policies, and practices are developed, implemented, and sustained.

These entities often undertake policy analysis; conduct research; work to change development and political processes to expand the inclusion of disadvantaged groups; advocate for changes in governmental and multilateral polices; and undertake advocacy campaigns, protests, and boycotts against government, multilaterals, and companies. Some NGOs focus largely on campaigns, whereas others also play an important role in the change process and monitor the adoption and progress of new practices. Both play a vital function in society.

Research and Consulting

NGOs that have research or consulting as their core business often play an intermediary role with both advocacy and operational NGOs as well as with businesses, governments, and multilaterals. These entities—think tanks, academic institutions, and consulting firms:

- Conduct vital policy, social, economic, and environmental research and analysis.

- Provide third-party monitoring and certification (e.g., Social Accountability International).
- Work with entities to spearhead or support changes within companies like BSR.
- Serve as brokers among entities with conflicting objectives.

Operations and Service Provision

Operational NGOs implement programs or provide services through three main mechanisms. First, they may provide social, economic, or environmental services to clients or members. Second, they work with individuals or community groups to build their capacity to demand access to social, economic, or environmental quality services. Third, they work with local institutions to build their capacity to provide better access to high quality services.

Some NGOs, such as World Education, have a single-sector focus. Other NGOs may be multi-sectoral, focusing on many sectors such as agriculture, education, health, and microfinance (e.g., CARE or Plan International). Although these core businesses are described separately here, many NGOs are strong in several core business areas. All of these core business areas can be utilized by both MBOs and CBOs. It should be noted that the local operating environment, including local laws, policies, donors, security, and the issues being addressed (e.g., girls' education, agriculture) greatly affect how the core business strategies are implemented. Table 3.1 provides some examples of membership-based and constituency-based NGOs by their primary core business.

NGO Trends

Seven key trends influence NGO partnerships with corporations. Those trends are (1) the growth of the NGO sector, (2) the increasing technical expertise and use of business methods in operations, (3) internal conflicts of interest, (4) technology advances, (5) changes in revenue streams, (6) greater accountability, and (7) a leadership vacuum.

Growth of the NGO Sector

The number of NGOs worldwide has mushroomed over the last few decades, from an estimated 23,600 in 1991 to 44,000 in 1999.[8] By 2007, it was estimated that there were between 4 and 5 million NGOs worldwide; India alone had between 1 and 2 million NGOs, and the United States had about 1.8 million.[9] The number of NGOs operating internationally, sometimes called "INGOs," is estimated at 40,000. In the United States, there is a surplus of

Table 3.1
NGO Function by Type of NGO Structure

NGO Structure	NGO Function: Advocacy and Policy Change	Research and Consulting	Operations and Service
Individual membership based	• *Advocate for their members or their interests* National Rifle Association, GreenPeace, trade unions	• *Support for their members*	• *Provides services to their members* American Automobile Association, American Association of Retired Persons
Organizational membership based	• *Advocate for their members or their interests* InterAction, CONGO	• *Support for their members* World Economic Forum, Ethical Trading Initiative, Business for Social Responsibility	• *Provide services to their members* The CORE Group
Constituency based	• *Advocate for clients* Population Action International, Children's Defense Fund	• *Support for clients* Aspen Institute, Transparency International	• *Provide services to clients* CARE, Save the Children, Médecins Sans Frontières

NGOs. A 2005 Stanford study found that there were about 27,500 NGOs in the San Francisco Bay Area, but only 36% (9,900) of these NGOs had annual revenues greater than $25,000, which requires them to file with the Internal Revenue Service (IRS).[10]

In general, U.S.-based NGOs are overwhelmingly small and relatively young; 42% of NGOs have been operational for less than 10 years, with median annual expenses of $100,000.[11] Over the next five years, there will probably be a consolidation phase among NGOs that will see (1) some mergers of NGOs or at least combined administrative structures to gain cost reductions, (2) transition of responsibilities from northern-based NGOs to southern-based NGOs, and (3) closure of some small NGOs.

Merging NGOs is usually quite complicated, with many board and managerial issues. In addition, a merger may not solve the economic issues at the heart of the matter. Two examples of this consolidation have already happened in California. First, the San Francisco Food Bank merged with the Marin Food Bank. Since 2008, the Marin Food Bank found itself unable to meet the increased demand resulting from the recent economic downturn, forcing them to increasingly rely on the San Francisco Food Bank for their food provision and distribution. As a result, they decided to merge with the San Francisco Food Bank to be able to continue to provide services to populations who greatly needed their services. In 2010, the Marin Community Foundation provided $200,000 to support the operational and planning costs to facilitate the merger and the relationship was finalized in 2010.[12]

Another example is the Walden House's acquisition of the historic Haight Ashbury Free Clinics, which provide world-class substance abuse and mental health treatment. In 2008, the Free Clinics suffered a 50% funding reduction from the city of San Francisco, so they could no longer go it alone, leaving many people without services. Walden House provides residential and outpatient substance abuse and mental health programs. Thus it made perfect sense for the two organizations to join forces.[13]

Increased Technical Expertise and Business Methods

There has been a rise in NGOs' technical ability to provide sophisticated analysis and information that can be crucial for key policy, trade agreements, and programmatic and business decisions. This has evolved because of (1) the increasing size of portfolios that NGOs manage, (2) higher education and skills of NGO staff, (3) increasing accountability required by stakeholders and donors, and (4) greater competition to secure funding.

As a group, NGOs now deliver more aid than the entire United Nations (UN) system. A growing share of development spending, emergency relief, and foreign aid passes through NGOs. Between 1990 and 1994, the proportion of the European Union's relief aid channeled through NGOs rose from 47% to 67%. NGOs have become "the most important constituency for the activities of development aid agencies."[14]

Conflicting Views Within NGOs

Many NGOs are worried that working with corporations will negatively affect their brand and credibility. Although it is true that there are risks to working with corporations, there are also benefits, which are further discussed in Chapter 5. Many NGOs do not have clear guidelines on how they want to work with corporations, such as engagement strategies or due diligence processes, to steer them through the process. More NGOs are starting to develop and refine their corporate engagement strategies, but this is still new for many NGOs, particularly southern NGOs. (Corporate engagement strategies and due diligence processes are further discussed in Chapter 9.)

Within NGOs, different departments often have varying reward systems for their staff. For example, development or fundraising staff usually have annual targets for raising funds and their incentives are based on these achievements. On the other hand, program staff may focus more on the nature of the partnerships such as how a partner may help them address climate change, regardless of funding levels. Incentives for these staff are based on the partnership's ability to achieve its results. These differences in reward systems may mean that there is limited cooperation between units in developing and implementing the partnership. As a result, there may be internal struggles regarding decisions about corporate partnerships. NGOs need to understand how these various incentives may affect partnerships with other organizations so these relationships can be maximized to achieve their results.

There may also be differences in perceptions between the NGO management and staff and their individual donors and members regarding how they think the NGO should operate. For example, a partnership was developed between the AMA and Sunbeam home products. The AMA staff thought this was a great opportunity and agreed to the partnership. However, once the partnership was announced, the AMA membership (individual doctors) and consumer groups were outraged and the AMA board chair revoked the partnership. (This case is further discussed in Chapter 5.)

Advances in Information, Communication, and Technology

The advancement in information, communication, and technology (ICT) has dramatically changed how NGOs operate. Now information can be dispersed quickly and relatively cheaply through new media, such as Facebook, text messaging, and Skype, creating new partnerships between different groups in developed and developing countries.

A survey of NGO mobile technology use found that 86% of NGO employees use mobile technology in their work, and 25% believe it has revolutionized the way their organizations work. The most common uses of mobile technology by NGO workers are voice calls (90%) and text messaging (83%). More sophisticated uses, such as mapping (10%), data analysis (8%), and inventory management (8%) also were reported.[15] Text messaging has also helped fundraising campaigns. Mobile giving is quite new. One of the first campaigns was a 10-second United Way public service announcement that played during the 2008 Super Bowl, raising a cool $10,000 in 10 seconds from $5 donations. In 2010, the American Red Cross raised $22 million through text message donations by appealing to the public for $10 donations in response to the Haiti earthquake.[16]

Technology has also played a key role in improved coordination among NGOs as well as with governments and businesses. NGO umbrella groups such as the Steering Committee for Humanitarian Response, InterAction, and Voluntary Organisations in Cooperation in Emergencies have served as forums for dialogue and information sharing, and as vehicles for joint advocacy that they could not have achieved without technology.

Another example is Microsoft's "Imagine Cup Solve This," a new program to provide inspiration for students looking to help solve the world's toughest problems. In the spirit of crowdsourcing, government agencies and NGOs now will be able to seek the help of the brilliant and passionate students competing in Microsoft's Imagine Cup, the world's premier student technology competition, to develop innovative solutions to real-world problems.[17]

Another type of technology that has helped coordination and implementation is "crowdsourcing," which is an act of outsourcing tasks traditionally performed by an employee or contractor to an undefined, large group of people or community (a crowd), through an open call.[18] For example, Ushahidi, created in Africa by Africans, used a crowdsourcing platform to gather information and report about disasters in real time.[19]

Changes in Revenue Sources

There is a large variation in the types and sources of funding that NGOs can receive, which are greatly influenced by the type of NGO and their modus operandi. Partners need to understand four key components of an NGO's resource base, including (1) where an NGO is registered, (2) type of funding and revenue streams that they can accept, (3) how operating (overhead) costs are calculated, and (4) new sources of revenue and capital that are being developed.

First, it is important to understand where an NGO is registered because it influences (1) the type of resources that it can accept, such as local versus foreign currency; (2) the way the NGO can operate, which may include ownership of property and licensing agreements; and (3) the types of activities and programs that can be undertaken.

Second, most NGOs receive funds from many different sources that are often accompanied by their own rules and regulations requiring a variety of accounting, monitoring and evaluation, and reporting mechanisms that can be very time consuming. Studies found that an NGO with an annual budget of $30 million can have as many as 20 different funding sources with different requirements in terms of billing, timing, eligibility, and reporting. These differences greatly increase the administrative burden of managing these programs. Some examples of funding sources include:

- Individual sponsorship programs such as Save the Children and Kiva
- Religious support like World Vision and Catholic Relief Services
- NGOs' self-generated revenues
- Multilateral grants through organizations like the UN and World Bank
- Bilateral grants from government agencies such as the U.S. government (USAID) or British government (Department For International Development)
- Private foundations such as the Bill and Melinda Gates Foundation and the Moore Foundation
- Corporations through foundation donations, licensing, and cause-related marketing campaigns
- Private individual donors

In addition, each different revenue stream or donor comes with its own set of financial and reporting requirements. In addition, some donors want to fund their own small projects rather than investing in larger, more cost-effective projects to achieve their results. Although reporting is important, the diversity of donor requirements and philosophies associated with the funding requires NGOs to spend more time doing administrative tasks that could be spent implementing program activities.

NGO self-generated and private grants usually offer the greatest flexibility, whereas contracts are more prescriptive. Usually, more self-generated or private funding—often called "unrestricted funding"—allows the NGO greater flexibility to innovate and quickly respond to a changing environment. Many donors only provide annual funding, rather than multi-year funding, which limits the ability to effectively plan and implement programs that often require several years to see results.

The Stanford NGO study found that 62% of California NGOs' funding came from program fees that include museum charges, university tuition, training fees, and medical clinic fees. Another 9% came from income-generation activities that were not directly related to their mission, such as sales through a café, selling souvenirs, or assets management.[20]

Third, there is often a significant misunderstanding regarding "NGO overhead." This is the cost of operating the NGO, which includes direct costs such as a portion of rent, utilities, and information systems. However, many donors do not see this as a business necessity, which limits the NGO's operating budgets and reduces their potential effect.

Fourth, although for-profit companies have several options to raise capital, such as loans, selling shares if publically traded, or tapping other types of investors such as venture capitalists, NGOs do not have access to these capital markets. There is greater recognition that this lack of access to long-term investment mechanisms places NGOs at a disadvantage. As a result, there is a growing interest in the private sector and investment community to develop new approaches, financial mechanisms, and alternative markets for NGOs and social enterprises to be able to access more reliable investment options based on financial and social returns.

Venture philanthropy or philanthrocapitalism and Social Impact Bonds are some of the new approaches discussed in the previous chapter. The term "patient capital" is often used to describe funding that seeks to bridge the gap between the efficiency and scale of market-based approaches (financial returns) and the social effect of pure philanthropy. Investor networks were developed as investment mechanisms to support companies that worked in low-income and distressed communities. One example is the Investors' Circle, a network of angel investors, venture capitalists, and foundations, that made investments, rather than donations, to social enterprises. Between 1992 and 2000, this group directed more than $130 million worth of investments to 200 companies.[21] Another example is the Community Development Venture Capital Alliance, which developed a network of venture funds that invest in companies in low-income communities that create jobs and support community development.[22] Since this time there has been a growth of organizations, both for-profit such as Good Capital and non-profit such as Acumen Fund.

Good Capital, established in 2006, is an investment firm that increases the flow of capital to innovative ventures, creating market-based solutions to deal with inequality and poverty. Good Capital uses a high-engagement model, investing in the most promising social enterprises as well as providing them the tools and guidance they need to succeed.[23] In addition, Good Capital actively leads the development of the emerging social capital market. They share a deep commitment to the creation of a new, informed, and passionate world of investing that strategically moves more capital to good. In 2009, Good Capital helped create the first social capital (SoCap) conference, which brought together the broad ecosystem of funders, foundations, and individual investors and donors with companies, NGOs, and social entrepreneurs who use business to develop market-based solutions to inequality, poverty, and other social problems.[24]

Greater Accountability

Although most NGOs operate within an ethical framework, the sector has also suffered from a number of scandals that have made many business people and the general public call for greater accountability. Most of these scandals have focused on mismanagement of funds. For instance, the 1992 investigation into the United Way chief executive officer's misuse of funds resulted in his jail sentence.[25]

Another type of scandal can occur when an NGO loses the trust of its supporters. For example, in 1998 the *Chicago Tribune* published its yearlong inquiry into four leading child-sponsorship organizations. The article stated, "sponsored children often received few or no benefits and, in the worst cases, children had been dead for years while unwitting donors continued to sponsor them."[26] Child-sponsorship agencies vigorously defended their approach, maintaining that their donors clearly understand that their money does not go to benefit a specific child, but to the broader community to support schools, water systems, and health services in which the children live.[27]

Even though NGOs are still very trusted, their reputation is falling along with trust in other parts of society. For example, the 2011 Edelman Trust Barometer asked the U.S. general public, "How much do you trust NGOs to do what is right?" The survey found a decline from 63% of respondents who replied that they trusted NGOs in 2008 to 55% in 2011.[28] NGOs need to practice what they preach, meaning managing their budgets, achieving their missions better, and contributing more to society.[29] As a response to concerns about NGO accountability, the American Enterprise Institute and the Federalist Society for Law and Public Policy launched NGO Watch to focus on "NGO and international organization's transparency and accountability."[30] An American Enterprise Institute press release stated,

> [T]he proliferation of international policymaking organizations has intensified and institutionalized the influence of global governance. Supra-state and non-state actors, such as the UN, NGOs, and international financial institutions, have risen in prominence

> and power, bringing with them internationalist agendas that are challenging the abilities of nation states to determine their own domestic policies and priorities.[31]

Most NGOs in the developed world have at least achieved financial transparency as a result of a mix of public and private oversight, regulation, and accreditation. For example, every NGO based in the United States must file its finances annually with the IRS and make these documents publicly available. If an NGO receives federal funds, it must be annually audited (Office of Management and Budget 133) by an independent accounting firm.

After 9/11, there was a fear that terrorists could use NGOs as a front for their operations. In addition, some highly publicized cases of NGO abuse have damaged the sector's credibility. Thus the limited transparency in the NGO sector is perhaps its greatest vulnerability and must be addressed to ensure the integrity and continuity of the work of NGOs.

The issue of funding and accountability becomes more complex when an NGO operates across national borders. It is much more challenging to accurately track the funding of NGOs based outside the United States, Europe, Japan, and Australia. However, some of the regulations that have been put into place have greatly constrained NGOs from providing any services, particularly small and local NGOs.

Accountability includes transparent information on accounting, governance, and management practices. NGO credibility is also needed to help create institutional arrangements for global governance in an interdependent world. For NGOs, there are four key accountability concerns: (1) misuse of resources, (2) response to beneficiaries, (3) greater advocacy role, and (4) ability to address the key problems. Currently, NGOs must comply with two aspects of the Sarbanes-Oxley Act: They must ensure whistle blower protection and financial documentation management and preservation.

First, it is clear that there have been cases of NGO misconduct—particularly, (mis)management of funds—that have brought into question the sector's legitimacy and congruency with the values they promote. Thus, they need to ensure adequate financial management systems to ensure accountability and transparency.

Second, some NGOs have also ignored the fact that they are stewards of funding, and are thus answerable to key stakeholders and the constituencies they serve. Although it can be a challenge to meet the needs of many diverse groups, NGOs must figure out how to be accountable to them. The expectations of NGOs vary based on the local context and type of intervention. For example, stakeholder expectations will be different for a human rights organization versus an environmental organization.[32]

Third, more vocal advocacy by NGOs has directly challenged the work of corporations, governments, and international organizations, which in turn has elicited counterattacks. NGOs need to ensure that they are implementing the same ethical principles that they criticize others for not implementing.

Fourth, concerns about the role and accountability of NGOs have been voiced from different quarters in recent years. Some donors, governments, corporations, and international agencies raise important questions about NGOs' effectiveness and the legitimacy of their advocacy. A greater focus on results enables NGOs to participate in the new funding models.

Several efforts have been undertaken to strengthen NGO accountability, as discussed in the following text.

- In 1995, the Commonwealth Foundation, with the support of the UN, published *NGO Guidelines for Good Policy and Practice,* the result of three years of research and consultation. It includes guidelines for governments dealing with NGOs, for NGOs themselves, for the policy and practice of funders, for northern NGOs and international agencies, and a plan of action for the implementation of the guidelines.
- In response to the *Chicago Tribune* inquiry, InterAction assisted the child-sponsorship NGOs to develop and adopt the *Social Accountability International's Child Survival Code of Conduct.*
- The draft Institute of Charity Fundraising Managers' *Donors' Rights Charter* sets out high professional standards for development professionals.
- In 1998, the South African National NGO Coalition adopted the *Code of Conduct for International Funding Agencies Working in South Africa.*
- The Sphere Project produced the *Humanitarian Charter and Minimum Standards in Disaster Response,* which guides behaviors during an international disaster response.

The international NGO Accountability Charter, established in 2003, grew out of deliberations among prominent civil society leaders. The Charter demonstrated the commitment of eleven leading international NGOs to uphold the highest standards of moral and professional conduct in all their policies, activities, and operations. In addition, they urged their partner organizations and networks to adopt the Charter.[33]

Four states have passed NGO integrity acts—Connecticut, California, Massachusetts, and New Hampshire. These laws focus largely on financial management and governance mechanisms rather than integrity per se. In addition, many NGOs have embraced the relevant aspects of the Sarbanes-Oxley Act in terms of good governance and financial management practices.

Although these codes are a step in the right direction, they have been adopted by only a relatively small number of NGOs. In addition, some of the international standards have allowed less legitimate NGOs to remain operational, undermining the effectiveness of credible NGOs. Thus accountability is still a work in progress, requiring a larger share of the NGO sector to accept these practices as normal operating procedures.

Leadership Vacuum

During the past decade, there has been a rising sense of alarm in the NGO sector about its future leadership. Studies point to an impending crisis, with roughly 75% of NGO executive directors reporting that they plan to leave their jobs within the next five years. A 2009 Bridgespan study found that over the next decade, NGOs will need to attract and develop some 640,000 new senior managers—2.4 times the number currently employed. In addition, by 2016, these organizations will need almost 80,000 new senior managers per year.[34,35] Although there is some interest among business professionals in working for NGOs, the difference in pay, up to 40% less than private sector salaries, can be a disincentive.[36] Leadership is and will continue to be a vital element for NGOs to successfully manage problems that are more complex, such as varied funding streams and diverse stakeholder issues.

Some creative solutions to address this leadership vacuum have included foundations supporting coaching of NGO executives to further their leadership skills. In addition, some companies "loan" their executives to work at NGOs. For example, United Parcel Service (UPS) loans executives to the United Way to expand solicitation efforts, reach new markets, and broaden the base of community giving. This keeps fundraising costs low by maximizing staff and volunteer efforts. In return, United Way provides a unique management program that develops sales and executive leadership skills and an understanding of community organization for UPS executives.[37]

Summary of NGO Trends

In summary, seven key trends influence NGO partnerships with corporations. Those trends are (1) the growth of the NGO sector, (2) increasing technical expertise of NGOs, (3) advances in ICT, (4) changes in revenue streams, (5) conflicting views about working with corporations, (6) greater accountability, and (7) a leadership vacuum.

- *Growth of the NGO sector:* Many NGOs are young organizations that are small, although the sector also has many very sophisticated, mature organizations with a large presence and asset base. This means that there is greater competition among a more diverse pool of NGOs for funding and partnerships. Thus NGOs need to better articulate the value that they can bring to cross-sectoral partnerships, particularly in terms of return on investment and relevant business benefits such as cost savings, access to markets, or innovations.
- *Increased technical expertise:* As the NGO sector has evolved, there has been a dramatic growth in financial resources, development of technical capacities, and efficiencies in operating structures and systems. Many NGOs manage large projects and portfolios across different sectors and locations, and have developed innovative approaches that have changed development models and market systems. This has created many more opportunities for NGOs to work with different partners, including companies, investors, and other stakeholders in new ways, which will continue into the future. There also has been a shift in the number and type of revenues streams for NGOs. NGOs have many different revenue sources, which is important for their sustainability. However, these revenues often have different reporting requirements, which can be time-consuming for the NGO. As government funds have become more limited, with greater requirements for matching funds, many NGOs have sought a greater role with the private sector. Although many NGOs traditionally had philanthropic relationships with companies, there has been a growing interest in developing partnerships that extend beyond philanthropic gifts to include access to skills, technologies, and networks.

- *Advances in ICT:* Advances in ICT have greatly helped NGOs, particularly smaller NGOs in less developed countries, to communicate with their stakeholders, mobilize resources, report on activities, and hold others accountable for their actions. For example, NGOs have been able to use new technologies such as geographic information system mapping to find people after disasters, such as the Haiti earthquake, or track health cases in an epidemic such as swine flu. Technologic advances, such as cell phones, have allowed less developed countries to leapfrog over older technology. Two examples of cell phone use include (1) providing access to market information to poor rural farmers who previously never had access to this information, and (2) programming health protocols to assist health providers in giving care to their clients in remote areas. Although new technologies are being developed at a rapid pace, there is often not equal access to these advances. NGOs can play a vital role in ensuring that new technologies can be adapted so that disadvantaged groups who may be less educated or who do not have access to financial capital or electricity can benefit from these new developments.
- *Changes in revenue streams:* NGOs have to manage a variety of funds from many different sources that often have different reporting and administrative requirements. Although reporting is important, these differences can be very time consuming and distract from program implementation and achieving results. NGOs need to articulate these concerns to their partners to streamline these efforts across revenue streams to ensure that their focus is on achieving results while ensuring accountability and good stewardship.
- Many hybrid organizational models and new funding opportunities are being created, including access to longer-term capital. NGOs need to evaluate these different options to see what makes the most sense for their organizational objectives. In addition, NGOs need to learn how to participate in these opportunities, such as Social Impact Bonds, which will probably require a greater focus on financial as well as social and environmental results.
- *Conflicting views about working with corporations:* One of the key issues that influence NGO-corporate partnerships is an NGO's

culture and its view about working with corporations. Some NGOs are concerned that working with corporations will damage their reputation or will result in them being perceived as "selling out." This may be of particular concern among NGOs that either campaigned against business or that have little experience with business as they transition to develop closer relationships with the private sector.

- Conflicting views about working with corporations can be held by employees, beneficiaries, members, and donors. Even if an NGO has a clear policy of working with corporations, management needs to understand that individuals within the NGO or partner NGOs may have differing views about this strategy, which can influence NGO-corporate partnerships. It is important for NGOs to allow their staff to air their differences and work through these issues to ensure that effective partnerships can be developed. As previously mentioned, units within NGOs may have different drivers and incentives that may benefit or hinder NGO-corporate partnerships. This is an area that each NGO will need to review to understand how personnel and systems can be aligned to support effective partnerships.
- Individual members and donors also have views in terms of how they think an NGO should operate. These expectations can jeopardize partnerships if not appropriately managed. This suggests that the NGO needs to clearly and regularly articulate its strategy to various stakeholder groups.
- *Greater accountability:* In light of all these issues, many stakeholders have called for greater accountability among NGOs, which is an important area that NGOs need to pay greater attention to in the future. Efforts are underway in many states to develop integrity acts or codes of conduct to guide NGO operations. NGOs need to ensure that they are accountable to their various stakeholders and ensure transparency of their actions. In terms of NGO-corporate partnerships, more companies are conducting "due diligence" processes on the NGOs that they are considering working with and the expectations of NGOs are likely to increase in the future.
- *Leadership vacuum:* A key factor in whether NGOs will be successful in managing all these trends is the availability of the NGO sector's leaders. The NGO sector is facing a significant

leadership gap. Although many business people are interested in working in the NGO sector, the difference in salaries is often a disincentive. This could be a limitation of NGO-corporate partnerships because substantial partnerships require involvement of senior management of the key organizations.

Notes

1. David Korten, *Getting to the 21st Century: Voluntary Action and the Global Agenda* (Bloomfield, Conn.: Kumarian Press, 1990).

2. Norman Uphoff, "Why Are NGOs Not a Third Sector? A Sectoral Analysis With Some Thoughts on Accountability, Sustainability and Evaluation," in *Beyond the Magic Bullet: NGO Performance and Accountability in the Post-Cold War World,* ed. Michael Edwards and David Hulme (Bloomfield, Conn.: Kumarian Press, 1996).

3. Ibid.

4. Ibid.

5. Ibid.

6. Ibid.

7. Ibid.

8. Helmut Anheier, Marlies Glasius, and Mary Kaldor, eds., *Global Civil Society* (Oxford, UK: Oxford University Press, 2001).

9. "Non-governmental Organization," *New World Encyclopedia,* http://www.newworldencyclopedia.org/entry/NGO.

10. Denise Gammal, Caroline Simard, Hokyu Hwang, and Walter Powell, *Managing Through Challenges: A Profile of San Francisco Bay Area Non-Profits* (Palo Alto, Calif.: Stanford Business School, August 2005).

11. Ibid.

12. Ruth McCambridge, "Merger Fever in San Francisco," *Nonprofit Quarterly,* January 7, 2011, http://www.nonprofitquarterly.org/index.php?option=com_content&view=article&id=8616&Itemid=136.

13. Ibid.

14. "Anybody Who's Anybody Is an NGO These Days," *Economist,* January 29, 2000.

15. Sheila Kinkade and Katrin Verclas, *Wireless Technology for Social Change* (Washington, DC, and Berkshire, UK: UN Foundation, and Vodafone Group Foundation Partnership, 2008).

16. Joanne Fritz, "Text-to-Give Fundraising Campaigns Take Off: Haiti Earthquake Propels Mobile Giving to New Highs," *About.com,* http://nonprofit.about.com/od/fundraising/a/mobilegivingtakesoff.htm.

17. "Inspired by Crowdsourcing, Imagine Cup Solve This Enables Students to Help IGOs, NGOs and Nonprofits," *PR Newswire,* http://www.prnewswire.com/news-releases/inspired-by-crowdsourcing-imagine-cup-solve-this-enables-students-to-help-igos-ngos-and-nonprofits-109872079.html.

18. "Crowdsourcing," *Wikipedia,* http://en.wikipedia.org/wiki/Crowdsourcing.

19. Ushahidi, http://www.ushahidi.com.

20. Gammal, Simard, Hwang, and Powell, *Managing Through Challenges: A Profile of San Francisco Bay Area Non-Profits.*

21. Investors' Circle, http://www.investorscircle.net/.

22. Community Development Venture Capital Alliance, http://www.cdvca.org/.

23. Ibid.

24. Acumen Fund, http://www.acumenfund.org/about-us/what-is-patient-capital.html.

25. Margaret Gibelman, "Very Public Scandals: An Analysis of How and Why NGOs Get in Trouble: A Working Paper," Paper presented at the Fourth International Society for Third-Sector Research Conference, Dublin, Ireland, July 7, 2000.

26. Lisa Anderson, "Child Sponsorship Programs—Idea of Saving One Child Is Marketing Myth," *Chicago Tribune,* March 16, 1998.

27. Ibid.

28. 2011 Edelman Trust Barometer, http://www.edelman.com/trust/2011/.

29. Jem Bendell, *Debating NGO Accountability: NGLS Development Dossier* (New York: UN, 2006).

30. American Enterprise Institute, *Dictating Norms: Who Decides What Is Right for the World? The Inauguration of Global Governance Watch* (Washington, DC: American Enterprise Institute, April 14, 2008).

31. Ibid.

32. Lisa Jordan and P. van Tuijl, eds., *NGO Accountability: Politics, Principles and Innovations* (London: Earthscan, 2006).

33. NGO Accountability Charter, http://www.ingoaccountabilitycharter.org.

34. Thomas Tierney, *The Nonprofit Sector's Leadership Deficit* (Boston, Mass.: Bridgespan, 2009).

35. Laura Otting, *Transitioning to the Nonprofit Sector* (New York: Kaplan, 2007).

36. Andrea Kay, "Nonprofit Groups Pay Competitive Salaries," *Hartford Business Journal,* November 1, 2007, http://www.hartfordbusiness.com/news3546.html.

37. "United Way and UPS Revolutionize CSR Partnerships," *Justmeans,* http://www.justmeans.com/United-Way-UPS-Revolutionize-CSR-Partnerships/24256.html.

4

Business Trends

Overview of the Business Sector

Before discussing the key business trends, it is useful to have a common understanding of the core underlying business objectives. These are determined by (1) the business's size, (2) where the business operates, and (3) the type of funding the business receives. Businesses are often classified as small (0–100 employees), medium (100–250 employees), or large (>250 employees), although this varies by country. These organizations can operate at the local, regional, and national levels within one country, often called "domestic companies," or "multinational corporations" (MNCs) can work in countries outside their headquarter country. The United Nations (UN) refers to these entities as "transnational corporations." Lastly, companies can be privately held or publically traded through stock markets. Publically traded companies (estimated around 60,000 worldwide) are usually larger in terms of employees, assets, and revenues. In contrast, privately held companies (estimates are around 10 million worldwide) are smaller in size, although they have a larger share of the global market.[1] One factor that has changed over the last decade is who owns these companies. In 2008, the Center for Women's Business Research found that 40% of all businesses based in the United States were women-owned. These entities generated $1.9 trillion in annual sales and employed 13 million people in 2008.[2]

Five key business trends include (1) the growth of the private sector, (2) investing priorities, (3) changes in consumer expectations and buying practices, (4) growth of corporate social responsibility (CSR), and (5) greater accountability.

Business Trends

Growth of the Private Sector

There has been a dramatic growth of the private sector relative to other sectors in society. In addition, the growth of MNCs (12.5%) has been sixfold that of the rest of the private sector (2.5%). Most MNCs are headquartered in eight developed countries: the United States, Japan, Germany, Great Britain, the Netherlands, France, Switzerland, and Sweden. The growth of MNCs has occurred in terms of the number of companies, from 1,572 in 1999 to 4,008 in 2008, as well as in terms of total sales, increasing from $50 billion in 1999 to $200 billion in 2008.[3] Estimates indicate that the revenues of 300 MNCs represent 51% of the largest 100 economies.[4] Some key facts about MNCs include:

- MNCs control 50% of all oil extraction and refining processes, and a similar proportion of the extraction, refining, and marketing of gas and coal production.
- Six companies account for 63% of the aluminium mine capacity, 66% of the refining capacity, and 54% of the smelting capacity.
- MNCs control 80% of land worldwide that is cultivated for export-oriented crops, often displacing local food crop production and small farms.
- More than 30% of global trade is "intra-firm," meaning it occurs between units of the same corporation.[5,6]

Much of the private sector's growth has been through mergers and acquisitions (M&As), resulting in the consolidation of the industries described previously. In 2006, the United States set a record with M&As totaling $1.2 trillion, a 23% increase from 2005. In 2008, there were almost 2,000 M&As, and between January and October 2009, an additional 1,800 deals were made despite the economic downturn. The average size of these deals was between $300 and $350 million.[7]

This concentration of wealth and power in the hands of a few companies in key industries is worrisome for three reasons. First, it has resulted in less competition rather than more, which was the promise of globalization. Second, studies show that 50% of all the acquiring companies paid more for the target firms than they were worth, ignoring important warning signs about the deal. Third, the current failure rate of M&As is between 50% and 80%. If companies continue to use M&As as their main growth strategy without addressing key structural and integration issues, the results will continue to be significantly below expectations.[8]

Changing Investor Roles and Priorities: Socially Responsible Investing

In the past few decades, investors have expected companies to do more than just make a profit. They have integrated their personal values and societal concerns into their investment strategies. Socially responsible investing (SRI) is a way for an investor to support companies that positively address environmental and social factors as well as provide financial returns.

There is a sizable and fast-growing number of "socially responsible" investors, both individual and institutional. SRI-managed assets grew from $639 billion in 1995 to $2.29 trillion in 2005, increasing faster than all other types of investing. In 2008, SRI funds composed 11% of the $25.1 trillion professionally managed assets.[9]

Three key SRI strategies have evolved over the years: screening stocks, shareholder advocacy and resolutions, and community investments to either reward or punish corporate practices.

"Screening stocks" uses key social and environmental criteria, as well as financial performance, for the inclusion or exclusion of companies in investment portfolios. Socially concerned investors generally seek to own profitable companies with (1) respectable employee relations, (2) strong records of community involvement, (3) excellent environmental impact policies and practices, (4) respect for human rights around the world, and (5) safe and useful products. Conversely, they often avoid investments in those firms that fall short in these areas. Some investors avoid specific industries altogether, such as alcohol and tobacco, which are perceived to have a negative effect on society. Studies have found that 80% of Americans said they would refuse to buy the company's stock if a company was found to have negative practices.[10] The number of socially screened mutual funds in the United States grew from 55 in 1995 to 260 in 2007.[11] The 2010 Social Investment Forum report showed that SRI topped $3 trillion, reaching $1 out of every $8 under professional management, growing by 13%, whereas overall assets only increased by 1%.[12]

Pension funds have traditionally shied away from SRI funds on the grounds that negative screening conflicts with their fiduciary duty to act in investors' best interest. By excluding investment into arms, pornography, gambling, or tobacco, which is what many SRI funds do, the investment pool is reduced, risking inferior returns. Rather than addressing environmental, social, and governance (ESG) issues via asset allocation, larger institutional pension funds prefer to engage with their existing assets, influencing corporate behavior through their major shareholder status. This approach has been favored by pension funds such as the California Public Employees Retirement System (CalPERS), the Dutch ABP fund, and Norway's government pension fund, but this is starting to change. A 2005 Freshfields Bruckhaus Deringer report found that that fiduciary duty requires ESG factors to be considered in cases in which there is the potential for material and financial effects from those factors. According to Matt Christensen, executive director of the European Social Investment Forum, "many pension funds are starting to 'take a toe dip' on SRI by including only one screen, often weapons, and leaving it at that. Right now there is a lot of breadth, but no real depth to SRI commitments from pension funds."[13]

In recent years, shareholders have had more influence on corporate practices through "shareholder advocacy." Studies have found that 80% of Americans would consider selling their existing stock if a company is identified as having bad practices.[14] Thus actions by shareholders, using their status as part-owners of companies to influence corporate behavior, has proven to be a powerful tool to improve a corporation's social and environmental records.

Historically, very few resolutions have achieved majority shareholder votes at corporate annual meetings. In fact, many votes only include 5% to 25% of shareholders.[15] However, even those seemingly low numbers represent a significant number of unhappy shareholders. Resolutions are often coordinated with consumer and media campaigns. Thus they may represent damage to a company's reputation and branding, and a potential loss of revenue through negative publicity, consumer boycotts, and loss of investor confidence. In fact, the mere act of filing a proposal has prompted some companies to amend their policies.

One important NGO coalition that has influenced social investing and shareholder resolutions is the Interfaith Center on Corporate Responsibility (ICCR). ICCR has 300 member organizations with equity market investments of over $130 billion. This 40-year coalition influences other social investors who represent $1 trillion in corporate equity.[16] In 2010, ICCR filed a total of 308 shareowner resolutions with corporations in their investment portfolios, addressing issues across the ESG spectrum. In addition, ICCR members engaged in 345 corporate dialogues with 248 companies and withdrew dozens of resolutions following positive engagements with corporate management.[17]

"Community investment" addresses the many communities around the world that lack affordable housing, childcare, health care, and jobs that pay a living wage. Several laws, such as the Community Reinvestment Act, have been created to mandate and incentivize investments in underserved communities as a strategy to address economic disparity by providing lower income people with access to capital, credit, and training that they might not otherwise have.

Community investment institutions use investor capital to finance or guarantee loans to individuals and other organizations that have historically been denied access to capital by traditional financial institutions. Loans are used for housing, small business development, workforce development, and education. These institutions also often provide training, financial management, business development, and other types of support to the loan recipients to ensure the success of the loan and its returns to the investors. Often governments require extractive or infrastructure projects to develop a social fund as part of their licensing agreement to create opportunities for people who might be displaced or be disadvantaged.

Community investing is not charity; it is a sound investment practice. These investments earn competitive financial returns, but they also have a social return that is attractive to investors and helps communities become stronger.[18]

Concerned Citizens and Consumer Expectations

In the 1980s, studies found that customers bought largely for convenience, and they wanted high-quality goods and services at a lower price. In the early 1990s, they focused on improved access, quicker response time to products, and more personal services. In the late 1990s, consumers looked for "wisdom-added" features seeking connections beyond the transaction. These consumers purchased goods and services that were aligned with their values, and they wanted to make a difference in the world with their spending patterns.

Over the last decade there has been growing consumer awareness about how products are made, where they are made, and the associated working conditions. In 2007, 80% of Americans said that corporations that support a social or environmental issue win their trust, a 21% increase since 1997.[19] This is reflected in an increased consumption of organic foods and cotton, fair-trade coffee and chocolate, and local sourcing of products.

It is estimated that 19% (about 41 million) of the adult U.S. population is classified as a "lifestyles of health and sustainability" (LOHAS) consumer, meaning that they have a profound sense of environmental and social responsibility.[20] These consumers are the most likely to buy environmentally and socially responsible products. Estimates of the LOHAS market in the United States ranges from $290 to $355 billion in revenues annually. This is expected to grow with the development of clean technologies and other environmental products and services. About two-thirds of LOHAS consumers indicate a willingness to spend more on the initial purchase price for products that will save them money in the future, such as energy efficient appliances and hybrid cars.[21] In addition, the 2007 Cone study found 18- to 25-year-olds were significantly more likely to consider a company's citizenship practices when making purchasing, employment, and investment decisions.[22]

Despite this positive response, there is a gap between positive attitudes, awareness, and buying practices. The UN Environmental Program describes a "40/4" gap in which 40% of consumers say they want to buy green products but only 4% actually make these purchases. Although many factors affect consumer buying practices, it is clear that there is a growing awareness of social and environmental issues and consumer expectations.[23]

There is a strong correlation between negative attitudes and purchases. Studies have found that if U.S. consumers learn that a company has negative or alleged negative practices, (1) 90% would consider switching to another company's products or services, (2) 73% would boycott that company's products or services, and (3) 81% would speak out against that company to their family and friends. Thus accusations of negative practices—even if they were later found to be untrue—can cause major damage to a corporation's reputation.[24]

It seems that consumer concerns are growing worldwide. For example, the 2005 GlobalScan opinion poll found that a large majority of populations in 21 countries hold companies accountable for the safety of their products, fair treatment of employees, responsible use of raw materials, and not harming the environment. In addition, a GlobalScan multi-year review of worldwide public opinion found that consumer expectations are rising and their ratings of company performance have dropped.[25] The Reputation Institute found that there is a large variation between countries in terms of the proportion of people who think that companies are socially responsible, ranging from 35% in Mexico, 26% in Canada, 16% in the United States, 11% in the United Kingdom, and 9% in Japan.[26] The recent "Occupy" movement—whether on Wall Street, in Oakland, or in other cities throughout the world—is a clear signal that stakeholders are not happy with current corporate practices, and this is an important trend that companies will need to monitor.

Corporate Social Responsibility

As previously discussed in Chapter 1, the definitions of "corporate social responsibility" (CSR), "sustainable development," and "triple bottom line" all embrace three key components: economic (profits), environment (planet), and social (people) practices described in the following list.

- Economic issues are associated with how profits are made. Key issues include providing a living wage; avoiding forced overtime and child labor; and allowing for freedom of association, workplace safety, and other labor practices.
- Environmental issues relate to the type of raw materials used, the way materials are used during industrial processes, reduction of pollution and greenhouse gases, and recycling options for

products. In addition, companies have become more concerned about their carbon footprint, climate change, and biodiversity.
- Social practices can be internal in terms of how the business treats its employees and suppliers or external in terms of how the business engages with key stakeholders, such as indigenous communities.

As part of the response to corporate scandals such as Enron and WorldCom, corporate governance became an important CSR element. As described in Chapter 1, "corporate governance" is defined as a set of processes, policies, and institutions that affect the way a corporation operates, including their relationships with their stakeholders.[27] The 2004 UN Global Compact *Who Cares Wins* document states that "sound corporate governance and risk management systems are crucial pre-requisites to successfully implementing policies and measures to address environmental and social challenges." Corporate governance issues include:

- Board structure and accountability
- Accounting and disclosure practices
- Audit committee structure and independence of auditors
- Executive compensation
- Management of corruption and bribery issues[28]

A 2006 McKinsey study of 4,000 executives from 116 countries found that 84% agreed that business should generate higher returns to investors, but that those returns should be balanced with contributing to a greater public good.[29] Initially, CSR efforts focused around philanthropy to gain "goodwill" deal with damages after the fact, or comply with regulation. This was in part because the role of business in society was not clear. For example, many business people quote Milton Freidman, who stated that "the business of business is business," meaning the only purpose of business is to "maximize shareholder value" regardless of its effect on society.[30] A contrasting, less commonly cited view is from James Rouse, who stated that "profit is not the legitimate purpose of business[;] its purpose is to provide for society."[31]

As mentioned in Chapter 1, Michael Porter and Mark Kramer introduced the concept of "shared value" in 2004. They articulate four limitations to the current CSR approach as described in the following list.

- Corporations narrowly define "value" as optimizing short-term financial performance. However, they often miss their customers'

most important needs and ignore broader influences that affect their long-term success.
- Economic efficiency and social progress have been at odds with each other for decades; however, data has shown that addressing societal issues can be beneficial for society and profitable businesses.
- Companies often do not think about CSR efforts as the core to their business strategy but rather they are seen on the periphery of their business.
- Companies must recognize that markets are defined by societal needs as well as economic factors.[32]

Porter and Kramer argue that the principle of "shared value" involves creating economic value in a way that also creates value for society by addressing its needs and challenges. The differences between CSR and shared value are articulated in Table 4.1. Some companies view CSR efforts as part of their core business strategy, and they may challenge Porter and Kramer's assumption

Table 4.1
Differences Between CSR and Shared-Value Approaches

Corporate Social Responsibility	Shared Value
• Doing good	• Economic and social benefits, relative to cost
• Citizenship, philanthropy, sustainability	• Joint company and community value creation
• Discretionary or in response to external pressure	• Integral to competition
• Separate from profit maximization	• Integral to profit maximization
• Agenda is determined by external reporting and personal preferences	• Agenda company-specific and internally generated
• Effect limited by corporate footprint or CSR budget	• Realigns the entire company budget
• Fair trade purchasing	• Transform procurement to increase quality and yield

Source. Michael Porter and Mark Kramer, "Creating Shared Value: How to Reinvent Capitalism and Unleash a Wave of Innovation and Growth," *Harvard Business Review*, January–February 2011.

that CSR is peripheral to their operations. There is certainly some momentum behind this concept, so I wish to include it in this discussion. However, there is very limited research on the implementation of the "shared value" concept, so the existing CSR research is reviewed in the following sections to understand how companies perceive, manage, and implement CSR efforts and its potential for NGO-corporate partnerships.

Corporate Social Responsibility Drivers

It is important to understand what motivates businesses to be involved in CSR efforts and the range of efforts that are under the rubric of CSR activities. As consumer, investor, and governmental awareness and expectations have increased, many companies have been forced into situations in which they must act responsibly, such as when public outrage was launched against Nike for the sweatshop conditions in their supplier factories in Asia.

As the business case for CSR has been developed and tested, there is a growing awareness among many businesses that what is good for society can also be good for business. Thus businesses are moving away from solely philanthropic and compliance activities to include broader CSR efforts into their overall corporate strategies.

Growing expectations, as described previously, is one main reason for companies to embrace CSR efforts. Three other key factors influencing CSR efforts are the desire to (1) maintain a good corporate reputation and image, (2) ensure a social license to operate, and (3) recruit and retain high-quality employees.

Corporate Reputation

Social capital is important for both businesses and NGOs. In today's international markets, a company's reputation and the quality of its human capital have overtaken factories, equipment, and property as its most valuable assets. There appears to be a direct correlation between corporate reputation and share price, making firms acutely vulnerable to scandal and accusations of wrongdoing. A study by Columbia University found that 33% of shareholder value in many industries is derived from the company's reputation.[33] Another study by Ernst and Young found that 66% of the total market value for ICT companies was due to intangible assets such as skills, relationships, and reputation.[34] In addition, a Hill and Knowlton Corporate Reputation Watch survey found that 30% of chief executive officers (CEOs) believe that CSR significantly affects their reputation. They also indicated that reputational benefits can dramatically enhance their company's ability to recruit and retain employees and generate additional sales.[35]

Companies such as Shell, Nestlé, and Nike have all experienced this effect. Regardless of their veracity, it takes time for claims to be investigated and reported on. Campaigners are slow to forgive and allegations of complicity in human rights violations can often be hard to fully refute. Even if an allegation is found to be untrue, it can take years to repair the damage caused by the original claim.[36] These scandals can also weaken the ability of companies to attract and retain top talent, especially among Generation Y staff who look at work as part of a cause to join.

License to Operate

Companies are increasingly realizing the need to develop a "license to operate" within society. Companies generally have a formal license to operate from the government but they may not have developed sufficient informal relationships with other local stakeholders in terms of the corporate practices within their local communities. Often the local communities are left out of this process and can cause major issues for businesses, particularly in the extractive (mining) sector. Businesses need continued support of their stakeholders to enable them to prosper. If they do not have the support of the local stakeholders, there can be serious consequences for corporate operations and performance.

To attain and protect its license to operate, a company needs to maintain the confidence of the government, NGOs, local communities, and the general public. Governments are increasingly looking at responsible business practices as a selection criteria when choosing corporate contractors. For example, many governments require companies bidding on extractive and infrastructure projects, such as mines or dams, to conduct environmental assessment and establish social funds to support the local communities.

By engaging with local community leaders in the planning and development of facilities or operations, companies are better placed to identify and respond to local needs and interests. Building trust and confidence among local stakeholders sets a solid foundation for the long-term security and effectiveness of an operation.

Many scandals have occurred when a company was not able to maintain its license to operate, losing the trust of its stakeholders, such as Shell in Nigeria. There are fewer examples in which a license to operate generated enough community goodwill to protect a company. One example is McDonald's during the Los Angeles uprisings in 1992. McDonald's had a long-standing relationship with the community through cash and volunteer support of the Ronald McDonald Houses. Many businesses were damaged and looted during this time but none of the 60 McDonald's locations were harmed because the community protected them.[37]

The 2011 Edelman Trust Barometer found that respondents believe that corporations should create shareholder value in a way that aligns with society's interests, even if that means sacrificing shareholder value. Rates vary by country, including 82% in the United Kingdom, 61% in both the United States and India, and 49% in Germany.[38]

Employee Recruitment and Retention

Competition for high-caliber employees is a challenge in today's business world. Companies need to deploy all strategies at their disposal to recruit and retain the best talent to ensure future performance. A GlobalScan survey asked the public about the most important thing a company can do to be seen as socially responsible. The most important factor globally is treating employees well.[39]

A Reputation Institute survey found that most people polled in 25 countries would prefer to work for a company that is known for its social responsibility practices. This is true across countries, accounting for 62% of respondents in the United States, 69% in India, 77% in South Africa, and 79% in China.[40] A 2003 study of MBA graduates from 11 top American and European business schools found that more than 97% of respondents were willing to give up some financial compensation (14%) to work for a company reputed to be socially and ethically responsible.[41] A 2007 Cone study showed that 85% of companies supported charitable causes to improve employee morale as well as providing volunteer opportunities.[42]

In addition, studies indicate that companies with superior workplace practices and that are committed to human rights have been shown to receive over 45% more unsolicited employment applications than other companies.[43] Thus responsible business practices can be a source of competitive advantage for companies in attracting and retaining quality employees.

Corporate Social Responsibility Strategy and Structures

Over the last decade, more corporations have worked to incorporate CSR efforts within their core business strategies and structures. However, many companies are trying to figure out how to operationalize CSR efforts in a more meaningful manner into their business practices.

Corporate Social Responsibility Strategies

The 2010 Profile of the Practice found that 60% of companies surveyed have a corporate citizenship strategy. Of these, 55% identified protecting the environment as the top goal, followed by community and local economic development

(52%) and employee well being (43%). These strategies are crafted to produce results in improving corporate reputation (66%); employee morale, recruitment, and retention (59%); and establishing a strong license to operate (38%). The 2010 Profile of the Practice found that corporate citizen strategies included community support and philanthropy (96%); environmental impacts and sustainability (74%); ethics (56%); workplace issues, including diversity (55%); and environmental health and safety (53%).[44]

The business case for social responsibility strongly indicates that CSR efforts are most successful when they are aligned and part of a company's overall strategies and business objectives. Evidence suggests that more companies are including CSR issues in their strategies, but there is still room for improvement. For example, less than half of the CEOs interviewed indicated that they incorporate CSR into their vision statements (54%), strategic plans (41%), business unit goals (36%), or employee performance appraisals (36%).[45]

A 2007 McKinsey Survey of UN Global Compact companies found that 72% of CEOs thought that their CSR efforts should be embedded into business strategy and operations, but only half thought their firms did so. In addition, 60% of CEOs thought that CSR should be integrated into the global supply chain, but only 27% said this was the case.[46]

Corporate Social Responsibility Structures

Companies vary in terms of how they manage CSR efforts. Many companies, particularly in Europe and Japan, have separate CSR units. The 2010 Profile of the Practice found that executive-level corporate citizenship councils increased from 18% in 2008 to 31% in 2010.[47] These councils are cross-functional committees that reach across the boundaries of operations, human resources, public relations, and finance. The study also found that the number of companies that had a senior executive position leading the CSR efforts increased from 27% in 2008 to 45% in 2010. In addition, almost one-third of respondents had a board-level CSR committee, up from 15% in 2008. Although these studies show progress in terms of CSR units and positions, there are still areas that need to be strengthened. For example, only 26% of respondents say their board members are well-informed about their CSR efforts.[48]

Corporate Social Responsibility Activities

CSR efforts can be internal to the company, focusing on core business units, or external to the company, working with colleagues and stakeholders. Corporations provide resources through three main mechanisms: (1) philanthropy through corporate foundations, regional offices, employee matching grants, in-kind donations, and volunteerism (45%); (2) community engagement and social investment (35%); and (3) business integration through operational units such as marketing and research and development units (20%). However, these rates vary greatly by industry. For example, health care companies provide almost half of their support through their business units and only 22% via their foundations. In contrast, utility companies give the majority of their contributions through their foundation and only 17% via business units.[49] This is important information for NGOs to understand when thinking about how to engage with corporations.

Corporate Foundations

As previously mentioned in Chapter 2, corporation foundations provide a relatively small portion of overall philanthropic funding. A 1950 Supreme Court decision reversed written codes that limited corporate contributions; thus in the 1960s corporations felt more pressure to demonstrate their CSR programs, primarily through philanthropy. In the 1970s and 1980s, corporate philanthropy efforts had little to do with the company's business objectives. By the 1990s people began to question if there should be more alignment between the business and foundation objectives.

In 1994, Craig Smith's *Harvard Business Review* article, "New Corporate Philanthropy," articulated a longer-term commitment to social and environment issues, with more resources, particularly more funds from business units. In addition, the article advocated a strategic fit between foundation activities and business objectives called "strategic philanthropy."[50] Carly Fiorina, Hewlett-Packard CEO, stated at the 2003 Business for Social Responsibility Conference,

> For many years, community development goals were philanthropic activities that were . . . seen as separate from business objectives, not fundamental to them; doing well and doing good were seen as separate pursuits. But I think that is changing. Many organizations are learning that cutting-edge innovation and competitive advantage can result from weaving social and environmental consideration into business strategy from the beginning.[51]

With the economic downturn, companies are becoming even more focused on strategic giving. They are embracing alternatives to cash to support their charitable activities, and increasing donations of corporate products and services, as well as employee volunteer efforts, are increasingly popular.

For more than 40 years, the Reader's Digest Foundation dutifully handed over a $40,000 check to the Boys & Girls Clubs of America with no strings attached and no questions asked. So when in 1993 a check didn't arrive, Kurt Aschermann, the chief marketing officer of the Boys & Girls Club, decided to find out why. He called the foundation, and they said they wanted to have a discussion with him about how their relationship could provide value to Reader's Digest. That was the day Aschermann realized that the world of corporate giving was changing. This meant that his organization needed to make some hard decisions about what they would and would not do for corporate money.[52]

Volunteerism

The era of scarce resources is encouraging companies to embrace alternatives to cash to support their charitable activities. Corporate employee volunteer efforts and pro bono services are increasingly popular. Companies have learned that employees highly value philanthropy, which helps companies attract and retain valued workers.

A survey of U.S. companies found that more than 90% of Fortune 500 companies include some type of volunteering in their overall business strategies.[53] The National Council on Workplace Volunteerism reported that its member companies involved 463,000 employees in over 9 million hours to programs in the United States and abroad in 2006.[54] *Talent Management's* April 2009 cover story states,

> Organizations should encourage, value and support extracurricular volunteer efforts, not just because it is the right thing to do but because these volunteer activities will increase employee engagement, underscore the employer brand, support recruitment and retention initiatives, and develop valuable workplace skills that ultimately will help the employer succeed.[55]

Besides improving employee morale and community relations, these companies believe that corporate volunteer efforts contribute positively to business performance. For example, 74% of companies with volunteer programs (paid or unpaid) said volunteerism increased their employees' productivity and 97% said it helped build teamwork.[56]

Although volunteers have always worked locally, there is an emerging trend of international corporate volunteering. For example, General Electric has 140 volunteer councils that allow each office to set its own volunteering agenda. Companies that have ventured into international volunteering include

Accenture, Cisco, Ernst & Young, HSBC, Pfizer, PricewaterhouseCoopers, and Starbucks. About 10% of Fortune 100 companies have service fellowships that allow an employee to volunteer with an NGO or government agency for 3 to 6 months.[57]

Like philanthropy, volunteering efforts have not been very strategic in the past. The focus had been on the quantity of activities rather than the results of activities, although this is starting to change. Many NGOs rely heavily on volunteers; however, most managers do a poor job of managing them. As a result, more than a third of those who volunteered did not donate any time the next year. That adds up to an estimated $38 billion in lost labor for NGOs. To remedy this situation, NGO leaders must develop a more strategic approach to managing this overlooked and undervalued talent pool. The good news is that new waves of retiring baby boomers and energetic young people are ready to fill the gap.[58]

Community Engagement

Studies have found that 67% of companies include community involvement in their strategic planning process.[59] Businesses stated that most of their NGO-community relationships met business and social goals. In addition, corporations are beginning to realize that NGO boards provide good leadership opportunities for employees. However, to be the most successful, candidates need to be carefully matched and trained. A 2004 study found that 44% of NGO board members who came from the corporate world found being on the NGO board to be more complex than they anticipated.[60]

Engagement with Business Units

Companies undertake CSR efforts through a variety of activities, some related to internal processes, whereas others include engaging with stakeholders. Companies vary greatly in how they manage their CSR efforts and which units are involved in decision-making and implementation. Thus it is important for NGOs to research how different corporations manage their CSR efforts. Table 4.2 provides illustrative CSR activities and the business units that may manage the activity as well as the potential activities that NGOs may be able to work with the identified business unit.

In many developing countries supply chains are quite weak, but strengthening small- and medium-sized entities to effectively participate in these supply chains can create economic development at multiple levels. And if they are done in a sustainable manner, they can contribute to better environmental and social conditions as well.

Table 4.2
Illustrative Corporate Social Responsibility Activities and Business Units

Business Unit	CSR Activities	Engagement with NGOs
Accounting and Finance	• Comply with reporting standards	
Environment and Engineering	• Raw material selection, product design, recycling, packaging, ensuring safe work environment for workers, management of hazardous waste, transport, environmental reporting	• Certification, technical advice, recycling, biodiversity and climate change efforts
Communications	• Environmental and social reporting, strategy dissemination	
Human Resources	• Ethical practices, employee compensation and benefits, matching grants, volunteer opportunities	• Volunteers, recipients of matching grants, health and wellness policy, employee training
Marketing		• Cause-related marketing, sponsorship
Research and Development	• Product design	• Community discussions, product testing
Legal	• Compliance with regulations	• Joint ventures, licensing agreements
Procurement	• Supplier code of conduct	• Auditing, assistance with remediation plans

Shared value is not about a wealth redistribution approach; it is about expanding the total pool of economic and social value. Companies have overlooked opportunities to meet fundamental societal needs and misunderstand how societal harms and weakness affect value chains. Porter and Kramer argue that companies will make real strides on a specific issue, such as the environment, when they treat it as a productivity driver rather than a feel-good response to external pressures. This approach requires different thinking and development of new skills for companies as well as NGOs and government officials.[61] Companies can create shared value by:

- Reconceiving products and markets to meet their customers' needs by incorporating better health, education, and other societal benefits
- Redefining productivity in their value chain by strengthening suppliers, reducing and reusing materials, and opening local plants
- Building supportive industry clusters at the company locations that embrace pro-poor growth, develop infrastructure, and build local capacities[62]

Corporate Social Responsibility Reporting

In 2007, 64% of the Fortune Global 100 published a CSR report outlining their economic, environmental, and social performance.[63] In Japan, the number of companies that have released CSR and sustainability reports has jumped significantly. Today, more than 70 Japanese companies are using Global Reporting Initiative guidelines to draw up CSR reports.[64]

Greater Corporate Accountability

Over the past decade there have been many corporate scandals, including the recent British Petroleum (BP) oil spill and mismanagement of financial firms in the mortgage market, that have eroded the public's trust. Historian and author Jeremy Brecher has argued,

> The recent quantum leap in the ability of transnational corporations to relocate their facilities around the world in effect makes all workers, communities and countries competitors for these corporations' favor. The consequence is a "race to the bottom" in which wages and social conditions tend to fall to the level of the most desperate.[65]

Although MNCs are collectively the world's most powerful economic force, no intergovernmental organization is charged with regulating their behavior. In 1974, the UN established the Centre on Transnational Corporations as a way to monitor and to some extent address MNCs' effects. However, with changes in the economic and political climate in the 1980s and 1990s, the Centre on Transnational Corporations was dismantled and a new UN division on Transnational Corporations and Investment emerged with the aim of promoting foreign direct investment.[66] As previously mentioned, UN Secretary-General Kofi Annan launched the UN Global Compact in 2000, a voluntary partnership between the UN, the private sector, and NGOs to incorporate ESG principles. Other UN agencies have been drawn into these efforts, as issues of MNCs' profits and free markets have run into specific interests of less developed countries, such as their wish to buy low-cost antiretroviral drugs to treat HIV and AIDS.

The unwillingness or inability of national governments to control MNCs in a period of deregulated global trade and investment does not bode well for people's health or the environment. MNCs' operations routinely expose workers and communities to an array of health, safety, and ecological dangers. All too often these operations erupt into disasters such as the gas release at the Indian subsidiary of the U.S.-based Union Carbide in Bhopal, the 2010 BP oil spill in the Gulf of Mexico, or the 2010 Pacific Gas and Electric pipeline explosion in northern California.

The limitations of the regulatory framework fueled activists groups. For example, in 1996 San Francisco–based CorpWatch was established to expose corporate malfeasance and to advocate for MNC accountability and transparency. They began by blowing the whistle on working conditions in Nike's operations in Vietnam, ultimately helping secure greater oversight of their factories and changes in their corporate practices.

As a result of the Enron, WorldCom, and Tyco scandals, the Sarbanes-Oxley Act was established. In 2002, the Sarbanes-Oxley Act required publicly traded companies to adhere to governance standards to strengthen corporate board members' responsibility for financial oversight. Despite these efforts and other regulations to contain poor corporate practices, the financial and mortgage crises demonstrate that there are still poor practices being continued. While more regulations are in store for these companies, their loss of trust among customers and the rise of the "Occupy" movement may be more effective in changing their behavior than regulations alone.

Summary of Business Trends

Five key business trends include (1) growth of the private sector, (2) changes in investing priorities, (3) changes in consumer expectations and buying practices, (4) CSR, and (5) greater accountability.

- *Growth of the private sector:* The private sector is the driver behind the last decade of significant economic growth. However, much of that growth has come through consolidation of industries into the hands of a few as a result of M&As. The private sector will continue to grow but probably not at the same rate as in the past. In the future a large part of this growth will come from emerging economies such as China, India, and Brazil. NGOs can play a key role in working with corporations to enhance their social and environmental practices. Society has growing expectations of corporate behaviors, particularly as they expand their work in emerging markets. These expectations are exhibited by investors and key stakeholders such as consumers and employees, as well as by communities and the society at large. Although many CSR efforts began with philanthropic efforts, these efforts are being more closely aligned with the businesses' core competencies and objectives. In addition, many companies are working to integrate their CSR efforts into their corporate strategies and business units. NGOs can assist corporations in developing inclusive and forward-reaching business strategies that build markets and enhance the living conditions of the poor as consumers, producers, and suppliers. In light of recent corporate scandals and poor practices, corporations need to find significant value in implementing and establishing mechanisms to gain the trust of shareholders, investors, consumers, employees, and the general public to ensure their growth.

- *Changes in investing priorities:* The growth of SRI funds has skyrocketed over the past decade. As societies question business practices, these trends continue to grow into the future, rewarding socially responsible companies and punishing those not perceived as "making the grade." This expanded view of investors—both institutional and individual—will continue to push companies to address ESG issues. In addition, with the growing recognition of 4 billion poor people as an untapped market, companies now view community investing as a source of competitive advantage and growth opportunities. Thus with greater interest among businesses to address ESG issues, there is a growing scope for NGO-corporate partnerships.
- *Changes in consumer expectations and buying practices:* As expectations grow among society as a whole as well as among consumers and employees, corporations are continually looking for ways to meet these growing expectations. The more NGOs can

develop innovative solutions to help companies meet these expectations, the more likely they are to be able to find common ground for partnerships.

- *Corporate social responsibility:* The growth of CSR efforts and the recent concept of shared value provide many opportunities for corporations and NGOs to work together. Platforms such as the UN Global Compact and World Summit on Sustainable Development have created opportunities for NGOs and businesses, as well as other sectors, to work collaboratively on addressing ESG issues. NGO-corporate partnerships work best when they can leverage the core competencies of the different sectors to address multifaceted, complex issues.
- *Greater accountability:* As the public's trust in corporations is falling, businesses are being required to be more transparent and accountable to a variety of stakeholders, not just their shareholders. Many companies have embraced a variety of ways to engage with stakeholders, including employees, consumers, suppliers, communities, and NGOs. This is an area in which partnerships with NGOs may be beneficial to corporations.

Notes

1. "Transnational Corporations," *Library of Halexandria,* http://www.halexandria.org/dward318.htm.

2. "Key Facts About Women-Owned Businesses," *Center for Women's Business Research,* http://www.womensbusinessresearchcenter.org/research/keyfacts/.

3. Martin McCauley, "Multinational Companies Will Outwit The G20 Regulators. You Can Bet On It," *Stirring Trouble Internationally,* April 14, 2009, http://www.stirringtroubleinternationally.com/2009/04/14/multinational-companies-will-outwit-the-g20-regulators-you-can-bet-on-it/.

4. Ibid.

5. Ibid.

6. Joseph Stiglitz, *Making Globalization Work* (New York: WW Norton and Company, 2006).

7. "Mergers and Acquisition," *Businessweek,* November 23, 2009.

8. "Why Do So Many Mergers Fail?" *Knowledge @ Wharton,* March 2005, http://knowledge.wharton.upenn.edu/article.cfm?articleid=1137.

9. "Socially Responsible Investing Facts," *US SIF,* http://socialinvest.org/resources/sriguide/srifacts.cfm.

10. Cone Communications, http://www.coneinc.com.

11. "Socially Responsible Investing Facts."

12. Ibid.

13. Rikki Stancich, "Pension Funds See Potential in Climate Investment," *Climate Change Corp,* September 22, 2008.

14. "Socially Responsible Investing Facts."

15. Ibid.

16. Interfaith Center on Corporate Responsibility, http://www.iccr.org/.

17. Robert Kropp, "ICCR Publishes 2011 Proxy Resolutions Book, *Sustainability Investment News,* January 21, 2011, http://www.socialfunds.com/news/article.cgi?sfArticleId=3130.

18. "Socially Responsible Investing Facts."

19. Cone Communications.

20. "Reaching the LOHAS Consumer," *The Essential Orange,* http://www.theessential orange.blogspot.com/2009/12/reaching-lohas-consumer.html.

21. Ibid.

22. Cone Communications.

23. United Nations Environmental Program, *Talk the Walk: Advancing Sustainable Lifestyles Through Marketing and Communications* (New York, United Nations Environmental Program and UN Global Compact, 2005).

24. Cone Communications.

25. Center for Corporate Citizenship at Boston College, *What Do Surveys Say About Corporate Citizenship?* (Chestnut Hill, Mass.: Center for Corporate Citizenship at Boston College, 2007).

26. Ibid.

27. "Corporate Governance," *Wikipedia,* http://en.wikipedia.org/wiki/Corporate_gover nance.

28. UN Global Compact, *Who Cares Wins: Connecting Financial Markets to a Changing World* (New York: UN Global Compact, 2004).

29. Center for Corporate Citizenship, *What Do Surveys Say About Corporate Citizenship?*

30. Milton Friedman, "The Social Responsibility of Business Is to Increase Its Profits," *The New York Times Magazine,* September 13, 1970.

31. Kenneth Mason, "Responsibility for What's on the Tube," *Businessweek,* August 13, 1979.

32. Michael Porter and Mark Kramer, "Creating Shared Value: How to Reinvent Capitalism and Unleash a Wave of Innovation and Growth," *Harvard Business Review* (January–February 2011):2–17.

33. Jem Bendell, *Terms of Endearment: Business, NGOs and Sustainable Development* (Sheffield, UK: Greenleaf, 2003).

34. Ibid.

35. Hill and Knowlton, *Reputation and the War for Talent: 2008 Corporate Reputation Watch Survey,* http://www2.hillandknowlton.com/crw/downloads.asp.

36. Lucy Amis et al., *Human Rights: It Is Your Business: The Case for Corporate Engagement* (London: International Business Leader's Forum, 2005).

37. Alice Korngold, *Leveraging Good Will: Strengthening Non-Profits by Engaging With Business* (San Francisco: Jossey-Bass, 2005).

38. *2011 Edelman Trust Barometer,* http://www.edelman.com/trust/2011/.

39. Center for Corporate Citizenship, *What Do Surveys Say About Corporate Citizenship?*

40. Ibid.

41. Ibid.

42. Cone Communications, http://www.coneinc.com.

43. Amis et al., *Human Rights.*

44. Center for Corporate Citizenship, *What Do Surveys Say About Corporate Citizenship?*

45. Ibid.

46. "Global Survey of Business Executives," *McKinsey Quarterly,* January 2006.

47. Center for Corporate Citizenship, *What Do Surveys Say About Corporate Citizenship?*

48. Ibid.

49. Committee for Encouraging Corporate Philanthropy, *Giving in Numbers* (Washington, DC: Committee for Encouraging Corporate Philanthropy, 2010).

50. Craig Smith: "New Corporate Philanthropy," *Harvard Business Review* (May–June 1994):1.

51. Philip Kotler and Nancy Lee, *Corporate Social Responsibility: Doing the Most Good for Your Company and Cause* (Hoboken, NJ: John Wiley and Sons, 2005).

52. Rebecca Gardyn, "Handling the Ethical Dilemmas that Corporate Partners Can Bring to a Charity," *Chronicle of Philanthropy,* February 13, 2003. http://philanthropy.com/article/Handling-the-Ethical-Dilemmas/52545/.

53. Points of Light Foundation: "The National Council on Workplace Volunteerism Achieves Important Milestone," *CSR Wire,* http://www.csrwire.com/press_releases/16770-National-Council-on-Workplace-Volunteerism-Achieves-Important-Milestone.

54. Ibid.

55. "Do it Pro-Bono: Getting the Most Benefit from Time off to Volunteer," *Benefits Buzz,* April 20, 2009, http://www.benefitsbuzz.net/2009/04/do-it-pro-bono-getting-the-most-benefit-from-time-off-to-volunteer.html.

56. Points of Light Foundation: *Business Leadership Forum Monograph: Senior Executives at Award-Winning Companies Share Keys for Successful Employee Volunteer Programs* (Washington, DC: Points of Light Foundation, 2005).

57. David Eisner et al., "New Volunteer Workforce," *Stanford Social Innovation Review* (Winter 2009):32–37.

58. Ibid.

59. Center for Corporate Citizenship at Boston College, *Community Involvement Index 2003* (Chestnut Hill, Mass.: Center for Corporate Citizenship at Boston College, 2003).

60. Ibid.

61. Porter and Kramer, "Creating Shared Value: How to Reinvent Capitalism and Unleash a Wave of Innovation and Growth," *Harvard Business Review.*

62. Ibid.

63. Center for Corporate Citizenship, *Community Involvement Index 2003.*

64. Center for Corporate Citizenship, *What Do Surveys Say About Corporate Citizenship?*

65. David Korten, *When Corporations Rule the World,* 2nd ed. (Bloomfield, Conn. and San Francisco, Calif.: Kumarian Press and Berrett-Koehler, 2001).

66. Manuel Contreras, ed., *Corporate Social Responsibility in the Promotion of Social Development* (Washington, DC: Inter-American Development Bank, 2004).

5

Partnership Options

Should NGOs and Businesses Partner?

Partnerships between non-governmental organizations (NGOs) and corporations are unique because they are both private-sector entities, but their missions, motives, and desired results are quite different. As previously mentioned, these relationships are important for three key reasons. First, globalization and the technology revolution have made the world smaller, but our problems are more complex and global in scope. For example, climate change has many sources, with widespread effects, requiring actions at multiple levels. There are no silver bullets. The more interconnected the world becomes, the broader the ripple effect individual actions have on the entire interdependent system. Second, more people are affected by these problems. Income inequities are growing throughout the world as evidenced by a widening gap between the "haves" and the "have-nots." Third, the current development approaches have received inadequate resources resulting in limited systematic effects.

In the 1960s and 1970s, relationships between NGOs and businesses were quite confrontational, particularly among environmental NGOs. A variety of tactics, such as campaigns or boycotts, were utilized to force businesses to change their practices. Many of these confrontations grew out of NGOs' frustrations with businesses that refused to listen to their concerns and governments that were unable or unwilling to protect workers, consumers, and the environment. During this time, some NGOs had philanthropic relationships with corporations. However, these philanthropic activities were largely unrelated to business objectives and practices. Also during this time, many NGOs completely avoided working with corporations because they believed corporations were a large part of the problem.

In the late 1980s and 1990s, NGOs were instrumental in raising public awareness and mobilizing responses against poor environmental practices. As a result, there was a growing understanding among consumers and governments regarding environmental issues.

In the late 1990s, some NGOs began directly engaging with businesses to improve their practices. For example, in 1994 the first fairtrade-certified product, Green and Black's Maya Gold Chocolate made with cocoa from Belize, was launched. This was followed by Café Direct's coffee and Clipper's tea. Then in 1997, the Fairtrade Foundation launched a pilot project to work with British companies in developing codes of conduct to guide relationships with their southern suppliers.[1] These relationships differed from the past because philanthropy was not the main driver. In addition, there was significant involvement of direct business units in these efforts. More of these partnerships are being designed to tackle both internal operational issues, such as codes of conduct or environmental policies, as well as external effects of corporate activity.

The 2004 Sustainable Assessment Management survey found that 45% of the 554 companies that responded had a variety of ongoing partnerships with NGOs.[2] The survey also found that although there are a number of partnerships, the idea of cross-sectoral partnering is still at the early phase and many focus on "project alliances."[3]

Both NGOs and businesses are beginning to understand that the only way to address the growing complexity of problems that affect more people is to create new paradigms that maximize core competencies of each sector—NGO, private, and government—to develop innovative and sustainable solutions. There is also a growing recognition for the need of new approaches among government agencies and foundations. In addition, more and different types of resources—money, skills, technology, and networks—are required to address existing and emerging issues.

True partnerships are about common agendas as well as shared resources, risks, and rewards. They are voluntary collaborations that build on the respective strengths and core competencies of each partner, optimize the allocation of resources, minimize risks, and achieve mutually beneficial results over a sustained period. Partnerships can increase resources, scale, and effect, if effectively designed and executed.[4]

Partnership opportunities require a strong incentive for all the partners to place a higher value on working in partnership than working for themselves. The level of the partnership benefits (value added) must be significantly higher than the costs and risks of the partnership; otherwise, there is no rationale to participate in the partnership. Rewards may include development of new approaches, increased access to markets and networks, or increased funding and visibility. Risks could be perceptions by other stakeholders, potential loss of revenue, or loss of independence.

What Are the Benefits of NGO-Corporate Partnerships?

Opposites can attract. It is the differences that exist between NGOs and businesses—both in resources and in organizational objectives, structures, and competencies—that make NGOs attractive partners for companies seeking to address environmental, social, and governance (ESG) issues and make the transition to sustainability. It is important that these differences, particularly the ability of NGOs to offer independent advice, are not compromised as a result of a partnership.

NGOs and businesses have many assets, both tangible and intangible, that they can offer each other through these relationships. Many NGOs do not fully understand or value, particularly in quantitative and monetary terms, their assets, which can include their:

- Field presence such as (country) office infrastructure
- Expert understanding about the local context, conditions, and relationships with local communities that can provide useful information and connections that could help companies appropriately access new markets and suppliers
- Ability to test new products and pilot innovative market solutions
- Technical and scientific expertise
- Access to networks such as consumer groups
- A strong, credible brand
- Policy advocacy and mobilization skills

Businesses can offer their:

- Ability to plan and work at scale
- Ability to design systems and structures
- Access to networks such as ministries of trade and chambers of commerce
- Technical expertise in areas such as marketing and communications
- Strong brand
- Access to employees and volunteers
- Access to other resources such as financial support, meeting room space, and distribution systems

Table 5.1
Benefits of Cross-Sectoral Partnerships

Benefits for NGOs Working With Business	Benefits for Business Working With NGOs
• Operational and organizational strategy enhancement and implementation at scale	• Improved image and credibility with customers and employees
• Access to human resources and skills	• Volunteer opportunities that can improve employee morale and retention of staff • Skills development and technical expertise
• Access to new product development and technology	• Product innovation and new perspectives of consumers
• Access to networks and greater visibility	• Access to markets and new networks

Source. Jem Bendell, *Terms of Endearment: Business, NGO and Sustainable Development* (Sheffield, UK: GreenLeaf Publishing, 2000).

Table 5.1 outlines the benefits that NGOs and corporations can gain from working with each other.

NGO Benefits of Working With Corporations

Although some NGOs may need financial resources from external sources, such as individuals or businesses, many of the best NGO benefits of working with corporations are the nonfinancial contributions of the relationship as articulated by David Grayson, of the National Council for Voluntary Organisations:

> There was remarkable consensus among NGOs that the real benefit of partnerships with business is not company cash, but the time, expertise and sometimes the political and commercial influence that business can bring. At the same time businesses can learn a great deal about the way in which successful civil society organizations can motivate and enthuse volunteers and build human resources.[5]

The four key benefits of NGOs partnering with corporations are described here.

- *Strategy enhancement and scale:* As mentioned in Chapter 3, NGO programs are often constrained by small amounts of funding that may only be renewed on a yearly basis. This may force the NGO to limit its efforts in terms of scale and effect. On the other hand, businesses have access to capital markets that allow them to secure adequate upfront investments to design efforts at scale and develop the necessary systems to support their efforts. These are important skills that can address multifaceted problems that require more collective efforts. There are many new funding mechanisms that have been developed over the last decade, such as Acumen and Domini Funds, and more are being tested such as Social Impact Bonds and other types of venture philanthropy approaches that blend financial returns with social and environmental results. This provides opportunities for NGOs, but it also implies that managers will need to evaluate the different options to understand the implications and select those that will be the most beneficial for the organization and its partners.
- *Access to human resources and skills:* Many businesses can provide various human resources, such as pro bono services or employee-volunteers, to support NGO efforts. Skills that are useful to NGOs include strategic planning, pricing goods and services, financial management, website development, marketing, and communications, to name a few. Some businesses, for example, Accenture Development Partners, have established separate departments to specifically provide services to NGOs at a reduced rate. Several organizations, such as UniversalGiving, facilitate NGOs' access to corporate skills and human resources, and vice versa. As previously mentioned, corporations now view participation on NGO boards as useful training grounds for their employees.
- *Access to new product development and technology:* Many new products have improved development approaches for consumers. Examples are the development of water purification filters, creation of clean technology stoves to reduce pollution, and the use of solar powered products such as cell phone chargers.

    In addition, there has been an explosion in technology that has improved the ways NGOs operate their programs. This ranges from new applications for global positioning systems that assist with better data collection, the use of text messaging for

contributions, and other platforms to facilitate coordination. NGOs need to be actively involved so that they can influence the evolution of technology to meet their needs as well as be appropriately adapted to their clients, whether they are mentally or physically challenged, less well educated, or lack the infrastructure to access the technology.
- *Access to business networks and greater visibility:* Businesses have large networks with other businesses, suppliers, and consumers globally. In addition, they often have strong relationships with ministries of trade, economics, and finance that often have more influence and resources in a country than some of the social-sector ministries, such as education or health.

The 2010 Cone Nonprofit Marketing Trend survey found that more than three-quarters of Americans believe that a partnership between an NGO and a company they trust makes a cause stand out. Consumers (75%) want to hear about the results of partnerships, including the effect on the social issue or the money raised for the cause.[6] The 2010 Cone study found that Americans reward NGO-corporate partnerships as demonstrated by the following:

- Fifty-nine percent of Americans are more likely to buy a product associated with the partnership, as in the case of a cause-related marketing (CRM) campaign.
- Fifty percent are more likely to donate to the NGO.
- Forty-nine percent are more likely to participate in an event for the NGO.
- Forty-one percent are more likely to volunteer for the NGO.[7]

Business Benefits of Working With NGOs

The 2004 Global Corporate Citizenship Initiative asked companies how they engage in partnerships for development. Companies reported that they conducted the following activities:

- Build frameworks for good governance by spreading industry-wide or global standards for accountability, transparency, and responsible business practice, and strengthening public institutions and administrative capacity.
- Expand economic opportunities to ensure that local communities benefit from major development projects, support small and

microenterprise development, invest in youth entrepreneurship and employment, and engage in integrated approaches to poverty reduction.

- Invest in physical infrastructure by preserving and providing access to clean water and energy as well as leveraging logistics and transportation competencies.
- Improve access to and quality of education by building national business coalitions for education, mobilizing private resources and technology, and preventing child exploitation.
- Provide better health care and affordable treatments by assisting to build the capacity and infrastructure in public health systems, supporting global and national alliances for health.
- Invest in training and experiential learning programs.[8]

A British partnership broker reports,

> European companies have taken the lead in meaningful engagement with NGOs. In the U.S. NGOs are seen as radical. Corporations don't spend nearly as much time as they should on this. . . . For example, after Hurricane Katrina some U.S. companies said they wished that they had partnerships in place before the hurricane so they could have acted more quickly.[9]

The five key benefits of corporations partnering with NGOs are as follows:

1. *Enhancing image and credibility:* It is clear that some companies that have not managed their social issues, such as Nike's sweatshop conditions in their supplier contracts or Denny's refusal to serve African Americans in their restaurants, have suffered major losses. This is also true for companies who do not manage their environmental responsibilities, such as the recent British Petroleum (BP) oil spill. All these companies have had to make major changes in their business practices with sustained investments over many years to recapture the trust of their consumers and rebuild their brand. Both Nike and Denny's have worked with NGOs to help them address these issues and regain the trust of their consumers. BP is still in the process of addressing the ESG issues resulting from the oil spill.

Research shows that social and environmental reports by companies continue to suffer from a credibility gap in the eyes of stakeholders. The UN Environment Program argues that "faced with this credibility challenge, active dialogue and stakeholder partnerships assume unprecedented importance. Northern-hemisphere retailers of products from the south need credible information in order to reassure consumers, as do southern exporters."[10] Thus NGOs can work with businesses in a variety of ways to address ESG practices ranging from consultation, facilitation with community groups, certification, and remediation of issues. However, one of the greatest fears of NGOs is that they will be "used" by a corporation to gain a better image without actually making any real changes, tarnishing the NGO's image in the process, which is further discussed later in this chapter in "NGO Challenges for Working With Business."

2. *Improving employee morale and retention:* As discussed in Chapter 4, a key corporate social responsibility (CSR) driver for companies is to attract and retain high-caliber employees. Both employees and consumers view corporations that support social and environmental causes more positively. Thus NGOs can provide volunteer opportunities and community engagement platforms for corporations to achieve their objectives in this regard if they are effectively implemented. As previously mentioned, NGOs need to find an appropriate fit and manage these highly competent volunteers. Otherwise, they will become frustrated and less likely to volunteer for any NGO in the future.
3. *Technical expertise and skills development:* NGOs have a wealth of scientific, technical, and community-level expertise in sustainable development issues. For example, in the partnership between the Nature Conservancy (TNC) and Georgia Pacific, TNC brought 400 world-class scientists together to develop strategies to protect the wetlands. It would have been difficult for Georgia Pacific to gather these scientists without the partnership with TNC. Another example is the Environmental Defense Fund's (EDF) expertise in helping McDonald's identify their solid waste problem and develop economically and environmentally feasible solutions. Other NGO efforts have included employee training on HIV and AIDS, diversity, and cultural competencies for company employees.

4. *Access to new products and markets:* Businesses are always looking for new markets to tap and products to produce. There has been growing attention among the business community on accessing "emerging markets." Another key market segment that businesses are interested in are the poor, whom C. K. Prahalad coined the "bottom of the pyramid." Tapping this market requires a new way of marketing and distributing products, and, most importantly, a new way of thinking about the role of business in society. Although some companies have implemented these innovations, it is often difficult for them to realize results independently; thus there are opportunities for businesses to partner with NGOs that often better understand the needs of this population.
5. Marketing to the poor is challenging. "It's not as simple as finding a low price point. Company executives need to understand not only what poor consumers can afford but also what they want and can use," says Richard Brown, marketing vice president for VIA Technologies. Motorola's vice-president, Allen Burnes, "says the company went through four redesigns to develop a low-cost cell phone with battery life as long as 500 hours (for villagers without regular electricity) and an extra-loud volume for use in noisy markets. The poor need innovative models of financing too."[11]

   As a result, more firms have sought partnerships with NGOs that have local knowledge and can help facilitate access to and develop distribution capacity in less developed markets. NGOs are in a key position to help businesses to understand these issues and make appropriate modifications to ensure that local communities and businesses both thrive in these new relationships.

   One example is a relationship between World Vision India and Eureka Forbes Limited. World Vision had been unable to find a suitable water purification system to remove high levels of fluoride in some villages. Because people couldn't afford the water transported by carriers from a nearby town, they had no choice but to drink the local polluted water, which resulted in many negative health effects. World Vision conducted a collaborative process with the community, including the local government and women's self-help groups to help Eureka Forbes better understand the local conditions and challenges. The community's involvement provided valuable information to Eureka Forbes to design a water filtration plant that was effective under the local conditions, affordable, and owned by the community—a win for all parties.[12]

- *Access to NGO networks:* Many NGOs often have strong relationships with ministries of education, health, agriculture, and environment. They also have very strong relationships with traditional community leaders and often local elected officials, as well as other key community members such as teachers, religious leaders, and farmers.
- Businesses often have strong relationships with ministries such as commerce, trade, agriculture, and chambers of commerce, as well as with national and state elected officials.

What Are the Challenges of NGO and Corporate Partnerships?

Of course, these new partnerships are not a panacea. They are not easy and can be messy as new approaches are tested. A 2004 study found that the success rate for cross-sector partnerships was only 53%.[13] To be successful, these partnerships must overcome mistrust; build new competencies, skills, and attitudes; and address resource disparities among parties while creating additional value. In addition, these partnerships have to balance:

- Economic competitiveness while achieving social and environment returns
- Short-term interests and long-term investments
- Power sharing among partners

Although all partnerships have challenges, NGO-corporate partnerships have a unique set of issues because they bring together diverse philosophies and capacities described in this section. These differences can be strengths, if successfully managed, but often they are the reasons that partnerships fail. Paul Gilding, the former executive director of Greenpeace International, states, "When it comes to market transformation, the problem is that NGOs are almost completely ignorant of how markets and business work, while business is largely ignorant of how to work with NGOs."[14]

Partnerships are not viable unless they add more value than a single organization can achieve on its own. Otherwise there is no reason to make the investment. This is true for any type of partnership. Because NGOs and businesses have different drivers, it may be difficult to identify benefits for both parties that would make the relationship a success. Some relationships may have benefits, but they are outweighed by unanticipated additional costs, particularly staff time that is key for the partnership's success.

NGOs and businesses have five key differences:

1. *World views:* There are major discrepancies between the time horizons of the business case (e.g., quarterly earnings) and the development approach (e.g., consensus-building). These differences shape implementation approaches, measures of success, and decision-making styles of the respective organizations.
2. *Languages:* Communication is often a challenge because the partners have different technical languages that may lead to miscommunication.
3. *Status:* There is often a vast difference in organizational size and resources that influences the power dynamics between the partners, which can make the partnership unbalanced.
4. *Expectations:* These groups often have different expectations of each other that can reinforce old attitudes and may jeopardize these relationships. Research indicates that there is still a huge amount of distrust among the private, public, and NGO sectors. For example, the International Business Leadership Forum found that businesses often:
    - Expect NGOs to provide value in specific business terms, such as cost savings, without social benefit
    - Feel that NGOs are not very effective
    - See NGOs as fostering dependency
    - View NGOs as highly political

    On the other hand, NGOs often:
    - See corporations as the problem and distrust their motives
    - View them only as check writers
    - Expect businesses to help further their social missions without any business benefits[15]

    In addition, NGOs often think that corporations will make decisions quickly and have a great deal of money. However, many corporations don't have clear strategies for working with NGOs so it may take them a relatively long time, requiring months to years of discussions, to decide what they want to do and with which NGO. In addition, corporate foundations only compose 10% of all philanthropic dollars in the United States. It should be noted that corporate volunteers and funds from business units are not included in the corporate foundation figure. Businesses usually give small ($10,000–$100,000) single-year grants to begin the process of working with an NGO. Building trust between the partners is essential. If a company is able to build trust with an NGO, then it may provide more funds in the future.

A 2005 Ethical Corporation survey found that attitudes on both sides are changing. NGOs are becoming more flexible, less dogmatic, and more eager to seek solutions from businesses. Businesses have also started to see the potential of working more closely with NGOs to develop a better working environment in which to operate and to gain credibility and improve their reputation within society.[16]

5. *Measures of success:* Success in part depends on time. Businesses may define success as increased visibility, enhanced employee morale, or increased sales, objectives that can be achieved in relatively short timeframes. NGOs often measure success in terms of changes in human conditions that require several years to demonstrate results, such as reduction of infant mortality. Partnerships require three measurement levels:
   - Results of the partnership activities on society (project effect)
   - Value created by the partnership for the individual organizations (organizational effect)
   - Effectiveness (costs and benefits) of the partnership approach[17]

   Most partnerships measure the first level of the partnership—project effects. However, less attention is directed toward measuring the costs and value added by the partnership approach, particularly in quantitative terms.

   As a result of these five differences, there has been limited interest or trust on either side. NGO-business relations have been (1) confrontational, using a variety of tactics such as boycotts to make businesses change; (2) philanthropic, with a fundraising focus; or (3) nonexistent. In the past decade, these relationships have started to change but much more work is needed.

NGO Challenges for Working With Businesses

Reputational risk from partnerships is openly recognized by both businesses and NGOs. NGOs are fearful that companies may not be serious about supporting the NGO's effort, and only want to work with the NGO to gain credibility within society. This could affect the NGO's credibility with key stakeholders such as members and donors, and jeopardize its ability to raise funds.

NGOs have three main concerns in regard to reputational risk: (1) guilt by association, (2) being considered a "sell-out," and (3) losing their independence. "Guilt by association" is an NGO's concern that by working with a company its reputation will be tainted just by being associated with that company. James Austin has written,

> This perception impeded some of the early collaboration between Timberland and City Year: "When we initially tried to do advertising with City Year," reported [Timberland vice president Ken] Freitas, "they refused saying, 'No, that's not us; it's the wrong kind of thing.' "[18]

Timberland's CEO Jeff Swartz recounted the objection of Michael Brown, City Year CEO: "You are commercializing something that is sacred to us." The risk and concern declined over time because the two partners developed greater trust and understanding. However, later in the partnership, an overseas Timberland factory was accused of dumping environmentally damaging waste disposal. Even though the City Year partnership had nothing to do with this factory, they were criticized for their affiliation with Timberland.

Another example is the Columbus Children's Hospital. When the hospital agreed to rename itself Nationwide Children's Hospital, to acknowledge a $50 million gift from Nationwide Insurance, everyone was all smiles. But there was public outrage by the Campaign for a Commercial-Free Childhood, several pediatricians, and Parents for Ethical Marketing when the hospital agreed to name a new emergency department and trauma center after locally based retailer, Abercrombie & Fitch, in exchange for a $10 million donation. They contended that naming the center after Abercrombie & Fitch, a clothing company known for its highly sexualized marketing that targets teens and preteens, sent a grievously wrong message. Thus NGOs need to carefully weigh the implications of partnering with different corporations. At issue is what serves the long-term interests of children better: Having a new emergency department or protecting them from negative marketing?[19]

NGOs are also afraid that they will be labeled as a "sell-out." A recent *Washington Post* article described how TNC, Conservation International, and EDF are facing a potential backlash because of their ties to BP and its actions in the recent Gulf Coast oil spill. For organizations such as TNC, which protects ecologically sensitive spots by buying them or persuading others to set them aside, businesses are a big source of income. For example, TNC has had a successful partnership with BP for almost a decade, the details of which were available on their website. When the BP oil spill occurred, TNC was bombarded by complaints from their members about working with BP. This example suggests that the members based their support for TNC on what they thought the organization should do and not what TNC actually does. NGOs have many stakeholder concerns that need to be considered when selecting partners.[20] Roger Cowe cites the *Nordic Report*:

> While most businesses want some visibility of their efforts, this should not be the main objective of the partnership. [The *Nordic Report* states,] "For business, it's undeniable that partnering with NGOs has positive effects on their image. However, if this benefit is misused and not underscored by a willingness to actually work with NGOs towards shared goals, it will quickly lose its value, as NGOs [*sic*] credibility diminishes, along with that of business."[21]

It is important for NGOs to be able to maintain their independence. The BP oil spill has raised questions about whether NGOs should accept money for the advice they give to companies. Greenpeace's website is full of reminders that it never accepts money from companies. Ironically, this policy has prompted questions from some large individual donors, who asked why firms as rich as Walmart should be the ultimate recipients of their charity.[22]

NGOs are thinking more strategically about how to engage with companies. Some NGOs have a sense that if you are helping a company be more profitable, that devalues the work of the NGO. But there is a new breed of NGOs that understand that successful partnerships with corporations need to result in some benefits to the company—cost savings, increased sales, or improved citizenship—as well as social and environmental effects, or they will not be interested in participating. For example, some companies might think it is not cost-effective to serve millions of small poor farmers who use drip-irrigation systems. Local NGOs, citizen groups, and Ashoka fellows in Mexico were able to convince Amanco, a large producer of water-conveyance products, that this was a worthwhile market. They worked together to create a new irrigation technology market worth about $56 million a year that enabled the poor farmers to double their income.[23] Other challenges for NGOs working with businesses include:

- *Inconsistent company behavior:* Business units may have differing objectives. For example, the CSR unit may be working with an NGO to improve working conditions in factories, which may focus on reducing overtime. On the other hand, the designers might not realize that their requests do not provide their suppliers adequate lead time to ensure that overtime is not required, thus undoing the NGO's efforts with the CSR unit. There also may be differences in approach and limited communication between the corporate foundation, business units, and offices in different locations, which can challenge partnerships.
- *Internal conflicts:* In addition to differing NGO management and staff attitudes about working with corporations, structural and procedural issues may make partnering with corporations more challenging. For example, in many NGOs the marketing departments are rewarded by how much money they raise while incentives for program and technical staff may be based on the development of innovative relationships. These differences in incentives often cause conflicts within NGOs, particularly if they do not have a framework to identify how they want to engage with corporations, requiring senior management involvement to guide the process. This can also result in missed partnership opportunities and frustrating potential partners with the process.

Business Challenges Working With NGOs

- *Addressing the broad sustainability development agenda:* Traditional business indicators are largely quantitative and fairly well defined. Sustainable development is a multifaceted, long-term endeavor with less developed indicators that are affected by more actors. In some cases, there is a direct relationship (attribution) between a corporation's action and its effect on society, such as pollution from a factory into a river. However, many times a corporation's effect on a problem (contribution) is less clear, such as addressing biodiversity, because there are many contributing factors. This presents many measurement challenges for companies and their partners. In addition, there are tremendous pressures on business to produce short-term results, which are at odds with a sustainable development approach.

- *Credibility of NGOs:* Because there are so many NGOs with different missions and approaches, business often do not know whom they can trust. In addition, some companies think that NGOs are not strategic or results-oriented, and they are slow to make decisions. Corporations want to work with NGOs that are credible, understand their business, and will produce results. The 2005 Ethical Corporation survey found that this was a top challenge expressed by businesses.[24] Often NGOs are selected based on informal relationships that may exist between individuals, including NGO executives and board members, which may or may not be a good fit for either organization. The growth of NGO rating agencies, such as Guide Star and Charity Navigator and facilitating organizations such as UniversalGiving, provide useful information to corporations about NGOs and vice versa.
- *Confidentiality of information:* Businesses have concerns about sharing confidential information with NGOs. Several businesses have been "burned" when they shared information with one unit of an NGO, such as a program unit that they were working with, only to have the information used against them by a different unit in the same NGO.

The long-term potential of these partnerships, as a tool for problem-solving and policy-making, depends critically on the partners' ability to (1) successfully overcome obstacles; (2) develop new skills, competencies, and attitudes; (3) be flexible and learn throughout the process; and (4) measure the value created by the partnership to society as well as to the partners.

Stakeholder Engagement Framework

Partnerships generally imply that there are positive relationships among the parties. As previously mentioned, the relationships between NGOs and corporations have not always been positive. Engagement encompasses a range of actions that vary in terms of the (1) type of partnership, (2) level of involvement of each party, (3) timeframe, (4) strategies, and (5) expected outcomes.

Some NGOs view relationships with corporations solely as the exchange of financial resources, which limits the opportunities that NGOs could engage in with a business. One example is between an agro-business company that was courting an NGO that worked with local farmers in many developing countries. There was great concern within the NGO about working with the company because of issues related to how their genetically modified organisms (seeds) were developed and marketed to local farmers. After many months of heated internal debate, the NGO decided not to take any money from the corporation. Unfortunately, they were not able to develop an alternative mechanism other than funding to continue their engagement with the business about the farmers' issues. As a result, the voices of the local farmers were not available to the corporation.

Because NGOs can employ a variety of approaches to influence and engage with the corporation, SR International (my company) has adapted several stakeholder engagement and partnership models to fully capture the breadth of interactions between NGOs and corporations. This framework is divided into two components as presented in Table 5.2.

- *Engagement without exchange of resources:* These interactions usually require a lower level of involvement and often have a short timeframe. Their main aim is to influence business practices, but there is not a shared objective. Thus they are *not* partnerships.
- *Engagement with exchange of resources between the parties:* These are deliberate actions between parties to work on a common goal with the exchange of some form of resources such as money, skills, and technical expertise. The organizations share both the risks and rewards of the relationship. These are NGO-corporate partnerships.

Before proceeding, it is important to define some important partnership terms. "Bilateral NGO-corporate partnerships" are direct partnerships between an NGO and a corporation. Other organizations may be involved, but the primary relationship is between the NGO and corporation. A meta-analysis of 25 bilateral partnerships is discussed in Chapter 6.

"Tri-party partnerships" are among three parties: an NGO, a corporation, and a government department, often a donor agency. A meta-analysis of ten tri-party partnerships is discussed in Chapter 7.

"Multi-stakeholder initiatives" (MSIs) bring together partners with diverse interests and typically include governments, multilateral organizations, foundations, NGOs, businesses, academia, trade unions, and other civil society groups in order to achieve common goals. These groups may organize

Table 5.2
Stakeholder Engagement Continuum

Level of Involvement	Engagement *Without* Exchange of Resources (Influence)	Engagement *With* Exchange of Resources for Common Purpose (Partnerships)
Minimal	• *Consulting and advising* may encompass NGOs providing technical expertise or representing voices of their clients and members.	• *Resource exchange (philanthropy)* includes the exchange of financial resources (money), skills (people), in-kind goods/services (things).
Moderate	• *Consumerism and procurement sourcing* involves rewarding corporate practices by buying practices.	• *Transactional (fee for service)* includes fee for a specific service with clearly articulated deliverables (audit, research).
Medium	• *Socially responsible investing and shareholder resolutions* are petitions brought by the shareholders against corporations to change their practices.	• *Joint programming* builds on the strength of the organizations to create new value that benefits both (licensing, cause-related marketing).
Intensive	• *Campaigning* includes protests, media campaigns, and boycotts against bad corporate or government practices.	• *Integrative Partnerships* occur when organizational missions become interdependent.

Source. Adapted from J. Austin, *The Collaboration Challenge: How Nonprofits and Business Succeed Through Strategic Alliances* (San Francisco: Jossey-Bass, 2000).

around a common theme or around an industry-specific issue such as improving conditions for workers in footwear and apparel suppliers.[25] A meta-analysis of 11 MSIs is discussed in Chapter 8.

Ruggero Bodo, of the Italian non-profit Sodalitas, states,

> Partnerships do not just happen by chance. Leadership and motivation play a major role, especially in an environment where there is neither an established culture nor policy fostering the coalition

of different actors to address complex social and environmental issues.[26]

Two key misused partnerships terms must be clarified: *public-private partnerships* and *strategic alliances*. "Public-private partnerships" (PPPs) involve a contract between a public-sector (government) authority and a private entity in which both parties assume substantial financial, technical, and operational risk in a project. Either party can provide capital, and the other usually gets some equity in the venture. Common types of PPPs include infrastructure and defense contracts.[27]

PPPs have become quite the buzzword. Some people include NGOs when they describe PPPs, which in reality are tri-party partnerships between government, NGOs, and business. Thus for our purposes the term "PPP" is not used because there is no NGO involvement. This text uses the term "tri-party partnerships," which more accurately describes partnerships among an NGO, a business, and a government department.

"Strategic alliance" is probably one of the most over-used partnership terms. Many of the organizations interviewed for this book reported that they had a large number of strategic alliances. Although these relationships were described as being "strategically" important to both organizations, very few had established or measured criteria that articulated the value being delivered by the partnership, making it a strategic alliance. For many, the meaning of "strategic" indicates that they intend to work with the organization for a long time, but there is no formal plan or process to further the relationship. Although the desire to work with an organization for the long term may be useful, this does not mean the relationship automatically adds value.[28] Thus this book focuses on integrated programming that has clearly defined objectives, processes, and measurements as outlined by James Austin's framework,[29] rather than strategic alliances.

As outlined in Table 5.2, there are four mechanisms that NGOs can use to influence corporate practices without the direct exchange of resources.

Engagement Without Resource Exchange

Consumerism and Procurement Sourcing

As a collective, NGOs buy a large amount of equipment and supplies such as computers, paper, vehicles, and other materials. However, NGOs often don't realize the effects of their purchasing power. Imagine the effect that NGOs could have as a collective if they harnessed their purchasing power of $1.6 trillion a year to reward companies that support their objectives. For example, many NGOs standardize the type of computers they buy, often based on price and service agreements. However, NGOs could also make their procurement decisions based on a company's environmental practices or in support of gender initiatives, thus rewarding companies with good practices through their buying practices.

Consulting and Advising

Many NGOs, particularly environmental NGOs, have strong technical capacities. These groups are often consulted for their scientific expertise, as well as their understanding of issues affecting indigenous people. Many relationships have grown from one-time consulting efforts to deeper relations with the exchange of technical expertise, which is further discussed later in this chapter in "Joint Programming." Bruce Freidrich, of People for the Ethical Treatment of Animals, states, "We've found that we change a lot by standing outside a business shouting at the top of our lungs, but we can often change even more by sitting down with that same business's leaders to address both sides' concerns in a cooperative spirit."[30]

Socially Responsible Investing and Shareholder Resolutions

As previously mentioned, socially responsible investing and shareholder resolutions can greatly be influenced by NGOs. One important NGO coalition is the Interfaith Center on Corporate Responsibility (ICCR), which has 300 faith-based institutional investors with a combined portfolio worth an estimated $100 billion. This 40-year coalition influences other social investors that now represent $1 trillion in corporate equity. In 2010, ICCR filed 258 shareholder resolutions.[31]

Campaigning

Many NGO campaigns have been highly visible and successful in changing corporate practices. Some well-known examples include efforts to (1) improve working conditions in apparel and footwear factories (stop sweatshops), and (2) stop testing products on animals.

Not every so-called success story has a happy ending, however. For example, pressure from environmental groups influenced Rio Tinto's decision to sell its equity stake in Freeport, the company behind the controversial Grasberg mine in West Papua, Indonesia. However, the mine remains open and may be operated by another mining company that may be far less accountable than Rio Tinto. If a high-profile company is badgered into pulling out of a controversial project, rather than working through issues and setting new environmental standards, the decision tends to benefit the lobbyists' public profile more than it benefits local communities or the environment.[32]

Engagement With Resource Exchange (Bilateral Partnerships)

As outlined in Table 5.2, there are four mechanisms for bilateral NGO-corporate partnerships.

Resource Exchange

Resource exchanges are philanthropic efforts that include grants, pro bono services, employee volunteering, and in-kind donations. Generally, there are low expectations about the outcome, minimal levels of investment from either party, no future commitments, and no break-up issues. Key questions for NGOs and businesses to consider include:

- What levels of resources are available?
- Why are you doing this?
- What is the objective of the resource exchange?
- What effects will partnering with you have on my reputation and business?
- What is the ideal outcome?
- What do we do if something goes wrong?

Pharmaceutical and information and communication technology (ICT) companies are the leading industries that provide "in-kind product contributions." For example, TechSoup, itself an NGO, is one of the most comprehensive technology resources for NGOs in the world. Working with corporate donors, including Microsoft, Adobe, Cisco, and Symantec, TechSoup provides NGOs, libraries, and community-based organizations with the latest hardware, software, and technical services. By June 2010, TechSoup Global had served more than 127,000 organizations, distributed more than $6.3 million worth of technology donations, and enabled NGO recipients to save more than $1.8 billion in ICT expenses in 33 countries.[33]

A survey of 1,000 NGO executives directors found that 77% wanted corporate volunteers to help them with business strategies and operations on a voluntary or pro bono basis, yet only 12% actually used volunteers in this capacity.[34] Pro bono services seem to be the most successful when the NGO (1) is clear about what pro bono services are required, (2) prioritizes the project and can adequately support the volunteer to succeed, and (3) structures the effort like a consultant agreement with a realistic timeframe.[35]

Most Fortune 500 human resource executives (91%) saw tangible benefits with their employees from skills-based volunteerism and pro bono work with NGOs, but only 16% felt there was a formal connection between the corporate pro bono programs and their human resources work.[36] A 2006 Deloitte–Points of Light Foundation study of white-collar workers found that 74% of those who volunteered reported that it had a positive effect on their careers. In a survey of professional women by Woman's Way, 83% reported that volunteering helped them develop leadership skills, 78% reported that it developed communication skills, and more than half reported development in other workplace skills.[37] Thus, resource exchanges can benefit both NGOs and businesses if they are well designed and executed.

Transactional Services

Businesses often have specific needs that can be met by NGOs. Usually these contracts are narrowly defined by the business, but NGOs may also be the hiring entity. A company may hire an NGO to conduct a certification process or an environmental impact assessment. On the other hand, an NGO may hire a business to do an audit or assist with market research.

One innovative example is the EDF Climate Corps. Many U.S. companies lack simple energy-saving strategies or efficiency investment plans for their facilities and equipment, which means money is wasted and greenhouse gas emissions are emitted into the atmosphere. As a result, EDF launched the Climate Corps, which trains students working on their Master of Business Administration degree from top business schools. The participating companies pay them as interns to help develop energy efficiency plans that will reduce the companies' environmental footprint and save money. In 2010, the Climate Corps interns worked on a variety of efforts. For example, one intern worked with Intuit to develop an energy conservation plan with a potential savings of $500,000 for the company. Another intern, working with Cisco, identified that installing "smart power distribution units" in their labs could save the company $24 million over five years and could reduce their carbon footprint by nearly 300 million pounds over the same time period.[38] These companies greatly benefited from the technical expertise shared by the EDF and the interns.

In these transactional relationships, each organization gets what they want within a specific scope. Break-up is not difficult as long as each party fulfills its obligations. Key questions for NGOs and business to consider include:

- What are the key deliverables of the relationship?
- What are the benefits for each organization?

- What is the timeframe for the agreement?
- What is the ideal outcome?
- What happens if something goes wrong?
- What are the decision-making processes used by the organizations?

Joint Programming

Value creation is key in these relationships; both entities are involved in the design, execution, and evaluation of the joint activities. These partnerships are like a courtship. They are reciprocal among the partners; are implemented over a moderate to long-term timeframe; have a shared sense of risks and rewards; and require a greater level of involvement, communication, and commitment among all the organizations, particularly by senior management. For businesses, these activities connect more directly with their business objectives and there may be more involvement of the operational business units. Key questions for NGOs and business to consider include:

- What are the expectations of the partners?
- How will the partnership create value for society and the individual organizations?
- Do we have adequate financial, managerial, and technical capacity to invest in the partnership?
- Who needs to be involved (level of staff, departments) to make the partnership a success?
- How will decisions about the partnership be made?
- What might be the perception of key stakeholders—board members, staff, other NGOs or businesses—toward the partnership?
- How will the partners communicate with each other?
- How will the partnership be shared with the public?
- What permissions are required?

CSR efforts no longer consist merely of "nice" things a company might do with its profits. Increasingly, CSR is directed toward how a company makes its profits in the first place. In the late 1990s there was a growing trend in which development NGOs in the northern hemisphere promoted sustainable development among companies working in the south such as the Forest Stewardship Council. More recently there is more interest in making industry value chains more inclusive or "pro-poor," such as strengthening the capacity of small and medium enterprises to be more effective suppliers, organizing farmers and women-owned businesses to sell to the formal supply chain in a

Table 5.3
Potential CSR Activities by Business Unit

Type of Partnership	Potential Business Unit
Licensing	• Legal
Cause-related marketing	• Marketing, legal, communications, public affairs and relations
Community involvement in product development	• Research and development, product development
Value chain improvements	• Procurement, sourcing
Changes in internal practices	• Product development such as changes in packaging to reduce waste • Distribution and supply chain such as changes in transportation and inventory management • Procurement and supply chain such as sourcing and supplier relationships • Human resources such as HIV/AIDS policies, elimination of pregnancy testing for female applicants

variety of industries. NGOs have techincal expertise in many of these areas, which can be a significant assest to businesses interested in developing an inclusive business model.

Examples of joint programs include licensing and CRM campaigns. Many of these partnerships work more closely with direct business units than a corporate foundation, which is often the main contact for resource exchanges. Table 5.3 summarizes the types of partnerships with NGOs and the potential business units that may be involved, although this varies greatly by industry and company.

"Licensing" is when a business pays a fee to use an NGO's name or some other asset for their business to market their product. By 1998, businesses had paid more than $535 million to license the name or logo of NGOs.[39] For example, the Sierra Club granted Milton Bradley a license to use its name on several of Milton Bradley jigsaw puzzles. A similar partnership was developed between the National Audubon Society and Bushnell Binoculars. This helped to raise public awareness about environmental issues and enhanced the market for green products. In addition, it provided a new revenue stream and greater visibility for the NGOs.[40]

Endorsements by NGOs are highly valued by business, but they need to ensure that appropriate processes are undertaken to solicit the NGO's approval. For example, SmithKline Beecham marketed Nicoderm, a smoking cessation patch, in a way that suggested that it was endorsed by the American Cancer Society (ACS), which was not true. As a result, they had to pay $2.5 million to the ACS for damages.[41]

Sometimes, one part of the organization may be interested in a partnership, but there is not buy-in from the whole organization. This was the case between the American Medical Association (AMA) and Sunbeam. The AMA agreed to endorse Sunbeam's home health care products. In return, Sunbeam would pay a percentage of sales to the AMA to support research education programs. For Sunbeam, the AMA's seal of approval would have provided a competitive advantage that could significantly boost sales. However, the proposal did not establish a mechanism to test the effectiveness of these products. Although the AMA staff was fine with the relationship, there was an immediate outcry from consumer groups, medical professionals, and the AMA board. A few days after the deal was announced, the AMA's board chair revoked it. Sunbeam responded by suing the AMA, which had to pay $9.9 million for breach of contract.[42] Key questions for NGOs and business to consider before entering into a licensing agreement include:

- Under what conditions can the name or logo be used with what level of permission?
- Does the value created by the partnership outweigh any risks of being associated with the company or the NGO?
- Do we have adequate financial, managerial, and technical capacity to invest in the partnership?
- Who needs to be involved (e.g., level of staff, departments) to make the partnership a success?
- What might be the perception of key stakeholders—board members, staff, other NGOs, or business—be toward the partnership?
- How will communications and publicity be handled?
- What are the legal implications of these partnerships?
- What happens if something goes wrong?

In the 1980s, a new form of marketing was born. "Cause-related marketing" (CRM) is a hybrid of product advertising and corporate public relations. CRM aims to link corporate identities with NGOs and good causes. As a tax-deductible expense for business, this form of brand leveraging seeks to connect with the public beyond the traditional point of purchase and to form long-lasting and emotional ties with its consumers. However, what might seem like a fair exchange between a corporation's search for goodwill and an NGO's search for support also raises a range of social, political, and ethical questions.

CRM takes on many forms, such as requesting customer donations at checkout, auctioning special items online, walkathons, inviting consumers to "vote" for charities to receive grants, and more. The most common type of CRM campaign is purchase-triggered donations in which a company pledges to contribute a percentage or set amount of a product's price to a charitable cause or organization.[43]

The first CRM effort in the United States was conducted by American Express in 1983. The company provided 1 cent for every card transaction and $1 for every new card issued. Over a four-month period, they were able to raise $1.7 million for the restoration of the Statue of Liberty. In addition, card usage grew 27% and new applications increased by 45%. In 1994, McDonald's raised $9 million for the Ronald McDonald Houses. To date, Avon has generated over $300 million to fight breast cancer worldwide. In 2004, American companies were expected to spend nearly $1 billion on CRM campaigns.[44]

Consumers have been a major driver in making CRM a success. According to Cone's 2010 Cause Evolution Study, 83% of Americans wish more of the products, services, and retailers they use would support causes. The study also found that 80% of consumers are willing to switch from one brand to another brand that is about the same in price and quality, if the other brand is associated with a good cause. In addition, 61% of consumers are willing to try a new brand or one they've never heard of if it's associated with a cause. The Edelman's Good Purpose Study 2010 found that 64% of global consumers believe it is no longer good enough for corporations to give away money; they must integrate good causes into their everyday business.[45]

In the early days people were more concerned about the ethics of the CRM mechanism, meaning whether the use of marketing approaches would taint a good cause. This created some partnerships that now may be viewed in a different light. For example, in the early 1990s, the Boys and Girls Club received a $60 million, 10-year agreement with the Coca-Cola Company to put vending machines in 2,000 clubs.[46] The debate at the time was whether CRM was a good approach, with less discussion about selling soda to children. Today, the argument might not be over the use of CRM as an approach, but the ethical related to providing soda to children and its links to the childhood obesity epidemic. The current partnership between the Boys and Girls Club and the Coca-Cola Company has evolved to focus on healthy eating programs.

The average amount of funding given by a company through CRM depends on the cost of the item and its profit margin. For example, Denny's gave 10 cents on a low-cost breakfast (about $5); American Express gave 1 cent on every purchase; and Calphalon, which sells high-end cookware, gave $5 for every pan (about $50) sold. Although the total amount raised from CRM efforts vary, the average annual return is usually somewhere between $100,000 and $250,000, depending on many factors such as the topic and scale of the campaign as well as the credibility and networks of the organizations involved. Some companies provide funds up to an agreed-upon ceiling, whereas others donate the total amount of funds raised during a limited timeframe.

CRM programs have become a widely accepted business practice, with many of the world's largest companies running comprehensive CRM campaigns supported by substantial advertising and communications resources. Today's pioneers realize that it is no longer about being just loosely associated with a cause or partnering with an NGO. It is now about integrating the concern and commitment for a cause into their core business strategy.

There are often legal implications and considerations for an NGO when entering into a CRM arrangement. According to Ed Chansky, more than 40 states have charitable solicitation laws that generally define and regulate "commercial co-ventures." An excellent resource is "For Goodness Sake: Legal Regulation and Best Practices in the Field of Cause Marketing," which is available on the cause marketing forum website.[47] The major issue for NGOs is unrelated business taxable income (UBTI), which arises when an NGO engages on a regular basis in business activity that is unrelated to its charitable purpose. Thus actively promoting the sale of a commercial sponsor's goods or services—even if such sales help generate donations to the charity—is not considered part of an NGO's purpose. Too much UBTI can result in loss of tax-exempt status. An NGO can publicly acknowledge a sponsor's support, but the line between "acknowledgement" and "advertising" is not always clear. Thus to protect both partners, Chansky suggest the following steps:

1. Sign a written agreement including any statutorily mandated provisions.
2. Structure the promotion to avoid misleading consumers as to the effect purchases will have on any charitable donation.
3. Review advertising carefully for transparent disclosure of the per-unit donation amount and compliance with applicable state disclosure laws.

4. Confirm that the benefiting charity is registered for general fund-raising purposes in all states where the offer will be made.[48]

Some key lessons learned about CRM are presented here:

- Focusing solely on the consumer may limit the value that can be created by the CRM campaign. Involving other key stakeholders such as retailers, employees, and media can enhance the visibility of and support for the campaign.
- Companies that develop rewards programs are better able to engage their internal stakeholders such as employees, franchises, and suppliers.
- NGOs with a strong network of local organizations like Save the Children, Special Olympics, the American Red Cross, or the Boys and Girls Club have been very successful in CRM efforts.[49]

Kurt Aschermann, CRM guru and chief marketing officer at the Boys and Girls Club, shares some of his lessons on the cause marketing forum website. He recommends:

- Both organizations need to have a strong ability and commitment to promote the partnership.
- It is important for NGOs to understand the unique value of their brand, infrastructure, knowledge, and networks.
- NGOs need to articulate their value to their partners in business terms that they can understand.
- NGOs need to understand basic businesses concepts such as "market share" and "return on investment."
- CRM takes time, requiring an enormous initial effort that may not produce immediate results; for example, it took four years before the partnership between the Boys and Girls Club and Major League Baseball got off the ground.
- These relationships are not just the job of the marketing and development department. They need support from senior management as well as the other departments for the effort to be successful.[50]

Table 5.4 provides examples of how several different companies developed broad cause marketing programs.

Table 5.4
Examples of Corporate Support of Social Causes

	Description	Washington Mutual: Education	Dell: Environmental Recycling	McDonald's: Child and Youth Health
Cause promotion	• Supporting causes though promotion sponsorships, increase awareness and funding	• WAMU teacher recruitment program (marketing department)	• Recycles computers to donate to NGOs and government agencies (environmental and community relations)	• Sponsors the Olympic Youth Camp Program held in 2000 in Sydney, Australia
Cause-related marketing	• Cash contribution based on sales of product	• WaMoola for Schools ties support for local schools to Visa check card usages (marketing department)	• Offers 10% off selected new products when up to three used products are recycled online (sales and environment)	• Earmarked $1 for children's causes from the sale of Big Macs on World Children's Day, 11/02/02
Corporate social marketing	• Support behavior change communication	• WAMU sponsors bank days at elementary schools during which parents who are bank volunteers work with students to open savings accounts and make regular deposits (financial centers)	• Offers free and convenient return of used printers for recycling and reuse (vendor relations)	• Promotes timely immunization
Corporate philanthropy	• Direct contribution to cause	• Grants funds for professional development for teachers (foundation)	• Dell's Direct Giving programs with employees, employee donations are made to Earth Share, which supports multiple environmental projects	• Ronald McDonald House provides place for sick children to stay with their families
Community volunteering	• Provide volunteer services in community	• Employees volunteer in classrooms and on school grounds (human resources)	• Employees around the globe participated in Global Community Involvement Week	• Provided meals for professionals and volunteers at 9/11 site
Business practices		• Provides on-the-job training for high school interns (financial centers)	• Designs products and programs with specific environmental guidelines, policies and goals	

Source. Phillip Kotler and Nancy Lee, *Corporate Social Responsibility: Doing the Most Good for Your Company and Cause* (Hoboken, NJ: John Wiley and Sons, 2005).

Another key area of joint programming is improving value chain performance, sometimes referred to as "inclusive business models" or "pro-poor growth." A business aiming to reach low-income customers needs to do more than provide the same goods or services at a lower price. It requires innovation in what type of product or service is provided as well as how it is packaged, marketed, distributed, and financed. Companies are investing in understanding low-income clients. As a result, they are (1) redesigning products to fit these consumers' buying practices and available cash flow, (2) offering rental and leasing models rather than ownership mechanisms, and (3) leveraging or creating alternative distribution and payment options to bring goods to these consumers.

One example of a pro-poor growth value chain is the Rural Sales Program (RSP) in Bangladesh. Bangladesh is plagued by a highly informal and inefficient rural marketing and distribution system that does not include the poor, particularly women, either as producers or consumers, depriving them of access to many important products, information, and income-generating opportunities. To address these system failures, CARE developed the RSP that created a rural distribution system to generate income and employment opportunities for the rural poor, particularly women. The first companies to participate in the program were Bata, Unilever, and Square Consumer Products. The rural saleswomen, called "Aparajitas," go door-to-door to sell products to their neighbors. These women can decide how much time they want to spend selling these products in their community and they make a commission on their sales. On average these women make between 2,200 to 3,000 Taka a month ($30–$45 a month). These women had to face a great deal of criticism from their families and the general community in a society that greatly restricts women's mobility. This was a key area that CARE had to address to ensure the program's success. Thus the fact that women are allowed to visit their neighbors and have gained status within their community is an even greater achievement than the increase in their earning potential. From the corporate side, the program has greatly expanded corporate access to poor markets. In the first nine months of 2010, companies participating in the RSP had 60 million Taka ($857,000) in sales.[51,52]

Integrative Partnerships

Integrative partnerships are similar to a marriage. Legal arrangements outline the long-term nature of the relationship. Often the operational systems and structures are intrinsically linked and there are strong ties between the brands. These partnerships look like highly integrated joint ventures that are central to achieving the missions of each partner. There are usually a variety of partnerships types and mechanisms that are implemented within the broader partnership. Break-ups for these relationships are often difficult because the brands, operating systems, and structures are melded together.

These partnerships are few and far between because they involve huge investments in time, resources, and commitment at many organizational levels. There are two examples of this type of relationship: CityYear's partnership with Timberland and Rainforest Alliance's partnership with Chiquita are discussed further in Chapter 6. Although the content of the partnership differs, the level of the relationship is very integrated. For example, City Year headquarters is housed at Timberland headquarters. Rainforest Alliance and Chiquita conducted a large-scale co-branding campaign. Both of these relationships started with small projects that evolved into more integrated relationships.

In other cases, a new, separate organization has been created. One example is Grameen Danone Foods Limited, a joint social business between Granmeen Foundation and Danone Yogurt in Bangladesh. Launched in 2006, Grameen Danone Foods Limited aims to provide Bangladeshi children with key nutrients that are typically missing from their diet through fortified yogurt. Creating a separate business allows the organization to align its mission and structure, which can be a challenge between existing organizations, particularly when they are different types of organizations with diverse drivers. This relationship is only a few years old so results are still pending, but more of these arrangements are being developed.[53] Table 5.5 provides a summary of the four types of NGO-corporate partnerships.

Notes

1. "Fairtrade Labeling International History," *The Fairtrade Foundation,* http://www.fairtrade.org.uk/what_is_fairtrade/history.aspx.

2. Jane Nelson and David Prescott, *Partnering for Success: Business Perspectives on Multi-Stakeholder Partnerships* (Switzerland: World Economic Forum Global Corporate Citizen Initiative, January 2005).

3. Ibid.

4. Ibid.

5. Jane Nelson and Simon Zadek, *Partnership Alchemy: New Social Partnership in Europe* (Copenhagen, Norway: The Copenhagen Center, March 2002).

6. "New Research: Nonprofit Marketing Trend Tracker," *What Do You Stand For?* http://www.coneinc.com/nonprofit-marketing-trend-tracker.

7. Ibid.

8. Nelson and Prescott, *Partnering for Success.*

9. Ben Schiller, *Business-NGO Partnerships* (London: Ethical Corporation, December 2005).

Table 5.5

Types of Partnerships

Areas	Resource Exchange	Transactional Service	Joint Programming	Integrative
Timeframe	• Short-term; episodic • No strings attached	• Time bound; short-term	• Medium to longer-term	• Long-term
Business involvement	• Limited; low expectations • Project and finance staff, some senior management	• Business defines need • Minimal communication and reporting requirements • Project and finance staff, some senior management	• Dedicated commitment of staff and resources; both entities have input into design; greater communication requirements • Project, finance, communications, marketing staff and greater support from senior management	• Highly aligned missions and systems • Project, finance, communications, marketing staff and greater support from senior management
Business benefit	• Feel-good feeling • Tax exemption	• Specific need is met	• Aligned to business objectives	• Value creation
NGO involvement	• Carries out program • Project and finance staff, some senior management	• Provides service/skills/products • Project and finance staff, some senior management	• Moderate commitment of staff and resources. Both have input into design. Greater communication • Project, finance, communications, marketing staff, more support from senior management	• Highly aligned missions and systems • CEO, senior management, and staff at various levels
NGO benefit	• Gets needed resources • No strings attached	• Gets needed resources	• Increased visibility, access other skills	• Value creation
Value creation	• Very limited • Project outcomes	• Narrowly defined mutual benefit • Delivery of defined outcomes	• Greater value than the sum of its parts; mutual benefit • Project outcomes + greater visibility + funds	• Create new models and approaches • Project outcomes + more visibility + improved relationships
Flexibility	• Moderate to great	• Little; contract based	• Moderate	• Great
Dissolving partnership	• Easy	• Easy	• Moderately difficult	• Difficult
Mechanisms	• Sponsorship, volunteers, cash donation, product donation, pro bono services, grant	• Contracts	• Caused-related marketing • Licensing agreement	• Series of agreements over an extended period

10. "Opposites Attract," *BSD Global,* http://www.iisd.org/business/ngo/opposites.aspx.

11. Kay Johnson-Xanhon, "Selling to the Poor," *Time,* May 29, 2005.

12. "Rural Access to Clean Water through Cross-Sector Partnerships," http://www.worldvision.ca/Programs-and-Projects/International-Programs/Documents/ICP-CleanWater-Profile-icp1076.pdf.

13. Jari Ylitalo, Eerikki Mäki, and Kirsi Ziegler, *Building Mutuality and Trust in Strategic Partnership: Meaning of Early Stages in Relationship Formation: A Case Study* (Helsinki: Helsinki University of Technology/BIT Research Centre, 2004), http://www.ebrc.info/kuvat/2123_04.pdf.

14. SustainAbility, UN Global Compact and UN Environmental Program, *The 21st Century NGO: In the Market for Change* (London: SustainAbility, UN Global Compact and UN Environmental Program, 2003).

15. Shirley Sagawa and Eli Segal, *Common Interest: Common Good: Creating Value Through Business and Social Sector Partnerships* (Boston, Mass.: Harvard Business School Press, 2000).

16. Bill Drayton and Valeria Budinich, "New Alliance for Global Change," *Harvard Business Review* (September 2010):1–8.

17. Sagawa and Segal, *Common Interest.*

18. James Austin, *The Collaboration Challenge: How Nonprofits and Business Succeed Through Strategic Alliances* (San Francisco: Jossey-Bass, 2000).

19. Stuart Elliot, "When a Corporate Donation Raises Protests," *New York Times,* March 12, 2008.

20. "Reaching for a Longer Spoon: The Disaster in the Gulf of Mexico is Straining Ties Between Companies and Activists," *Economist,* June 3, 2010.

21. Roger Cowe, *Business-NGO Partnerships—What's the Payback?* (London: Ethical Corporation, April 2004).

22. Ibid.

23. Drayton and Budinich, "New Alliance for Global Change."

24. Schiller, *Business-NGO Partnerships.*

25. "Multi-stakeholder initiatives," http://www.csr-weltweit.de/en/initiativen-prinzipien/multi-stakeholder-initiativen/index.nc.html.

26. Nelson and Zadek, *Partnership Alchemy: New Social Partnership in Europe.*

27. "Public-Private Partnership," *Wikipedia,* http://en.wikipedia.org/wiki/Public-private_partnership.

28. Anna Claudia Pellicelli, "Strategic Alliance: Clusters and Global Value Chains in the North and Third World" (Paper presented at EADI Workshop, Nova, Italy, October 30, 2003).

29. Austin, *The Collaboration Challenge.*

30. Cause Marketing Forum, http://www.causemarketingforum.com.

31. Interfaith Center on Corporate Responsibility, http://www.iccr.org/.

32. Annalisa Grigg and Tim Knight, "Best of Both Worlds," *Fauna & Flora,* July 2005, www.oecd.org/dataoecd/36/15/35026474.pdf.

33. Techsoup.org, http://home.techsoup.org/pages/default.aspx.

34. *Social Enterprise Summit: Summary Report: The Revolution in Pro-Bono Professional Services* (New York: Harvard Business School Club, September 23, 2008).

35. Ibid.

36. Ibid.

37. Points of Light Foundation, *A Summary of the Current State of Knowledge: Using Employee Volunteering to Benefit HR Departments* (Washington, DC: Points of Light Foundation, June 2006).

38. EDF Climate Corps, http://edfclimatecorps.org/.

39. Ibid.

40. Dennis Rondinelli and Ted London, "Stakeholder and Corporate Responsibilities in Cross-sectoral Environmental Collaborations," in *Unfolding Stakeholder Thinking, Volume 1: Theory, Responsibility and Engagement,* ed. J. Andriof, S. Waddacok, B. Husted, S. Sutherland-Raham (Sheffield, UK: Greenleaf Publishing, 2003).

41. Austin, *The Collaboration Challenge.*

42. Associated Press, "American Medical Association to Pay Sunbeam $9.9Million," *Washington Post,* August 2, 1998.

43. Cause Marketing Forum, http://www.causemarketing forum.com.

44. Jessica Stannard-Friel, "Proving the Win-Win Strategy of Cause Related Marketing," http://www.fishamerica.org/images/projects/cmwin.pdf.

45. Rondinelli and London, "Stakeholder and Corporate Responsibilities."

46. Stuart Elliot, "When a Corporate Donation Raises Protests."

47. Ed Chansky, "For Goodness Sake: Legal Regulation and Best Practices in the Field of Cause," *NYSBA Inside* 28, no. 1 (Spring–Summer 2010):13–16.

48. Ibid.

49. Cause Marketing Forum.

50. "Cause Marketing Insights," *Cause Marketing Forum,* http://www.causemarketing forum.com/site/apps/nlnet/content2.aspx?c=bkLUKcOTLkK4E&b=6415417&ct=8971401.

51. Catherine Dolan and Linda Scott, "The Future of Retailing? The Aparajitas of Bangladesh," CARE Bangladesh and Said Business School, Oxford University, Oxford, UK, 2008.

52. Personal interview, Mr. Saif-Al Rashid, RSP Program Manager of CARE Bangladesh, May 5, 2011.

53. "Grameen Danone Foods Innovates as a Social Business," Danone, http://www.danone .com/en/what-s-new/focus-4.html.

6

Bilateral NGO-Corporate Partnerships

What Are Bilateral NGO-Corporate Partnerships?

This chapter provides a meta-analysis of 25 "bilateral" partnerships directly between a non-governmental organization (NGO) and a company. These partnerships may have participation of local governments and communities but the primary relationship is between the NGO and corporation.

Although many of these relationships started with a grant or donation, the cases selected focus on more in-depth relationships—transactional, joint programming, and integrated partnerships. The cases represent a range of large and small NGOs and diverse companies from a wide array of countries and industries. There were six integrative partnerships and the remaining 19 cases including a variety of joint programming initiatives. Table 6.1 provides an overview of the cases selected for review.

How Do NGO-Corporate Partnerships Work?

In general, the literature indicates that the key elements of successful partnerships are:

1. Mutual trust and respect
2. Shared goals
3. Clear alignment of objectives and expectations among all parties
4. Clearly articulated roles and responsibilities of each party
5. Effective communication and management structures
6. Well-defined and agreed-upon results and metrics to measure progress
7. Evaluation and learning to ensure value creation of the partnership

(*text continues on p. 144*)

Table 6.1
Examples of Bilateral Partnerships

NGO	Company	Site	Objective	Activities	Results
American Red Cross (relief and development)[a]	The National Restaurant Association (food retail)	United States	• Raise funding for Hurricane Katrina survivors.	• CRM: More than 17,000 restaurants from coffee shops to fine dining establishments joined "Dine for America" along with their employees and guests to raise money for survivors of Hurricane Katrina.	• $12 million raised for the American Red Cross's Gulf Coast programs.
CARE (multi-sectoral)[b] (1992–Current)	Starbucks (coffee)	United States, Ethiopia	• Raise funding to support programs that work with farmers who supply Starbucks.	• CRM: In 1992, Starbucks developed a coffee sampling from three countries where CARE worked, with $2 from each sale going to support CARE programs. Starbucks displayed posters and other materials about CARE programs in their stores. • Starbucks provided $100,000 to CARE for a land restoration project in Ethiopia and supported a series of Kenny G concerts with proceeds going to CARE. • In 1995, for CARE's 50th anniversary, Starbucks increased their funding amount to $500,000 to be implemented over three years. • Some of the CARE staff spent time at Starbucks headquarters to learn more about the company; several Starbucks staff visited CARE field projects.	• Generated $62,500 for CARE programs. • Increased visibility of CARE's programs. • CARE awarded Howard Schultz, Starbucks CEO, its Corporate Leadership Award. • In 1997, Starbucks hired a CARE staff to lead the Starbucks Foundation. • Starbucks senior vice president was added to CARE's Board. • By 1998, Starbucks had become CARE's largest corporate donor ($1.2M).

City Year (youth)[c] (1991–Current)	Timberland (retail)	United States	• Support community development efforts provided by City Year youth volunteers	• In 1991, Timberland sponsored one City Year location. In 1992 City Year created a service day for Timberland employees to renovate an adolescent treatment center. • In 1994, Timberland became City Year's major supporter, with a $5 million donation. City Year conducted leadership training for Timberland's staff. • In 1997, Timberland increased the employee paid time off to 40 hours/year, the highest of any corporation at the time. • In 1998, Timberland introduced City Year to other corporations to diversify their donor base.	• In 1993, Timberland became the official supplier of City Year uniforms, crystallizing City Year's brand in the public's mind. • City Year expanded to six cities. Timberland CEO became the chair of the City Year board. • City Year and Timberland headquarters are located together. The partnership is still going strong.
Dana Mitra Lingkungan (DML) (environmental)[d] (1993–1998)	PT Aqua Gold Mississippi (AGM) (water company)	Indonesia	• Reduce environmental pollution from PET water bottles through a market mechanism.	• AGM produces drinking water in Indonesia. As sales grew, so did the waste associated with the PET water bottles. In 1992, the company was criticized for the waste created by the bottles. The CEO agreed that he would address the problem. The AGM CEO selected DML because he had a previous good experience with the DML founder. • *Buy-Back Program:* DML organized and educated the scavengers and garbage pickers on how to clean and sell the bottles to the recycling program.	• AGM provided a grant of $811,429 and revenues of the recycling program. A third of this funding was provided through an endowment to DML. As of 2001, DML was earning about $160,000/year on the endowment. • By 1995, 30% of the bottles were recycled.

(*continues*)

Table 6.1 (*continued*)

NGO	Company	Site	Objective	Activities	Results
Dana Mitra Lingkungan (DML) (environmental)[d] (1993–1998) (*continued*)				• *Crusher Distribution Program:* Once the bottles were recycled, the next step was to crush the plastic into fibers that could be used in carpets, toys, and fabrics. DML distributed 26 crushing machines throughout the country, collaborating with other environmental groups and local communities.	• The crusher machines produced between 200 and 500 kilograms. The plastic flakes were sold to textile companies for $0.13–0.33 per kilo. • In 1998, a French company bought 40% shares of AGM and they did not have the same commitment so the partnership ended.
Endangered Wildlife Trust (EWT) (environmental)[e]	Eskom (electricity utility)	South Africa	• Protect bird life from electrical lines.	• EWT provided strategic guidance to Eskom on biodiversity risks and opportunities. • Developed a disk, attached to power lines, to improve line visibility so birds can avoid them.	• Established an internationally recognized biodiversity center. • Reduced bird collisions and electrocutions. • Reduced costs for Eskom.
EarthWatch, Fauna and Flora International (environmental)[f] (2001–Current)	British America Tobacco (BAT) (tobacco)	Multiple	• Protect biodiversity near BAT tobacco supplier farms.	• Developed and tested biodiversity risk and opportunity assessment, which was a core tool to drive change. • EarthWatch organized scientists to work with 75 partner organizations who trained over 200 people on biodiversity conservation; 96% of the people trained still work in biodiversity conservation. • Fauna and Flora worked with 50 partner organizations to strengthen their biodiversity conservation effect.	• Created an international supply chain of locally certified wild flowers in South Africa. • Developed a management plan for the Mount Mulanje Global Biosphere Reserve. • Developed a collaborative management system for orangutan conservation. • Brought over 1,000 hectares of native forest in Uganda under sustainable management.

Environmental Defense Fund (EDF) (environmental)[g]	McDonald's (restaurant chain)	United States	• Reduce solid environmental waste created by McDonald's packing materials.	• Established a joint task force to address the company's solid waste issue. • EDF helped McDonald's develop reusable and recycling programs.	• McDonald's switched from polystyrene foam "clamshells" to paper-based wraps, a 70% reduction in packaging volume; reduced paper use by 21%; incorporated 30% postconsumer recycled content; saved $6 million per year as a result of these packaging changes.
First Responder Institute (first aid)[h]	TUMS (consumer products)	United States	• Raise funds for fire departments to respond to emergencies.	• CRM: TUMS provided a $0.10 donation on every bottle sold. TUMS helped educate consumers about First Responder Institute's programs through point-of-sale displays, brochures.	• TUMS experienced a 16% sales increase; increased visibility for the Institute; generated $238,000 for the Institute, which awarded grants to 60 fire departments for breathing systems, thermal imaging cameras.
Food for the Hungry (faith-based)[i]	Sawyer Products (water filter)	Bolivia	• Field test a water purification filter in periurban settings.	• Conducted a randomized cluster trial of Sawyer Products water filter with four groups: (1) water filter alone, (2) water filter with care (support) groups, (3) behavior change with care groups only, and (4) control (no intervention).	• Improved design for use among periurban populations. • Demonstrated effectiveness of the water filter in removing key impurities that cause poor health.
Girls, Inc. (youth)[j]	Lancôme (cosmetics)	United States	• Raise funds for the empowerment of girls and women.	• Created a corporate camp where girls, 14–18 years old, are mentored by Lancôme executives. • CRM: Proceeds from Lancôme's specially created "She Shines" lip gloss go to Girls, Inc.	• Provided role models for girls that benefited the company as well as the communities where the girls live. • Generated funds for Girls, Inc., programs.

(*continues*)

Table 6.1 (*continued*)

NGO	Company	Site	Objective	Activities	Results
Grameen Bank (GB) (microfinance)[k]	Grameen Phone (GP) (mobile telecom)	Bangladesh	• Increase access to information for rural poor in Bangladesh, while creating economic opportunities for local women.	• Village Phone (VP) operators, women who had received a GB loan, were offered a phone through a lease program. The VP operator acts like a public call office; she sells phone calls, provides message services, and lets others receive incoming calls. GP provides the phone and trains the VP operators.	• VP operators grew from 28 in 1997 to 4,166 in 2001. • VP operators made an average profit (after loan payments) of $12 a week in 1998 that skyrocketed to $26 in 2000. • GP rapidly expanded rural access at a low cost, helping them to become the leading mobile phone company in Bangladesh.
Greenpeace (environmental)[l]	Foron (household appliances)	Germany	• Increase the use of hydrocarbon technology using market mechanisms to reduce greenhouse gases.	• Greenpeace provided a grant (DM27,000) to Foron in 1992 to support their use of hydrocarbon technology in the refrigerator market. Greenpeace led a grassroots campaign to increase awareness and educate consumers about the benefits of the new refrigerators. The new refrigerator was introduced in 1993, with much resistance from the chemical and refrigerator industries who launched their own misinformation campaign.	• Within three months, there were 700,000 orders for the new refrigerator. • By 1994, all German manufacturers switched or planned to switch to hydrocarbon technology.
Jumpstart (youth/ education)[m]	American Eagle Outfitters (retail)	United States	• Support the educational programs provided by Jumpstart youth volunteers.	• In 1996, tee-shirts were donated. • In 1997–1998 there were several joint events to build trust and clarify roles. The Jumpstart CEO facilitated a meeting between the CEOs of Timberland and AEO to learn about their experiences.	• Jumpstart network expanded nationally.

				• In 1998, Jumpstart received a $200,000 grant. Jumpstart introduced AEO to their network of socially minded companies.	• In 1998, AEO's CEO was named to the Jumpstart board of directors.
Kaboom (children)[n]	Home Depot (home décor/ repair)	United States	• Create safe play spaces in inner cities for children.	• Developed playgrounds in inner cities in the United States. • From 1996–98 Home Depot provided $2M in cash and $2M in in-kind constructions to Kaboom. Home Depot also shared their community connections with mayors and other companies that also supported Kaboom.	• From 1996–98 built 20 playgrounds. • More recently, Home Depot's commitment of $25 million supported the creation or refurbishment of 1,000 play spaces.
Kairos (community development)[o]	ColCeramica (home décor/ repair)	Colombia	• Create a new tile market for the rural poor. • Provide economic opportunities for poor rural women.	• Kairos worked with local NGOs to train and support local saleswomen. The saleswomen receive a 7% commission, the local NGOs get a 3% commission for hiring and managing the process, and Kairos gets a commission for overall management of the program.	• Supported 1,260 saleswomen who each earn $230 month, as well as greatly increasing the women's self-esteem.
				• ColCeramica changed its marketing, sales and distribution system to reach poor clients with a new line of lower price tiles. They allowed customers to pay for tiles in 12 monthly installments, providing $3 million in credit to its customers. • Introduced a network of 15 outlets to aggregate orders from the community organizations to maintain stock near the customer.	• ColCeramica's distribution costs fell by 30%. Sales grew from $90,000 in 2006 to $12 million in 2009. • By 2012, ColCeramica expects to sell $25 million in tile to more than 70,000 families.

(*continues*)

Table 6.1 (*continued*)

NGO	Company	Site	Objective	Activities	Results
MedShare (health)[p]	Kimberly-Clark (KC) (paper products)	Latin America, United States	• Provide paper and medical supplies to hospitals in less developed countries.	• Donated products to hospitals in Latin America that KC would have incinerated. • MedShare also warehouses KC supplies. • Provided volunteer opportunities for KC employees.	• Saved more than 1 million cubic feet of space in U.S. landfills, more than 3 million pounds of supplies and equipment. • Provided products valued at $6.2 million to more than 25 hospitals in nine countries. • KC vice president of marketing added to MedShare's board of directors
The Nature Conservancy (TNC) (environmental)[q]	MBNA (financial services)	United States	• Raise funds for conservation.	• CRM: MBNA generated royalty payments for TNC for each new account, renewed accounts, cash advances, and purchases.	• Since 1995, MBNA has contributed more than $5 million to support TNC's programs.
The Nature Conservancy (TNC) (environmental)[r]	Georgia Pacific (GP) (utilities)	North Carolina	• Protect the wetland through joint management.	• In 1994, TNC and GP developed an agreement to jointly monitor wetlands. • TNC provided access to 400 world-class scientists with expert knowledge on wetland management. • GP granted the land to TNC for strategic conservation, access to its network of environmentally conscious timber companies, and knowledge of forestry management.	• The land is now managed by a committee including employees of the two partner organizations, and nonvoting representatives from the Roanoke River National Wildlife Refuge, the North Carolina Wildlife Resources Commission, and the North Carolina State School of Forestry.
PCI (formerly Project Concern International) (multisectoral)[s]	Qualcomm (mobile phone chips)	India	• Test BREW-based software applications for cell phones to enhance access to market	• Developed BREW-based software applications for CDMA cell phones. • Worked with women microentrepreneurs who had received loans from Indian microfinance institutions (MFIs) to access market data,	• Created a CIDP application and established a web-based universal interface for MFIs. • Strong demand by entrepreneurs for access to market and financial data as well as nonfinancial information

			information for women microentre-preneurs.	financial data about their loans, and other types of information. • Worked with Indian MFIs to provide their customers with up-to-date financial information via cell phones. • Developed annual seminar on key topics.	such as vaccination campaigns. • MFIs increased their operational efficiency by improving communications with their customers. • Stronger relationship between PCI and Qualcomm.
Rainforest Alliance (RA) (environmental)[t]	Chiquita (agriculture) ($20M) Better Banana Certification	Colombia, Costa Rica, Guatemala, Honduras, Panama	• Develop a certification program for bananas.	• Conducted a company-wide assess-ment of farming and labor practices. • Developed a certification standard similar to Social Accountability 8000. • Identified key issues, trained farmers, and developed a timeline to monitor changes.	• By 2000, Chiquita certified 71,000 acres on 127 company-owned banana farms. • Reduced productions costs by • $100 million. • Recycled or reused 3,000 tons of plastic per year.
Save the Children (women/children)[u]	Denny's (restaurant chain)	United States	• Improve Denny's image and reputation by supporting programs for poor children in inner cities.	• In 1993, Denny's settled a lawsuit for refusing to serve African Americans in their restaurants. • Denny's developed a promotional video and TV commercial about the partnership featuring a diverse group of young children. • Save the Children ties, artwork that was designed by children, were worn by the Denny's employees. • CRM: $0.05 of the proceeds of baseball cards and $0.10 of a low-cost breakfast were sold with the proceeds donated to Save the Children. • Save the Children provided children with safe places, caring adults, and constructive activities in 8 cities and 42 rural areas.	• 30% of the Denny's franchises participated in the program. • Increased visibility in the selected communities for both Save the Children and Denny's. • In 1995, Save the Children honored Ron Petty, Denny's CEO, with their Distinguished Service Award. • Contributed $3M over 5 years and helped Save the Children get other corporate sponsors. • 96% of the youth who participated in the program in Duncan, Mississippi, improved their reading skills.

(*continues*)

Table 6.1 (*continued*)

NGO	Company	Site	Objective	Activities	Results
Share our Strength (SOS) (hunger)[v]	Calphalon (cookware)	United States	• Raise funds and awareness about hunger in the United States.	• Bloomingdales (NY) held a launch event for SOS's *Home Food Cookbook;* Calphalon purchased 2,000 cookbooks for customers who made a Calphalon purchase at the Bloomingdales event. • CRM: Co-branded a selected Calphalon pan every year with $5 of every sale going to support SOS's programs. • In 1998, created a Chef's Alliance to formalize the partnership (18 SOS chefs). The chefs showcased the Calphalon product through cooking demonstrations in key department stores. The department stores promoted the event and guaranteed a $5,000 donation to SOS.	• Increased visibility for SOS and Calphalon with retailers. • Increased sales of the Calphalon pan; achieved four times the sales of the previous year. • In the first year, SOS received $180,000. • In 1998, SOS received $400,000. • The company was bought in 1998 and the partnership ended.
Thai Business Initiative in Rural Development (community development)[w]	Bata (shoes)	Thailand	• Increase economic opportunities in rural Thailand. • Increase production of Bata shoes.	• Bata established four factories in rural Thailand and trained people to work in the factory.	• Created jobs for 140 people in the village that manufactured 8,000 shoe uppers a day. • Increased shoe production by 35,000 shoes a day.
Universal Giving (volunteering)[x]	Cisco Systems (information technology)		• Increase effectiveness of Cisco Systems' Civic Councils.	• Universal Giving used their Quality Model (10 stage) to vet potential NGOs to work with Cisco's Civic Councils. • Worked with the Civic Councils to improve their efficiency.	• Vetted over 500 NGOs to select those with the best fit with Cisco's 30 Civic Councils around the world. • Increased employee giving and volunteer rate.

World Vision (multisectoral/ faith-based)[y]	Eureka Forbes Limited (engineering)	India		• Worked with communities to understand their needs and test water filtration options. • Eureka tested several ideas before a suitable water purification system was developed.	• Filtration system is owned by a self-help group that supervises its operation. Communities paid for the water source. • Established more than 25 Eureka Forbes reverse osmosis plants and 40 ultraviolet water treatment plants in 35 rural and four urban communities. This opened a new market for Eureka.

a. Cause Marketing Forum, http://www.causemarketingforum.com.
b. James Austin, *The Collaboration Challenge: How Nonprofits and Business Succeed Through Strategic Alliances* (San Francisco: Jossey-Bass, 2000).
c. Ibid.
d. Tadashi Yamamoto and Kim Gould Ashizawa, *Corporate-NGO Partnerships* (Tokyo, Japan: Japanese Center for International Exchange, 1999).
e. Ibid.
f. "Biodiversity Partnership," *British American Tobacco,* http://www.bat.com/group/sites/uk__3mnfen.nsf/vwPagesWebLive/DO726H3V?opendocument&SKN=1.
g. "Better Packaging With McDonald's," *Environmental Defense Fund,* http://business.edf.org/casestudies/better-packaging-mcdonalds.
h. Cause Marketing Forum.
i. Personal interview with Tom Davis, senior director of program quality for Food for the Hungry, and Kurt Avery, president of Sawyer Products, October 23, 2010.
j. Girls, Inc., http://www.girlsinc.org/downloads/girlsinc_annualreport_03.pdf.
k. Shyamal Chowdhury, "Attaining Universal Access: Public-Private Partnership and Business-NGO Partnership," ZEF Bonn, Discussion Papers on Development Policy, Bonn, Germany, July 2002.
l. Jorg Andriof, Sandra Waddacok, Bryan Husted, and Sandra Sutherland-Raham, eds, *Unfolding Stakeholder Thinking, Volume 2: Relationships, Communication, Reporting and Performance* (Sheffield, UK: GreenLeaf, 2003).
m. James Austin, *The Collaboration Challenge: How Nonprofits and Business Succeed Through Strategic Alliances* (San Francisco: Jossey-Bass, 2000).
n. Shirley Sagawa and Eli Segal, *Common Interest: Common Good: Creating Value Through Business and Social Sector Partnerships* (Boston: Harvard Business School Press, 2000).
o. Bill Drayton and Valeria Budinich, "New Alliance for Global Change," *Harvard Business Review,* September 2010.
p. Personnel interview with A. B. Short, CEO of MedShare, and Dr. James Quayle, medical director of Kimberly-Clark, January 31, 2006.
q. Cause Marketing Forum.
r. Austin, *The Collaboration Challenge.*
s. Personal interview with Janine Schooley, senior vice president for programs for PCI, and Amy Waterman, director of public affairs and wireless reach for Qualcomm, December 9, 2010.
t. J. Gary Taylor and Patricia J. Scharlin, *Smart Alliance: How a Global Corporation and Environmental Activities Transformed a Tarnished Brand* (New Haven: Yale University Press, 2004).
u. Sagawa and Segal, *Common Interest.*
v. Ibid.
w. Deborah Leipzer, *Canadian Companies on the Cutting Edge: Bata Promotes Development Research Report* (New York: Council on Economic Priorities, July–August).
x. Personal interview with Pamela Hawley, CEO of Universal Giving, June 3, 2009.
y. World Vision Case, http://www.worldvision.ca/Programs-and-Projects/International-Programs/Documents/ICP-CleanWater-Profile-icp1076.pdf.

These seem rather straightforward; however, most people interviewed found these simple concepts are often hard to implement.

There are a variety of partnership frameworks. In 1995, Frederick Long and Matthew Arnold developed a matrix that identified nine key success factors of environmental partnerships between NGOs and corporations. Although the framework only looked at environmental partnerships, it provides a simple yet comprehensive approach to understanding a variety of types of NGO-corporate partnerships. Thus the Long-Arnold framework is used to review the bilateral cases outlined in Table 6.1, the tri-party partnerships in Chapter 7 (see Table 7.1), and the multi-stakeholder initiatives in Chapter 8 (see Tables 8.1–8.3). Table 6.2 presents the nine success factors of NGO-corporate partnerships articulated in the Long-Arnold framework.

The Long-Arnold framework is based on a Partnership Lifecycle that starts with a seed phase, which includes all the prepartnership activities, such as conducting an internal assessment, making the business case, selecting a partner, and negotiating a partnership agreement. If the organizations agree to develop a relationship, there are three partnership phases: (1) initiation, (2) execution, and (3) closure and renewal.[1]

Table 6.2
Long-Arnold Framework on Partnership Success Factors

Factors of Success	Initiation	Execution	Closure/Renewal
People	INCLUDE all critical stakeholders.	RESPECT each partner's needs and interests.	SHARE success and credit.
Goals	DEFINE a viable and inspirational shared vision.	STEWARD based on process learning and new science and technology.	EVALUATE results against goals and alternatives.
Capacity building	INVEST in relationships needed for long-term success.	TRANSLATE knowledge into signs of progress.	SUSTAIN progress by institutionalizing (partnership) arrangements.

Source. Fredrick Long and Matthew Arnold, *The Power of Environmental Partnerships* (Washington, DC: The Dryden Press, Harcourt Brace College Publishers, 1995).

In each phase, the Long-Arnold framework identified three key factors that influence the success of the partnership: people, goals, and capacity building. Based on this framework, people are the most important determinants of a partnership's success because they champion, sell, and coordinate its efforts. Goals, or the vision, is the key motivation of the partnership. If there is not consensus at this level, then it will be impossible to translate the goals into strategies and effective activities. Organizations need to have or build their capacity to convert goals into tangible efforts to achieve the partnership's objective. Capacity building may include securing financial resources, strengthening operational systems and personnel, improving technology, engaging with nonparticipating stakeholders, and creating institutional mechanisms to support the partnership.[2]

The Long-Arnold framework discusses two levels of partnership deficiencies: structural flaws and process breakdowns. Structural flaws usually occur at the beginning of the partnership and can lead to termination if they are not addressed because they are fundamental to the partnership.[3] One example of a relationship that was not able to deliver on its goals is the relationship between the American Medical Association (AMA) and Sunbeam. The AMA agreed to endorse Sunbeam's home health care products, but they did not establish a way to test the effectiveness of these products. Although the deal would have generated millions for the AMA to fund a variety of public health programs, consumer groups and the AMA membership denounced the relationship. This was a factor of both insufficient involvement of key stakeholders in the design of the partnership and the lack of clearly defined goals that would benefit both parties. As a result, the AMA broke the deal, Sunbeam sued, and the AMA had to pay $9.9 million in damages.[4]

Process breakdowns are relatively easy to address because they relate to implementation problems. These issues often arise from miscommunication between the partners, once again highlighting the need for regular communication between the partners.

Partnership Lifecycle

Seed Phase

Although the Long-Arnold framework does not identify specific success factors during the seed phase, prepartnership activities are vital because many discussions never make it beyond this stage. For this analysis, cases were reviewed based on three key components: (1) who initiated the partnership, (2) whether the NGO had a specific strategy for engaging with the corporation, and (3) whether the NGO and business were able to negotiate a successful partnership agreement.

Partnership Initiation

Based on the review of case studies in Table 6.1, in 13 cases NGOs initiated the relationship, and 12 cases were prompted by a business. Three of the cases occurred through random opportunities. For example, Monique Barbeau, a chef, happened to sit next to Dean Kasperzak, a Calphalon (high-end cookware company) executive, on a plane ride from Boston to Seattle. During the conversation, Ms. Barbeau told him about Share Our Strength's (SOS) Taste of the Nation, a series of food and wine benefits, catered by top-notch chefs, held in major cities to raise money for antihunger and nutrition programs. Mr. Kasperzak thought this could strengthen his relationships with the company's retailers and suppliers, so he decided to explore working with SOS.[5]

Another example is the case of CARE and Starbucks. One of the CARE fundraisers made a cold call to Starbucks that led to interest on both sides. This call led to David Olsen, Starbucks's senior vice president, being invited to a CARE-sponsored seminar in Indonesia with fellow academics, thought leaders, business people, and others. This helped the Starbucks executive understand CARE and how it works. Although Mr. Olsen was very interested in supporting CARE, Starbucks was losing money at the time, about $1 million in 1991. However, Howard Schultz, Starbucks's chief executive officer (CEO) and Mr. Olsen made a pledge that when the company was profitable they would support CARE. A year later Starbucks launched a cause-related marketing (CRM) campaign with CARE.[6]

Board members often play a critical link in initial introductions and fostering relationships. One example is the partnership between MedShare and Kimberly-Clark Corporation (KC). The spouse of a managing director in Latin America visited a local hospital. She was appalled at the conditions and how few supplies were available. She discussed this with her husband and asked if KC could do anything to help. A few months later, KC had a regional board meeting in this country. During the board meeting, the manager's spouse arranged a trip to the hospital for all the board members' spouses, who were just as concerned about the horrible conditions. This was a major factor influencing the board members' decision to start a program to assist hospitals throughout the region. As a result, they began to explore the possibility of working with an NGO and found a great fit with MedShare, another Atlanta-based entity.[7]

Although several businesses approached NGOs to develop partnerships, they were not always welcomed with open arms. For example, Lancôme launched a new fragrance, Miracle, with the philosophy that "it takes an empowered girl to become an empowered woman" and a tag line: "You Make It

Happen." The company wanted to develop a CRM campaign around women's empowerment with this product, so they searched for a partner that had a mission of empowering girls. Girls, Inc., was the clear and obvious choice for the company's partnership goals. However, Girls, Inc., was skeptical of working with a cosmetic company, so they grilled Lancôme with many questions before even considering partnering. Girls, Inc., made sure that the alliance would be true to the organization's belief that "Girls have the right to prepare for interesting work and economic independence." Fortunately, Lancôme passed the test because of its commitment to women as demonstrated by a significant number of female executives, supportive workplace policies, and willingness to take Girls, Inc.'s values seriously.[8] Another example is the case of Denny's and Save the Children. Several years before Denny's approached Save the Children, Susan Schneider, Denny's director of promotions and community affairs, explored the idea of working with a national NGO. She began calling well-known national NGOs that work with children, but she was not successful in finding a partner. She commented, "maybe I wasn't talking to the right people in the NGO, and in some cases I was passed to four or five different people at the NGO, but none of them followed up."[9] In 1993, Denny's settled a federal discrimination lawsuit in which six African American Secret Service agents went public with the allegation that a Denny's restaurant had refused to serve them. This made national headlines, resulting in significant damage to Denny's reputation and a crisis of morale among employees and franchises. Thus when they approached Save the Children there was quite a bit of concern.[10]

Partnership Strategy

Six of the cases studies were developed through a proactive strategy by the NGO approaching a company for a specific objective beyond philanthropy. This was confirmed in discussions with many NGO managers. NGOs that do not have a corporate engagement strategy are often placed in a reactive position. This means that they need to evaluate each corporate request individually, which makes the process more time consuming and less focused, particularly in large NGOs that work in many locations. In addition, NGO management and staff attitudes about working with corporations can vary greatly by department, location, and type of job. There may also be structural or procedural issues, such as incentives systems, procurement requirements, or other policies that may make it difficult for staff to partner with corporations. This can result in confusion, internal struggles, missed partnership opportunities, and potentially a negative image for the organization as being perceived as slow to make decisions or indecisive.

It was more common for environmental NGOs, such as Rainforest Alliance and the Environmental Defense Fund (EDF), to target a specific corporation or corporations to promote changes in their practices that negatively affected the environment or workers' rights. Many of these NGOs have well-defined strategies of how they want to engage with corporations because it is clearer how corporations are contributing to issues that these NGOs are concerned about, such as global warming, whereas some other issues such as a company's effect on or responsibility to communities may be harder to determine. Sometimes the companies were selected because they had a large market share, as in the case of McDonald's, Chiquita, and British American Tobacco (BAT). This is an efficient strategy for NGOs because if they can get market leaders to change their practices, these businesses can encourage, either directly or indirectly, their suppliers and competitors to adopt these new practices as well, which are better for both the environment and their bottom line. It should be mentioned that in some of these cases the NGO received funds from the corporation, as in the case of Rainforest Alliance and Chiquita. In contrast, EDF and Greenpeace do not accept any corporate funding.

Partnership Agreement

Many of the NGO and corporate managers interviewed indicated that they grossly underestimated the time it takes to develop and implement these partnerships. Many corporate managers felt frustrated because the process took much longer than they thought it should, based on their corporate experience. The biggest challenge for NGOs was the staff time required to develop potential partnerships. Because the lead-time to agree on a partnership can be quite long, NGOs often have to tap staff, who may be fully occupied by other projects, to develop the relationship until a partnership agreement is in place and funds are available to hire more staff. For example, the partnership between Denny's and Save the Children took eight months of discussions before an agreement was signed.[11]

A key component of this phase is negotiating a successful partnership agreement to start a partnership. Partnership agreements are discussed further in Chapter 9, but in general a partnership agreement should include (1) a well-articulated goal and objectives, (2) a clear definition of roles and responsibilities, (3) communication parameters including use of each other's brands, (4) relationship management structures and systems, (5) an articulation of the general principles of the partnership, and (6) a grievance policy.

Many initial efforts do not develop into a partnership because they cannot negotiate a favorable agreement for all parties. One example is a relationship between a large media corporation and small human rights NGO that wanted to create a music recording by famous pop stars that would include a children's educational curriculum on human rights. Control over the project became a key issue. An advisory board was created to assist the project, but it was not a neutral body. If the corporation didn't listen to the advisory board, it would withdraw from the project. The memorandum of understanding called for the NGO to be housed in the corporation, which wanted to have the final say over the hiring of the NGO's staff. As a result the final decision-making authority rested with the corporation. The NGO was a subcontractor, which meant that they could be terminated by the corporation at any time. Although the corporation needed the NGO to provide its knowledge and credibility in human rights and the NGO needed the corporation to widely disseminate its human rights message, in the end a partnership never took place because of the tensions created by their differing missions and lack of an acceptable partnership model.[12]

Initiation Phase

The Long-Arnold framework factors of success in the initiation phase include:

- Creating a well-defined partnership opportunity (value-proposition)
- Identifying key stakeholders
- Developing a clearly articulated rationale for working together (mutual benefits)
- Sharing a common goal and vision[13]

People

The Long-Arnold framework indicates that the key to the people component of the initiation phase is to identify all the critical internal and external stakeholders who need to support the partnership to ensure its success. Although it might take more time to listen to a variety of stakeholder groups, inclusion can increase legitimacy and credibility for the partnership.

Partnership champions are important at this phase, particularly if there is internal resistance within any of the organizations. For example, key stakeholders for the Denny's and Save the Children partnership were the Denny's franchises. It was clear that a significant portion of franchises needed to be involved to make the partnership a success. Initially, there was quite a bit of skepticism among the franchises so a representative, Marci York, was selected to learn more about the relationship. Involving Ms. York initially slowed down the process, but after her visit to the Save the Children headquarters, she became one of the biggest advocates of the partnership. She gave speeches to the franchises explaining how the partnership would benefit them. Thus although this approach required more upfront investment, it resulted in greater support and credibility for the initiative in the long run.[14]

Goals and Objectives

The Long-Arnold framework indicates that the key to the goals and objectives component of the initiation phase is to define a shared agenda that embodies the vision and goals that they want to achieve through the partnership. This shared vision allows the partners to translate the goals into strategies and then actions that are crucial for a successful partnership. It is important for the partners to develop work plans with realistic metrics that clearly articulate responsibilities of each organization that are owned by all.

The ability for an NGO to develop a successful partnership with a corporation varies greatly depending on the (1) alignment of the missions and objectives of the participating organizations, (2) identification of areas of mutual interest, (3) operating practices of the organization, and (4) perceptions of the corporation's commitment to key social and environmental practices.

For some issues it is easy for NGOs to find alignment with corporate goals—a "win-win" for all parties. For example, there is not much controversy for either entity around helping hurricane survivors or feeding the hungry. Thus the CRM initiatives of the American Red Cross with the National Restaurant Association and SOS with Calphalon were seen as highly beneficial, without any controversy.

For NGOs that have campaigned against businesses on topics such as environmental degradation, child labor, or worker rights, it has been more challenging for them to redefine how they can identify common ground with corporations to successfully undertake partnerships. However, over the last decade more NGOs and businesses have started to change their thinking, enabling them to find a shared vision in situations in which they may have utilized confrontational approaches in the past. For example, most environmental NGOs wanted to campaign against Chiquita for their poor environmental and labor practices. Instead, the Rainforest Alliance decided to approach them with an option to establish a banana certification program. Another example was when the EDF announced an agreement to help McDonald's with their solid waste issues. There was shock and dismay from activists and business alike. EDF was accused of "selling out," and the fast-food retailer, which had previously had a reputation for hostility to green causes, was chided by some of its peers for allowing "tree-huggers" into the boardroom. Gwen Ruta, EDF's senior vice president, stated, "At the time, it was heresy to say that companies and NGOs could work together; now it is dogma, at least for the Fortune 500."[15]

Lastly, some NGOs avoid working with specific industries because of their poor practices such as extractives and gambling or their products such as tobacco or alcohol. For example, in the 1980s and 1990s the extractive industry was seen as having quite bad practices. Since then there has been a great deal of work within these industries and with NGOs and multilateral agencies to improve their practices. Now many more NGOs are willing to work with these companies, preferably reputable entities in these industries.

Although working with these "taboo" industries, such as tobacco or alcohol, may pose many risks, some NGOs have found that they can also provide significant rewards. For example, tobacco farming occurs predominantly in parts of the world rich in biodiversity, including areas where there is conflict between agricultural land use and biodiversity conservation. Several countries, which are of particular importance to tobacco companies, are "biodiversity hotspots." BAT has one of the most vertically integrated agricultural supply chains in the world, obtaining most of its tobacco from 149,000 contracted farmers. The effects of BAT's supply chain on biodiversity and ecosystems are key issues for its stakeholders, and its reputation rests on being able to demonstrate responsible behavior. Thus for NGOs that want to address biodiversity issues, tobacco companies are key stakeholders. The EarthWatch Institute had a successful partnership with BAT, which grew into the BAT Biodiversity Partnership that includes EarthWatch as well as Fauna and Flora International and several local NGOs. For these NGOs the benefits of the BAT biodiversity partnership outweighs the risks of being associated with a tobacco company.[16]

Capacity Building

The Long-Arnold framework indicates that the key to the capacity-building component of the initiation phase is investing time and resources to develop relationships among the partners and key stakeholders to build trust and mutual respect. As previously mentioned, NGO and corporate managers interviewed indicated that they grossly underestimated the time it takes to undertake these partnerships; they also stressed the importance of building relationships to really understand each other. Organizations employed several different strategies to learn about their partners in addition to regular partner meetings. Some examples follow:

- *CARE and Starbucks:* Several CARE staff spent time at Starbucks headquarters to learn more about the company. Similarly, several Starbucks staff visited both the CARE headquarters and field projects to learn more about development issues and the intersection with their business objectives.[17]

- *City Year and Timberland:* In 1992, City Year created a service day for Timberland employees, including the Timberland CEO, Jeff Swartz, to rehabilitate an adolescent treatment center. This was a pivotal experience for Swartz, solidifying the value of community services by employees. In addition, City Year made a presentation at the Timberland sales meeting.[18]
- *Jumpstart and American Eagle Outfitters (AEO):* In 1998, the AEO and Jumpstart executive teams came together to broaden the interaction and personal relationships beyond the two CEOs. AEO paid for the Jumpstart staff to attend this meeting, which was crucial support for Jumpstart. In the same year, Jumpstart invited AEO to attend the National Forum on Education in Washington, DC. This provided AEO with a much better understanding of educational issues and access to Jumpstart's educational network.[19]

Another element of capacity building is how the partnership will be managed for each organization, including (1) which department will oversee the partnership, (2) whether there will be a designated person to manage the relationship, and (3) which department or person will be responsible for communication about the partnership. Answers to these questions vary based on the size and structure of the organizations and the nature of the partnership. Ideally it is best to have a relationship manager for each organization who keeps the partnership on track and communicates within the organization and with the partner organization. This may be challenging, particularly for smaller organizations. If it is not possible to have a full-time relationship manager, it is beneficial to identify a few key people who can regularly participate in the partnership to serve as contact people. This is particularly important during the initial phase when the partnership relies heavily on personal relationships to move it forward. For example, one of the initial challenges faced by City Year in their partnership with Timberland was the lack of a designated person to manage the collaboration. Several years into the partnership, City Year hired a dedicated person to manage the relationship, which greatly facilitated the partnership process. Upon reflection, they thought that not having an identified manager hindered institutionalization of the partnership.[20]

A large part of relationship building revolves around communication that needs to take place at three levels: (1) internally, to garner and sustain support for the partnership; (2) among the partners to plan, coordinate, and address issues; and (3) externally with stakeholders and peers. As previously mentioned, partnership champions are important in addressing internal resistance to the partnership, coordinating efforts of different units, and exciting people about the partnership's potential.

To maximize each partner's core competencies it takes time for the organizations to learn about each other and explore other areas that they might have in common. Many of these partnerships start small, until trust can be developed. In the partnership between SOS and Timberland, the SOS liaison spoke with the Timberland marketing manager monthly. These meetings provided an opportunity to monitor progress, addressed any challenges, and identified other ways they could support each other. As a result, another partnership opportunity was developed between Timberland's women's department and SOS's Operation Frontline program, which offers a series of cooking and nutritional classes for low-income women and their families.[21]

External communication is a key component of the partnership agreement because it can deal with the use of logos and releases to the media. Thus a clear process needs to be developed between the partners to ensure that they are both comfortable about the information that is released about the partnership.

Execution

The Long-Arnold factors of success in the execution phase include:

- Establishing ground rules to guide the partnership
- Ensuring a clear process for managing disputes (outlined in the initial phase)
- Securing adequate financing
- Regularly reviewing work plans, addressing issues, and making revisions based on discussions among the partners
- Continuing to build the relationship throughout the organizations (partnership)[22]

People

The Long-Arnold framework suggests that the aim of the people component of the execution phase is listening to key stakeholders who are required to have a successful outcome. A strength of these partnerships is the diversity of the organizations; however, this can be a challenge as well. As previously mentioned, NGOs and corporations have differences in timing, processes, expectation of results, language, and decision-making styles, which can cause frustration and misperceptions as well as spur innovation. Therefore, it is important that the partners be able to maintain an open mind and be respectful of each other's differences while focusing on the areas of mutual interest.

It is particularly important to solicit information from groups who may not normally be consulted, ranging from workers in supply chains, marginalized groups such as women, indigenous communities, the poor, or other specialized groups such as youth. NGOs have been more likely to include these groups in their consultations, and businesses now are also widening their reach to include other stakeholder groups. Although there are still some differences in how NGOs and businesses look at these groups, there is growing understanding that their input is valuable. For example, in the partnership between ColCeramica and Kairos it was important for ColCeramica to listen to the needs of the low-income customers and the community saleswomen. For example, the saleswomen did not trust the company and thought that the tiles were made from leftover high-end tiles. To build trust, Kairos facilitated a tour of the factory for the saleswomen. This way they could see that the tiles were newly made and were not from leftovers, demonstrating the company's honesty and commitment to the initiative. If this had not happened, the women may not have been very motivated to sell the tiles, or worse, they could have provided negative information about the product and the company. Kairos and the local NGOs were able to identify the saleswomen's and poor customers' concerns and transmit this information to the company. Based on this information, Colcermica made significant changes to their distribution, marketing, and financing systems to meet these customer's needs, resulting in positive outcomes for all.[23]

Another example was the partnership between Dana Mitra Lingkungan (DML), an Indonesian environmental NGO, and Aqua Gold Mississippi (AGM), a drinking water company that aimed to recycle plastic polyethylene terephthalate (PET) water bottles that were causing environmental harm. In 1992, the program was designed to have consumers pay a deposit for the bottles when they were purchased. Then when the consumer returned the bottles, they would receive double the amount of the deposit as an incentive for recycling. Unfortunately, the return amount was not a sufficient incentive to get many people to recycle the bottles. As a result, most of the bottles were scattered in the sea, threatening the mangrove plants along the shore. It became clear that this program would not be successful without the involvement of the scavengers and garbage pickers who would value a 10- to 20-rupee incentive. It should be noted that these individuals were not identified as a stakeholder group at the outset of the project. The program was redesigned and DML organized and educated the scavengers and garbage pickers about how to clean and recycle the bottles. By 1995, about 30% of the bottles were recycled using this strategy.[24]

One of the interesting things that has happened through NGO-corporate partnerships is that NGOs are using their established networks in different ways. For example, the Grameen Bank is known for its microfinance work with poor rural women in Bangladesh. When Grameen Phone wanted to expand their reach to the rural areas, it was a natural fit to tap this existing network of women, who had previously received a Grameen loan, to sell access to their airtime. As a result, the Grameen Bank staff selected women to serve as village phone operators based on their loan repayment history, financial solvency such as business income, literacy, availability of electricity in the house, and central location within the village. Because these women had previously repaid a loan, it was not difficult to develop this highly desired service. The operator acts like a public call office: She resells phone calls, provides message services within the village, and lets others receive incoming calls, all of which greatly improved rural people's access to information. By leveraging this network, Grameen Phone was able to efficiently, reliably, and rapidly expand its presence in the rural market without having to build an entire rural distribution by itself.[25]

In successful partnerships, participants share their knowledge and potential challenges with their partners early in the process. For example, when Starbucks was criticized by Guatemalan labor activists for not helping coffee workers, they sought CARE's counsel and experience to help them develop a code of conduct for their coffee suppliers. CARE's expertise and long-term presence in Guatemala provided valuable insights and credibility to Starbucks in response to this issue.[26]

People are key at this stage, because the partnership is largely based on the relationships of these key individuals; they are the drivers of the partnership. Most of the intangible information about the partnership—for example, how it started—is in people's heads, not on paper. These people are usually the partnership champions within their organizations and their professional networks. One of the key successes of the Rainforest Alliance and Chiquita partnership was the continued presence of the two partnership champions. This provided great stability for the partnership, deepening the relationship, which helped them weather many storms.[27]

Because people are crucial to this process, changes in personnel during this phase can significantly affect the progress of the partnership. In the Save the Children and Denny's partnership, the departure of Denny's CEO, who had made the commitment to undertake more strategic community development efforts, could have been the end of the partnership. However, because the relationship had reached a maturity level at which there was substantial involvement and support throughout both organizations, it was able to continue. To get buy-in, the Denny's senior staff quickly took their new CEO to meet the Save the Children CEO. This provided an opportunity for him to understand the importance and value created by the partnership.[28]

Goals and Objectives

The Long-Arnold framework suggests that the aim of the goals and objectives component of the execution phase is to translate the shared vision into clear and actionable interventions that the partners can implement to achieve the overall partnership goal. It is also important that the partners have a common understanding about the key causes of the problem and how their combined efforts will address the issue. Goals between NGOs and corporations can range from being very specific, by location and type of activity, to being very broad, such as addressing biodiversity.

Because most of the partnerships reviewed started small, it is not surprising that many focused on a single issue in a specific location, such as DML and AGM's work in Indonesia to reduce waste created by the PET water bottles. Although several of the partnerships began as a donation in a specific location, they grew to a national program, as in the case of City Year and Timberland. The CRM partnerships were usually done on a larger scale to enhance visibility and fundraising, as demonstrated by the partnership between the American Red Cross and National Restaurant Association.

Six of the partnerships aimed to have market-level changes, including:

1. Greenpeace and Foron to improve the use of hydrocarbon technology in Germany
2. Rainforest Alliance and Chiquita to improve banana farming practices in Latin America
3. DML and AGM to recycle PET water bottles in Indonesia
4. Grameen Bank and Grameen Phone to expand access to information in rural Bangladesh
5. ColCeramica and Kayros to develop a market for home repair/décor tiles in Colombia

6. World Vision and Eureka Forbes to develop an affordable water service in Indonesia

Most of these partnerships were good at identifying activities and developing work plans, sometimes jointly and at other times individually. Measurements of the outcomes of the partnerships activities were clearly defined and reported. This is further discussed later in this chapter in "Closure and Renewal." As previously mentioned, partnership champions or relationship managers play a vital role in ensuring that participants are focused on the goal, meet milestones, and address issues as they arise. In addition, they provide support for the partnership, such as providing internal and external communication, and help resolve disputes as needed. Many NGOs and even some corporations were not able to have a designated person to manage the partnership. It was usually assigned to someone who already had a full-time job or it was divided between a few staff people. The senior vice president of non-profit PCI Global said, "[W]e didn't have enough staff to fully engage with Qualcomm. We know there are a lot of other opportunities for us to work together, but we have not had the time or the staff to explore the possibilities."[29]

Challenges arise in partnerships. Some are minor and others are critical to the partnership. They may be caused by (1) internal issues within one organization limiting its ability to participate in the partnership, such as changes in senior management; (2) disagreements between the partners; or (3) changes in the external environment that negatively affect one or both of the partners, such as the recent financial crisis.

In 1994, several events challenged the partnership between the Rainforest Alliance and Chiquita. First, the European Union changed their quota and licensing policies to favor local producers, thus reducing the ability of large banana companies to sell their products in the European market. Second, a newspaper in Cincinnati, Ohio—where Chiquita is headquartered—featured an exposé alleging that Chiquita had horrible business practices, such as poisoning staff with pesticides. The article was found to be very inaccurate, but the retraction did not change the minds of the readers. Third, critics questioned Rainforest Alliance's credibility and expertise to conduct third-party certification processes. Fourth, a shareholder resolution was brought by the Interfaith Center on Corporate Responsibility, although it was later withdrawn. Both organizations agreed that these events "put the partnership to the test," but in the end it made the partnership stronger, increasing their commitment and trust, and leading to a cobranding effort.[30]

Capacity Building

The Long-Arnold framework suggests that the aim of the capacity-building component of the execution phase is to develop the adequate systems and skills to translate the vision into results. Building capacity also implies a learning process among the partners in which performance is regularly assessed and revisions are made based on the partner's knowledge and experience. A key component to building a partnership is communication.

The partnership agreement should clearly articulate how the partners will communicate, such as a monthly meeting to review progress. Organizations should not underestimate the amount of internal communication that is required to reduce criticism, gain support from various units, and motivate employee engagement. Because NGO-corporate partnerships are relatively new, there is a great deal of learning that needs to take place to figure out how these two entities can successfully work together. Communication must be two-directional for the partnership to be successful. For example, Food for the Hungry tested Sawyer Products' water filter in Bolivian communities. The two organizations needed to have regular dialogue to identify issues with the use of the filter and ways it could be improved. The information that Food for the Hungry provided to Sawyer Products enabled them to develop a more effective water filter design that has a greater likelihood of being used correctly by Bolivians.[31]

With the recent economic recession, one of the key questions is, will businesses continue to contribute to partnerships when their overall profitability and viability is significantly threatened? Social and environmental issues have business value, so if partnerships are designed to maximize this value they can help companies survive during a rough economy. Jeff Swartz, Timberland CEO, sums it up best. In 1995, when Timberland faced a liquidity crisis, its bankers demanded that Timberland get out of the community service business. Swartz's response was "[A]s long as I am running the company, values are central to who we are." Despite the fiscal difficulties, the company doubled the paid community service hours offered to employees. According to Swartz, that is what saved the company.[32]

Closure and Renewal

The Long-Arnold factors of success in the closure and renewal phase include:

- Evaluating results compared with the partnership goal
- Sharing credit among partners
- Identifying future value
- Institutional arrangements[33]

People

The Long-Arnold framework suggests that the aim of the people component in the closure and renewal phase is for the partners to share the credit of the partnership's success. For example, Rainforest Alliance and Chiquita conducted a co-branding campaign to share the results of their partnership, providing visibility to each organization. Two NGOs gave awards to their corporate partners—CARE to Howard Schultz, Starbucks CEO; and Save the Children to Ron Perry, Denny's CEO. Starbucks stores had posters about the partnership with CARE at their stores so their customers could learn about the partnership.

It is extremely important to acknowledge the contribution of the partners as well as other key stakeholders such as local governments in the partnership's success. EDF suffered some criticism for not giving enough credit to grassroots campaigners for making McDonald's realize that it had a solid-waste problem in the first place.[34]

Goals

The Long-Arnold framework indicates that the aim of the goal component during the closure and renewal phase is to evaluate performance against stated goals. It is vital that partnerships be evaluated based on the partnership goal outlined and agreed to in the initial phase. There are two components of this process. First, there is an evaluation of the value added by the specific activities. Second, there is a review of the partnership structures and processes to see if the partnership itself provided learning and value. Based on this information, the partners can determine if they want to renew the partnership, with some modifications, or if they want to end the partnership.

It appears that almost all the of the partnerships reviewed had defined metrics for the results of specific activities, such as the amount of money raised through CRM, the earned income for PET bottle crushers, and the number of certified banana farmers. However, it was less clear if these partnerships had metrics that measured the overall partnership process and approach. This is not surprising because the field is still evolving and the work is ongoing to find meaningful partnership metrics, which are further discussed in Chapter 9.

Capacity Building

The Long-Arnold framework suggests that the aim of the capacity-building component during the closure and renewal phase is to sustain the results of the partnership by deepening relationships, obtaining commitments, and identifying resources to institutionalize the partnership arrangements. Of the partnerships reviewed, five have continued for over 10 years, implying that they have been able to continue to create value through these partnerships. It is interesting to note that they all started with a relatively small discrete activity—donation of a product or grant, or CRM campaign—that grew into other areas of collaboration.

If the decision is to renew a partnership, then it is important to develop institutional arrangements to ensure that the partnership continues at an organizational level and not just among the key people who are directly involved in the partnership. For example, City Year is located within Timberland's headquarters, which provides easy access, communication, and ample opportunities to develop new initiatives. Another NGO strategy has been to elect business representatives to their board of directors, as seen in the cases of MedShare and Kimberly-Clark, City Year and Timberland, CARE and Starbucks, and Jumpstart and AEO. This provides opportunities at the most strategic level of the organizations to identify areas that can create commonly shared value. It is interesting to note that I am not aware of any businesses that have named NGO representatives to their board of directors.

Several of the partnerships were not able to continue because of structural changes in the business. For example, a French company bought 40% of AGM. It did not have the same commitment to environmental issues as AGM so the partnership with DML ended.[35] This is an important issue, considering the high rate of business mergers and acquisitions.

Another reason that a partnership may not be able to create more value is that the goal has been achieved or changes in the environment result in changes in the relationship between the NGO and the business. For example, once Greenpeace created a demand for the hydrocarbon technology in the German refrigerator market, accomplishing their goal, there was no reason for them to continue to work solely with Foron, so the partnership ended.[36]

Summary

Table 6.1 provides an overview of a diverse group of NGO-corporate partnerships. They range in terms of size, topic, location, and types of organizations. This diversity is both a strength and a challenge for the NGO sector. Table 6.1 demonstrates that many NGOs are successfully working with corporations and those that are not can learn from those that have gone through the process. The analysis of these case studies provides some insights that can improve NGO-corporate partnerships described here.

- *Begin at Home:* Some of the work to be a better partner has to happen internally. Organizations, both NGOs and corporations, need to:

- Know why they want to engage (e.g., visibility, raise money, or practice new approaches)
- Know the value they can bring to the partnership
- Know how they want to engage (e.g., CRM, joint venture)
- Know who they want to engage with and who they don't want to work with
- Know if they have the capacity, resources, and skills to partner (if not, they need to develop a plan to develop their capacity)

- *Focus on the Content, Not the Cash:* Partnerships are based on common interests. In the beginning, organizations do not fully understand all the ways they can work together. Although some NGOs may need financial support to work with corporations, focusing on this limits the potential of the partnership.
- *Spend Time Getting to Know Each Other:* It takes time to develop a relationship, which at times may seem more process than results focused. However, time and resources to develop a relationship are well-rewarded investments, even if a specific partnership does not develop.
- *Designate a Relationship Manager:* Partnerships require dedicated time and resources, particularly human resources, to be successful. If a part-time relationship manager is the only option, then the organization should ensure that it accurately calculates the time requirements needed to effectively support the partnership.
- *Communicate Regularly:* Partnerships require a regular mechanism to ensure communication and coordination among all the partners and stakeholders. This helps build trust, ensure transparency, and can greatly reduce misunderstandings or misperceptions.
- *Performance Measurement Is Key:* Partnerships are designed to create value, so it is important to assess whether the partnership is really adding value to both partners. This can be in terms of achieving results, sharing and learning information, or improving processes or products.

Notes

1. Fredrick Long and Matthew Arnold, *The Power of Environmental Partnerships* (Washington, DC: The Dryden Press, Harcourt Brace College Publishers, 1995).

2. Ibid.

3. Ibid.

4. "The American Medical Association to Pay Sunbeam $9.9Million," *Washington Post,* August 2, 1998.

5. Shirley Sagawa and Eli Segal, *Common Interest: Common Good: Creating Value Through Business and Social Sector Partnerships* (Boston: Harvard Business School Press, 2000).

6. James Austin, *The Collaboration Challenge: How Nonprofits and Business Succeed Through Strategic Alliances* (San Francisco: Jossey-Bass, 2000).

7. Personal interview with A. B. Short, CEO of MedShare, and Dr. James Quayle, medical director of Kimberly-Clark, January 31, 2006.

8. Bea Boccalandro, *A Helping Hand or a Hijacking: How Non-Profits Can Respond to Ever-Increasing Corporate Involvement in the Community* (Germany: Centrum fur Corporate Citizenship, 2005).

9. Sagawa and Segal, *Common Interest.*

10. Ibid.

11. Ibid.

12. Jorg Andriof, Sandra Waddacok, Bryan Husted, and Sandra Sutherland-Raham, eds., *Unfolding Stakeholder Thinking, Volume 2: Relationships, Communication, Reporting and Performance* (Sheffield, UK: GreenLeaf, 2003).

13. Long and Arnold, *The Power of Environmental Partnerships.*

14. Sagawa and Segal, *Common Interest.*

15. Chris Zwicke, "Corporate-NGO Partnerships: A Conversation With EDF's Gwen Ruta," *Triple Pundit,* March 4, 2010, http://www.triplepundit.com/2010/03/corporate-ngo-partnerships-edf-gwen-ruta.

16. "British American Tobacco plc," *EarthWatch,* http://www.earthwatch.org/europe/our_work/corporate/corporate_partners/bat/.

17. Austin, *The Collaboration Challenge.*

18. Ibid.

19. Ibid.

20. Ibid.

21. Center for Corporate Citizenship at Boston College, "Teaming Up to Brand and Bond: Timberland Partners with City Year, SOS and Skills USA," *In Practice: A Series About Integrating Business and Community Development: Center for Corporate Citizenship at Boston College,* no. 5, March 2004.

22. Long and Arnold, *The Power of Environmental Partnerships.*

23. Bill Drayton and Valeria Budinich, "A New Alliance for Global Change," *Harvard Business Review* (September 2010):1–12.

24. Tadashi Yamamoto, Kim Gould, and K. G. Ashizawa, *Corporate-NGO Partnerships* (Tokyo, Japan: Japanese Center for International Exchange, 1999).

25. Shyamal Chowdhury, "Attaining Universal Access: Public-Private Partnership and Business-NGO Partnership," ZEF Bonn, Discussion Papers on Development Policy, Bonn, Germany, July 2002.

26. Austin, *The Collaboration Challenge.*

27. J. Gary Taylor and Patricia J. Scharlin, *Smart Alliance: How a Global Corporation and Environmental Activities Transformed a Tarnished Brand* (New Haven: Yale University Press, 2004).

28. Sagawa and Segal, *Common Interest.*

29. Personal interview with A. B. Short, CEO of MedShare, and Dr. James Quayle, medical director of Kimberly-Clark, January 31, 2006.

30. Taylor and Scharlin, *Smart Alliance.*

31. Personal interview with Tom Davis, senior director of program quality for Food for the Hungry, and Kurt Avery, president of Sawyer Products, October 23, 2010.

32. Sagawa and Segal, *Common Interest.*

33. Long and Arnold, *The Power of Environmental Partnerships.*

34. Andriof, Waddacok, Husted, and Sutherland-Raham, eds., *Unfolding Stakeholder Thinking.*

35. Yamamoto, Gould, and Ashizawa, *Corporate-NGO Partnerships.*

36. Andriof, Waddacok, Husted, and Sutherland-Raham, eds., *Unfolding Stakeholder Thinking.*

7

Tri-Party Partnerships

What Are Tri-Party Partnerships?

The boundaries between the non-governmental organization (NGO), business, and public sectors are becoming increasingly blurred. These three sectors are becoming more interdependent, requiring involvement of one sector to achieve another sector's goals. As previously mentioned, public-private partnerships are usually contractual relationships between a government entity and a for-profit private business, often in the field of defense or infrastructure. They do not include any NGO involvement, so for this discussion the term "tri-party" is used to accurately reflect partnerships among an NGO, a business, and a government agency.

These sectors bring different resources, skills, and networks to these partnerships, which are both a strength and a challenge. NGOs have technical expertise in key areas, long-standing relationships with communities, and global and local networks. Businesses can provide skills, technologies, infrastructure, distribution systems, and networks through suppliers, employees, and consumers. Government agencies can bring technical expertise, funding, and policy formulation abilities, as well as their facilitation and convening power. Although there are many similarities between bilateral NGO-corporate partnerships and tri-party partnerships, the addition of a government department in the partnership changes the dynamic. They have different cultures, motivations, timeframes, and measures of success than NGOs or businesses.

Figure 7.1 presents the classic market segmentation model in which the population is divided into different economic strata, with "A" being the wealthy, "C" being the middle class, and "E" being the very poor. Historically, businesses have marketed luxury goods and service items to the A- and some B-class consumers and moderately priced goods to B- and C-class consumers. NGOs' target markets for goods and services have been the lower middle class

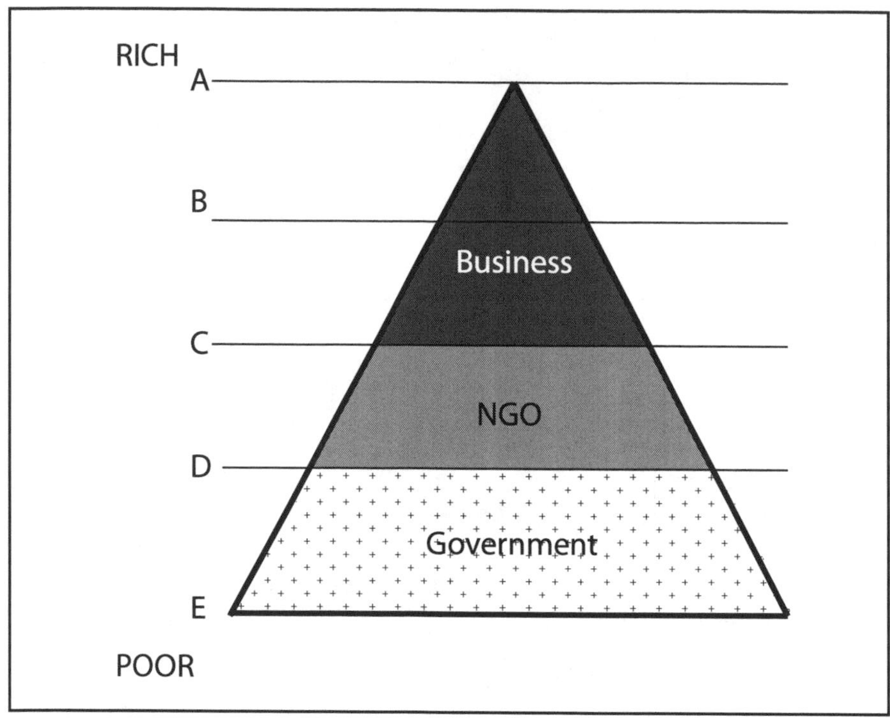

Figure 7.1 Traditional market segmentation.

(C) and the poor (D), while government safety nets focus on the poor (D) and the very poor (E).

There is a growing interest among the private sector to work with the base of the economy—an estimated 4 billion people who have a purchasing power of less than $3,000.[1] For example, through partnerships with NGOs and governments, businesses are now able to source from and sell to the poor in more effective ways than redistributing their profits through philanthropy. In addition, more NGOs are thinking of effective ways to work with higher income groups to diversify their revenue streams and cross-subsidize their efforts for those who cannot afford to pay for the goods or services. Lastly, governments are looking for better ways to design their social safety net programs. Thus all the sectors have expanded the market segments that they work with, increasing the overlap with other sectors, as presented in Figure 7.2. These changes suggest more commonalities among the sectors that could lead to more partnership opportunities.

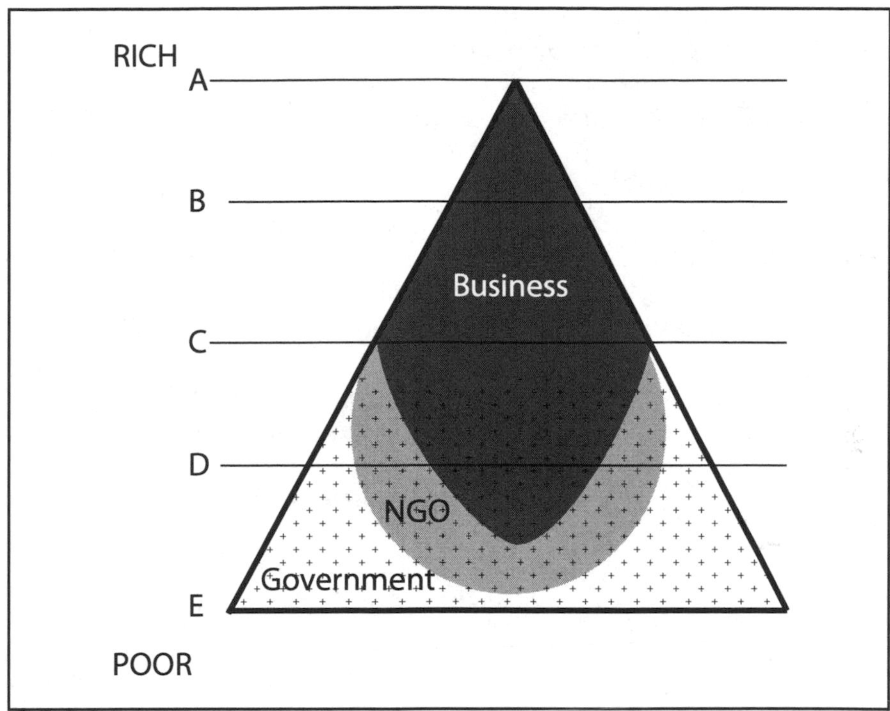

Figure 7.2 Overlapping market segmentation.

As governments at all levels—city, state, and national—are faced with increasing budget deficits, growing distrust among their constituents, and looming complex social problems, they are seeking innovative solutions that build on their strengths while tapping the resources and expertise of both the private and NGO sectors. In addition, since the late 1990s, there has been growing interest among international government donor agencies to leverage the resources, skills, and technology of the private sector. The 2009 *Partnering for Global Development* report identified 10 international development agencies from Europe, Japan, and the United States that were developing programs to involve the private sector.[2]

The British government has established several funds to foster partnerships among NGOs, businesses, and the United Kingdom's Department For International Development (DFID). DFID describes these partnerships as "the best approach to development enabling aid to deliver more direct benefits to the poor without excessive transaction costs."[3,4] DFID invested £14.7 million to establish the Business Linkage Challenge Fund, which provided funds to British companies engaged in innovative partnerships with businesses or NGOs in less developed countries to benefit the poor. This experience helped generate the £100 million Africa Enterprise Challenge Fund, supported by the DFID, the African Development Bank, and the International Fund for Agricultural Development, for similar types of partnerships in Africa. In 2010, DFID launched the Business Innovation Facility, which supports development and use of inclusive business models by companies in developing countries.[5]

In 1995, Vice President Gore announced the United States Agency for International Development (USAID)'s New Partnership Initiative to further the Agency's partnership approach with a variety of organizations. In 2001, Secretary of State Colin Powell established the USAID/Global Development Alliance (USAID/GDA) to be "an innovative public-private alliance model for improving social and economic conditions in developing countries. GDA combines the assets and experience of strategic partners, leveraging their capital, investments, creativity and access to markets to solve complex problems."[6] Initially, the focus was on leveraging private sector funds, but the strategy has evolved into strategically collaborating with the private sector to build on respective core competencies: financial, technology, skills, and networks. Between 2002 and 2004, USAID engaged new partners through nearly 300 alliances with an investment of more than $1.1 billion that leveraged over $3.7 billion from partners.[7]

Multilateral organizations have also become very interested in involving the private sector in development programs. In 1998, in response to a changing global environment, the World Bank facilitated the development of Business Partners for Development (BPD). BPD was designed as a three-year program to study, support, and promote strategic examples of tri-sector partnerships involving business, government, and NGOs. BPD had four clusters—natural resources, water and sanitation, global road safety, and youth development—that implemented about 30 projects with a network of over 120 organizations during the three-year period. To foster sustainable development, communities were at the center of these partnerships. The results of BPD showed that companies, through tri-sector partnerships, have an important role in development programming that can enhance their productivity and underlying profitability while addressing the needs of the poor.[8]

How Do Tri-Party Partnerships Work?

As previously mentioned, the Long-Arnold framework identifies nine key success factors of NGOs and corporate partnerships, further discussed in Chapter 6 and presented in Table 6.2. For purposes of consistency, the Long-Arnold framework is used to review the 10 tri-party cases presented in Table 7.1. The framework is based on a Partnership Lifecycle approach, which starts with a seed phase that includes the prepartnership activities. If organizations agree to develop a relationship, there are three partnership phases: initiation, execution, and closure and renewal. Within each phase, there are three key factors: people, goals, and capacity building.[9]

Partnership Lifecycle

Seed Phase

Although the Long-Arnold framework does not identify specific success factors during the seed phase, prepartnership activities are vital because many discussions never make it beyond this stage. For example, the BPD water and sanitation cluster found that this stage is often underanalyzed. They found that partners look at the benefits and challenges of working with others, but little attention is paid to the implications that the larger environment might have on the success of the partnership. The BPD water and sanitation cluster suggests that some of the key questions that should be considered are:

- Is the political, social, and economic climate conducive to the formation of a partnership?
- Is the private sector willing to take on additional risks in the current investment climate?
- Are communities and local government actors receptive to the notion of private sector participation?
- What are the dynamics between local politicians and poor communities?[10]

Thus actors should allow extra time to carefully consider and analyze all the factors that may affect the potential partnership and its likelihood of success.

Partnership Initiation

Any organization can initiate a partnership as evidenced by these case studies. Three of the NGOs—CARE, Concern Universal, and Institute for Sustainable Communities (ISC)—were already working on specific topics that led them to initiate a relationship with a business. For Gambia is Good (GiG), the process was facilitated by the fact that Concern Universal's executive director had previously worked for Haygrove and was close friends with the Haygrove directors.[11] In the case of the Rural Sales Program (RSP), CARE

(*text continues on p. 175*)

Table 7.1
Examples of Tri-Party Partnerships

Partners	Objective	Activities	Results
Business Partners for Development (natural resources cluster)[a]			
NGOs: Association for Social and Health Advancement (ASHA) (community development) and Suchetana (community development) **Company:** Integrated Coal Mining Limited (ICML) (mining) **Government:** World Bank and local Indian districts	• Effectively manage the resettlement of villages affected by the mine development. • Create livelihood opportunities for the affected villages.	• NGOs developed self-help groups to help the communities transition to new location. • Trained farmers on better utilization of the remaining land for agriculture production. • Provided training on alternative livelihoods such as crafts and trading.	• Communities developed livelihood skills, improved civic capacity through leadership and skills training. • Use of NGOs was more cost effective (25%) than if the company did it alone. • ICML secured "social license to operate" through an equitable resettlement plan.
Business Partners for Development (water and sanitation cluster)[b]			
NGO: ENDA (community development) **Company:** Senegalese des Eaux (SdE) (private water utility) **Government:** SONES (public water utility) and World Bank	• Create a water system (metered standpipes) in Senegal to serve poor households who used a polluted water source with negative health effects.	• SONES developed new infrastructure, regulated SdE, approved ENDA's work with communities. • SdE operated the water system, developed billing system. • ENDA worked with communities to mobilize financial contributions, form water committees, and train standpipe operators.	• Increased access to potable water for 200,000 people. • Reduced waterborne illnesses among children. • Standpipe operators received between 30,000 and 80,000 francs per month.

Gambia is Good (local Gambian NGO)[c]			
NGOs: Haygrove Development (company NGO) and Concern Universal (community development) **Company:** Haygrove (agriculture products) (donated £125,000 worth of business services) **Government:** DFID (£200,000 Business Challenge Fund)	• Develop a pro-poor marketing entity to improve Gambian farmers' yields and provide produce to tourist hotels, restaurants, and supermarkets.	• Created a farm to provide training and demonstrate best practices. • Created market linkages to ensure a regular supply of quality produce to hotels and restaurants.	• Won (2008) Virgin Holidays Responsible Tourism Award. • Farmers received £7.9 million for 500 tons of locally grown produce. • Women farmers earned up to £150 a month.
Global Alliance for Workers and Communities (1999–2005)[d]			
NGO: International Youth Foundation (IYF) (Youth) **Companies:** Nike ($7.7M) and Gap ($5.5M) (footwear and apparel) **Government:** World Bank	• Improve working conditions in subcontracted footwear and apparel factories in Asia.	• Conducted factory assessments of workers' issues. • Worked with NGOs and factory managers to provide access to health services, and other life skills. • Trained 740 factory managers in effective management and communication approaches.	• Nike and Gap gained a better understanding of their supply chains. • 175,000 workers in 50 factories received health care, reducing absenteeism. • Over 7,100 workers received life skills training. • Improved worker-manager relationships and higher productivity.
Guangdong Environment Partnership (GEP) (2009–2011)[e]			
NGO: Institute for Sustainable Communities (environmental and community development) **Companies:** General Electric (GE) Foundation and CitiBank Foundation (Financial) **Government:** USAID/GDA ($750,000), US-EPA, and China EPA	• Reduce greenhouse gas emissions, improve public health, and increase environmental accountability in Guangdong province.	• Created Environment, Health and Safety (EHS) Academy at Sun Yat-Sen University to train corporate EHS managers. • Developed certification protocol for EHS managers. • Worked with 100 factories in three communities to reduce energy use and waste.	• Trained 2,300 factory managers from 24 companies at EHS Academy. • Piloted certification protocol in 2011. • Saved 50 kilowatts of electricity. • Reduced greenhouse gas emissions by 100 tons.

(*continues*)

Table 7.1 (*continued*)

Partners	Objective	Activities	Results
Inclusive Marketplace Alliance Rural Enterprises (IMARE)[f]			
NGO: MercyCorps **Company:** Walmart **Government:** USAID/GDA	• Increase small Guatemalan farmers' ability to sell products to the formal supermarket sector.	• Trained 39 farmer groups to supply fresh vegetables to Walmart stores, meeting all standards of quality and volume. • Enhanced market linkages.	• Producer groups increased formal market sales by 45%. • Farmers increased their income by 59%. • Increased profitability per hectare planted by 25%. • Farmers hired over 1,300 people as their operations grew. • 63% of farm profits are used for family benefit, such as schooling, improved housing, and health care.
NetMark (1999–2009)[g]			
NGO: Academy of Education Development (AED) (multisectoral) **Companies:** Exxon Mobile Foundation ($700,000) (extractive), 42 African companies, and 9 MNC partners **Government:** USAID ($65M) 1995–2005	• Create a commercial channel for insecticide-treated bednets (ITNs) to reduce malaria.	• Developed a discount voucher system that paid for a portion of the ITNs distributed through ExxonMobil gas stations.	• ITNs protected 15 million people from malaria. • NetMark partners sold 60 million ITNs. • In Ghana, Nigeria, Senegal, and Zambia, the voucher redemption rate among users was 90%.

Pro-Planalto[h]			
NGO: CARE, World Vision, PLAN, Africare, Catholic Relief Services, and Save the Children (multisectoral) **Company:** Chevron Texaco ($4M) (Oil and Gas) **Government:** USAID/Angola ($3M)	• Help returned combatants rebuild farms and improve agricultural yields.	• Formed 150 farming cooperatives. Provided tools, seeds, technical support, and access to credit. • Rebuilt rural infrastructure and created market linkages so farmers could sell their products.	• Increased production of farmers' crop harvest from 245 kg in 2003 to 404 kg in 2005. • Rehabilitated 4,000 km of roads and 1,000 km of irrigation canals.
Rural Sales Program 2004–2011[i]			
NGO: CARE (multisectoral) **Companies:** Bata (shoes), Unilever/Square (consumer products), Lal Teer (agricultural seeds), and Bic (razors, pens) **Government:** USAID/Bangladesh	• Create a rural distribution system to provide economic opportunities for low-income women.	• Developed distribution system of 70 Hub managers (5% commission) and 140 service people to provide products to the 2,000 saleswomen (Aparajitas). • Aparajitas receive a commission from sales—about 3,000 Taka worth of product a week. • Trained Aparajitas on business skills, basic health and product-specific information. • Negotiated with companies for product sales. Companies pay CARE a commission (4%–8%) to manage the system.	• Aparajitas' average monthly income is about $20. • In 2010, CARE received about $178,000 from commissions.

(*continues*)

Table 7.1 (*continued*)

Partners	Objective	Activities	Results
Sakhalin Salmon Initiative (SSI)[j]			
NGO: Wild Salmon Center (environmental) **Company:** Sakhalin Energy (energy and utilities) **Government:** USAID/Russia and US Forest Service	• Conserve and manage wild salmon on Sakhalin Island.	• Established six Watershed Councils in an effort to fight poaching. • Educated 200 children in both Russia and the United States about the issues surrounding salmon. • Developed sustainable fisheries.	• Won first place at the 2009 Russia Corporate Donor Awards. • Organized the first international environmental salmon camp. • Fisheries expected to be MSC-certified in 2011.

a. Michael Warner and Rory Sullivan, eds., *Putting Partnership to Work: Strategic Alliances for Development Between Government, the Private Sector, and Civil Society* (Sheffield, UK: GreenLeaf, 2004).
b. Business Partners for Development, http://www.bpdws.org/web/w/www_57_en.aspx.
c. Helen Wadham, "An Exploration of Business and NGO Perspectives on Corporate Social Responsibility, Sustainable Development and Partnership," Manchester Metropolitan University Business School, submitted December 2007.
d. Rionda Zynia, *CSR Casebook* (Washington, DC: Catalyst Consortium and USAID, July 2002).
e. Institute for Sustainable Communities, http://www.iscvt.org/news/press_releases/article/?id=45.
f. Mercy Corps, "IMARE Project Fact Sheet," Mercy Corps, Portland, OR, March 9, 2011.
g. NetMark Alliance Brief, http://pdf.usaid.gov/pdf_docs/PDACL539.pdf.
h. Rani Parker, Mark Schlagenhauf, and Gail Spence, *The Public-Private Alliances of USAID in Angola: An Assessment of Lessons Learned and Ways Forward* (USAID/Angola, Sept. 2004).
i. Catherine Dolan and Linda Scott, *The Future of Retailing? The Aparajitas of Bangladesh* (Oxford, UK: CARE Bangladesh and Said Business School, Oxford University, 2009).
j. Sakhalin Salmon Initiative, http://www.wildsalmoncenter.org/programs/sakhalin/accomplishments.php.

had existing relationships with several donors, so the key was how to involve businesses in the program. CARE Bangladesh's introduction was fostered by discussions between CARE Canada and Bata Canada, although Bata Bangladesh was initially less enthusiastic about the partnership.[12] For ISC, it was easy to approach companies because the companies had been struggling to train environmental, health, and safety (EHS) managers as mandated by the government and thought that pooling their resources would be a great benefit to them, so it was a felt need of the companies.[13]

In the case of International Youth Foundation (IYF) and Nike, a Nike board member who knew that both organizations were looking for a partner facilitated the introduction.[14] The World Bank played a similar role in the two BPD case studies.

Although USAID/Angola had existing relationships with NGOs, ChevronTexaco approached them to fulfill a commitment made by David O'Reilly, the chief executive officer (CEO) of ChevronTexaco, who was asked by the president of Angola to make a substantial contribution toward rebuilding the country. ChevronTexaco was knowledgeable about Cabinda, where they operate, but they were not well positioned to make a significant contribution in the rest of Angola.[15]

For MercyCorps, the discussions began with both USAID and Walmart in Guatemala and were continued by their Washington staff with USAID/GDA and the Walmart government relations office.[16]

Lastly, NetMark was a competitive solicitation that was won by the Academy of Education Development (AED). One of the challenges to tri-party partnerships, discussed later, is that the solicitation identified the strategy and the timeline without any involvement of private-sector entities, which significantly affected the partnership options.[17]

Partnership Agreement

A key component of this phase is negotiating a successful partnership agreement to move into a partnership. A partnership agreement, further discussed in Chapter 9, should articulate goals and objectives, roles and responsibilities, communication and management structures, and the general principles of the partnership. Tri-party partnerships may have one joint agreement among all the partners that outlines the general principles and expectations of the partnership. However, the NGO often receives funding from both the business and government agency, so separate agreements are required. This means that the NGO has more financial and reporting requirements in these types of partnerships than in a bilateral partnership, as outlined in Table 7.2. In summary, Table 7.2 shows that out of the ten cases reviewed there were:

Table 7.2
Tri-Party Partnerships and Financial Agreements by Type of Organization

Partnership	Contract Between Government and Business	Contract or Grant Between Government and NGO	Contract or Grant Between Business and NGO	Comments
Business Partners for Development (natural resources)	• Contract between IFC, Indian government, and ICML	• None	• Grant between ICML, ASHA, and Suchenna	• Part of licensing agreement; • IFC and the Indian Government did not sign the MOU.
Business Partners for Development (water and sanitation)	• Contract between SONES (public) and Senegalese des Eaux (company)	• SONES (public water utility) and ENDA (NGO)	• None	
Gambia is Good (GiG)	• None	• DFID and Haygrove development (NGO) subgranted to GiG		• Haygrove provided business management support to GiG.
GEP	• None	• USAID/GDA and ISC	• GE, Citbank Foundation, and ISC	• ISC and University had agreement.
Global Alliance for Workers and Communities	• None	• None	• Nike, Gap, and IYF	• Joint agreement with World Bank
IMARE	• None	• USAID and MercyCorps	• Walmart and MercyCorps	• Joint agreement among all partners
NetMark	• None	• USAID and AED	• AED, Exxon, and other companies	
Pro-Planalto	• None	• Chevron and NGO Consortium (CARE, World Vision, PLAN, Africare, Catholic Relief Services, and Save the Children)	• USAID/Angola • NGO Consortium	• Joint agreement among all partners
Rural Sales Program	• None	• USAID and CARE	• Companies pay commission to CARE	
Sakhalin Salmon Initiative (SSI)		• USAID/Russia, U.S. Forest Service, and Wild Salmon Center	• Wild Salmon Center • Sakhalin	

- Two contracts between government and private sector entities: true public-private partnerships
- Eight agreements between an NGO and a government agency
- Seventeen agreements between an NGO and a company

These partnerships showed that the NGOs range from managing two agreements to having arrangements with six different organizations. One of the most involved partnership relationships was among the Angola NGO consortium, which was made up of five international NGOs, USAID/Angola, and ChevronTexaco. A memorandum of understanding (MOU) was developed that outlined roles, responsibilities, and activities for the USAID/Angola and ChevronTexaco partnership, but no funds were exchanged. Instead, CARE, as prime contractor of the NGO consortium, had two agreements, one with USAID/Angola and another with ChevronTexaco.[18] Funds were then subgranted to the four other NGO consortium members to implement their activities. In the Inclusive Markets Alliance for Rural Enterprises (IMARE) case, MercyCorps received funding from USAID and both corporate and foundation funding from Walmart. This has not been a problem, but it does require more communication and support for MercyCorps to manage these different funding sources. Thus NGOs play a pivotal role in implementing and managing tri-party partnerships.

Initiation Phase

The Long-Arnold framework factors of success include:

- Creating a well-defined partnership opportunity (value-proposition)
- Identifying internal and external key stakeholders
- Clearly articulating rationale for working together (mutual benefits)
- Sharing a common goal or vision[19]

People

The Long-Arnold framework indicates that the key to the people component of the initiation phase is to identify all the critical internal and external stakeholders who need to support the partnership to ensure its success. Engaging stakeholders can take time, but in the long run their involvement can identify the key issues to be addressed, foster local ownership, and give legitimacy to the partnership.

In response to a public outcry against factory sweatshop conditions, Nike launched an effort to change management practice by developing a code of conduct (CoC) for its subcontracted factories. However, it quickly became apparent that simply having a CoC was not enough. Nike needed to follow up the CoC with a major worker development program and they needed a partner who could help them implement this program on the ground. They began discussions with IYF, who suggested that they could learn how to improve the conditions by engaging the workers in the reform process, a strategy that had not previously been tried. As a result, the Global Alliance for Workers and Communities was predicated on worker and community engagement, which has proven to be a successful strategy.[20]

Goals and Objectives

The Long-Arnold framework indicates that the key to the goals and objectives component of the initiation phase is to define a shared agenda that embodies the vision and goals that they want to achieve through the partnership. The ability to develop a "win-win" partnership varies greatly on the participating organization's mission, modus operandi, timeframes, the issues and sectors to be addressed, and the potential effect for each partner. A key task during this phase is to agree on indicators that will demonstrate the partnership's success, both in terms of the key deliverables and the effectiveness of the partnership. Partners need to ask five key questions when selecting metrics to fully capture the partnership's efforts:

1. How will the outcomes be chosen?
2. How and by whom will the outcomes be achieved?
3. How will the outcomes be measured?
4. What is a fair measure of success for each organization and for the overall partnership?
5. Is there adequate capacity and are there enough resources to collect data to assess the selected metrics?

The NetMark partnership is a good example of organizations having different objectives and timeframes. AED won the USAID solicitation in September 1999 with the aim of creating a viable commercial market for insecticide-treated bednets (ITNs) in at least four countries within five years. AED approached SC Johnson, a global leader in the marketing of consumer insect control products, to develop a partnership. AED believed it was necessary to work with a company that had insect control as part of its core business as well as distribution and marketing capacity to take on a new product under an existing well-known brand. SC Johnson was not sure about the feasibility of the ITN market, but they agreed to conduct market research before they would make a final commitment. When the market research yielded mixed results, SC Johnson proposed launching a test ITN market in Nigeria before making a final decision to roll it out on a larger scale. SC Johnson was concerned about the viability of a commercial ITN market in an environment of low ITN demand, competition from highly subsidized and free ITNs, and uncertain tax and tariff policies. Although AED understood SC Johnson's concerns, their test market proposal would not help them meet their USAID commitment of creating viable markets in four countries in the given timeframe. As a result, SC Johnson decided that it was not a good business decision for them and they withdrew. This meant that AED had to rethink their entire partnership strategy.[21]

This example highlights two key points. First, it is important to involve stakeholders in the design of the partnership at an early stage. In this case, USAID and AED developed the strategy, measures of success, and timeframe without any input from SC Johnson, so SC Johnson had little commitment to achieving results. Second, it is necessary to understand the external environment in which the partnership functions. SC Johnson was concerned about the market conditions that could result in failure and they probably thought that the partnership had little influence over changing these conditions. Thus the risks outweighed the rewards of the partnership. As a result, AED and USAID had to reexamine their objectives and redesign their strategy for partnership with the private sector. This led to a new objective that provided a better balance between the development of commercial markets and improved access for the poor to ITNs. Because of this change, AED changed their approach to working with the private sector. Instead of trying to build a partnership with a few businesses, they aimed to develop a diverse pool of private-sector partners that could help them achieve their new objective.[22]

Capacity Building

The Long-Arnold framework indicates that the key to the capacity-building component of the initiation phase is threefold: (1) investing time and resources to develop relationships among the partners, (2) having or developing the requisite resources and skills to achieve the partnership goal, and (3) ensuring adequate structures and systems, including communication structures, in place to support the partnership.

As previously mentioned, building partnerships takes time. For RSP in Bangladesh, CARE spent almost two years having discussions with Unilever about joining their partnership with Bata. Unilever already had their own program, Joythi, through which they provided a discount to 1,200 rural women to sell their products, so they didn't see any reason why they should work with CARE. In addition, they were worried about competition with Bata. Unilever joined the RSP program in 2008. By 2010 Unilever decided that the RSP was more effective in reaching rural consumers. This was largely due to CARE's facilitation role and their support of the saleswomen to gain credibility in their communities. As a result, Unilever shifted the women in their Joythi program to become part of RSP.[23,24]

It takes time for the organizations to learn about each other and explore other areas that they might have in common. For the Guangdong Environmental Partnership (GEP), sharing best practices was key. The EHS Academy's innovative curriculum was shaped by collaboration among Chinese and Western experts, including trainers from corporations such as General Electric, Honeywell, SABIC Innovative Plastics, and Adidas.[25] This collaboration provided a more comprehensive curriculum in a shorter timeframe with significant corporate buy-in.

In terms of skills and resources, one of the key challenges in the partnership between Association for Social and Health Advancement (ASHA) and Integrated Coal Mining Limited (ICML) was that Suchetana, the local NGO, did not have enough staff to implement their portion of the partnership. Although this was identified as a potential problem during the initial NGO selection process, no plan was developed to address this issue. Fortunately, ASHA and ICML were able to take on additional responsibility to ensure the partnership's success, but it was a greater burden for them.[26]

Building capacity also includes communication with key stakeholders. It is important that this communication occurs both internally within each of the organizations, involving different departments and locations as well as externally with the organization's network.

Partnerships can range from informal associations to formal structures and processes. For GEP, there was a steering committee for the EHS Academy but not for the overall partnership. Two of the reviewed cases included the creation of new NGOs: GiG and Sakhalin Salmon Initiative (SSI) Center. GiG has a board of directors, while a coordinating committee oversees the SSI center. Because of the political importance of the Angola partnership, USAID/GDA in Washington negotiated the MOU directly with ChevronTexaco's corporate headquarters, which included a steering committee as a decision-making body.

These cases demonstrate that there are a variety of approaches to design and structure successful partnerships. Tools such as partnership agreements;

MOUs, which may or may not be legally binding; and steering committees can provide an organized way of dealing with partner tensions, fostering communication, ensuring accountability and transparency, developing institutional buy-in and ownership, and managing grievances. Each partnership needs to determine what approaches are the most effective to support the partnership's success.

Execution

The Long-Arnold factors of success include:

- Establishing ground rules to guide the partnership
- Developing a clear process for managing disputes (outlined in the initial phase)
- Securing adequate financing
- Regularly reviewing work plans to address issues and make revisions based on discussions among the partners
- Continuing to build the relationship[27]

People

The Long-Arnold Framework suggests that the aim of the people component of the execution phase is listening to key stakeholders whose participation is required to have a successful outcome. This can range from workers in supply chains; marginalized groups such as women, indigenous communities, and the poor; or other specialized groups such as youth.

A 2001 Concern Universal study found that even though Gambian tourist hotels, restaurants, and supermarkets were interested in buying local fruits and vegetables, they were not able to do so because of poor quality and an irregular supply. As a result, these businesses were forced to import produce from Europe and Senegal at a much higher price. Smallholder farmers were missing this market opportunity and had no incentive to increase their productivity or quality. By discussing the issues with all the key stakeholders, GiG was able to (1) work with the growers to provide quality produce that was desired by the buyers, (2) develop market linkages that would enable the growers to get their products to the buyers in quantities and a timeframe they required, and (3) get a commitment from the tourist industry to buy local produce. By understanding the issues of all the stakeholders, GiG was able to create value for each player in the supply chain.[28]

One of the key lessons that NetMark learned is that certain conditions needed to be in place before they could successfully launch a commercial ITN market. For example, NetMark's experience showed that to engage low-income markets there needs to be capable small and medium enterprises (SMEs) that can work effectively in a formal supply chain. At the beginning of the process NetMark did not identify SMEs as a key stakeholder group. NetMark initially approached multinational corporations (MNCs) for partnerships. This did not prove to be a very successful strategy because the SMEs were quite weak and thus the supply chain was not very efficient. As the partnership evolved, NetMark worked to build the capcity of the SMEs before they engaged with the MNCs.[29]

Goals

The Long-Arnold framework suggests that the aim of the goals component of the execution phase is to translate the shared vision into clear and actionable interventions that the partners can implement. It can be challenging for all partners to work toward the goal when the relationship is being criticized. This was a major factor that the Global Alliance for Workers and Communities had to contend with to handle the continuing criticism coming from three levels. First, Nike and Gap continued to be criticized for not addressing poor factory conditions. Second, the Global Alliance was criticized for the overall approach. Third, an even greater threat came from internal critics: the factory managers in Indonesia. The factory assessment found that many of the problems on the factory floor resulted from poor communication, poor supervisor training, and verbal abuse from supervisors. These factory managers were upset that the assessment focused more on harassment and other compliance issues rather than on worker development. Despite the concern of the factory managers, the partnership decided that they needed to publicly report these findings to protect its credibility. Through this process the partners learned that there were differing expectations about the assessment among the various stakeholders and priorities about the program. This highlights the need for the partners to ensure that the factory managers were more involved in the partnership and there was clear communication about the process.[30]

A partnership champion or relationship manager plays a vital role in ensuring that participants focus on the goal, meet milestones, manage day-to-day issues of the partnership, resolve disputes, and modify strategies as needed. The CEOs, senior management, and boards of Nike and Gap were highly committed to the Global Alliance for Workers and Communities program, investing their time and money and using their influence with Asian suppliers to support the program.[31]

Another challenge can be when multiple cultures are involved in the partnership. For example, the buyers participating in the Global Alliance for

Workers and Communities partnership were mostly headquartered in the United States. In contrast, many of the factory managers were Korean or Chinese men, who did not speak the local language such as Vietnamese, and the workers were young women who had migrated from rural villages. Thus communication was key and materials needed to be translated into the local language for the workers to understand the partnership.

Capacity Building

The Long-Arnold framework suggests that the aim of the capacity-building component of the execution phase is to develop adequate systems and skills to translate the vision into results. A critical component of GiG's success is its training and demonstration center. The GiG Farm, developed with the assistance of the ministry of agriculture and the National Agricultural Research Institute, demonstrates best-practice farming techniques for local communities and is one of the leading training centers in the country for agricultural innovation. This unique collaboration has resulted in immense knowledge sharing among the partners with mutual benefits for all. Through its action research-demonstration approach, the Farm provides growers with ways to produce new as well as traditional crops during the off-season, which helps the farmers maximize market opportunities. The Farm showcases environmentally sustainable technology and green farming practices so that local farmers and national NGOs have access to working examples of sustainable farming practices. In addition, the Farm has provided training for hundreds of farmers and technical agricultural trainers who have trained even more farmers throughout the country.

Often the capacity that needs to be developed is that of the poor to participate in the partnership. Unlike corporate-managed, base-of-the-pyramid schemes, in RSP, CARE Bangladesh plays a key facilitation role by identifying and supporting women to become sales people, "Aparajitas," the Bangla word for "women who never give up." This is vital to the success of this approach, because in patriarchal rural Bangladesh, women are typically homebound and secluded from the community. They are not allowed to work outside the home, unless it is in the fields, and women who do are not well regarded in their communities. So it is relatively easy to train women in sales, accounting, and business negotiations, but the challenge is how to empower them to want to do this work and how to create an enabling environment that will let them thrive. CARE Bangladesh had to devote significant time and effort to encourage and support these women to agree to be trained, let alone be saleswomen. In many cases their families and communities were not supportive and CARE's community facilitators had to gain their trust and support. Now, there are over 2,000 Aparajitas who are proud to move within and beyond their communities. They are building both social and business connections with other community members and have the respect of their peers. In addition, they have provided access to rural markets for the participating companies and are a trusted source of information and products within their communities, particularly among rural women who are often marginalized. Without this support, RSP would not be the success it is today.[32,33]

Organizations often manage partnerships differently. Some organizations are highly centralized, whereas others are more decentralized. This can be a challenge for the partners to manage. In the case of USAID/Angola and ChevronTexaco, the responsibility for planning and implementing the programs clearly rested with the USAID Mission in Angola. In contrast, ChevronTexaco headquarters retained the responsibility for the program and the local ChevronTexaco office had limited involvement in the program on the ground. As a result, USAID/Angola had a very limited understanding of how the local ChevronTexaco's business unit worked or its relationship to the headquarters, making the partnership more challenging. Fortunately, this did not seem to hinder the work of the NGO consortium that was implementing the program.[34]

Another challenge for these partnerships can occur when multiple levels of organizations are involved in the partnership, requiring substantial coordination efforts. For example in the IMARE case there were three different levels of the organizations and several locations involved in partnership, including:

- In Guatemala, MercyCorps's office, Walmart's office, and USAID/Guatemala
- In Latin America, Walmart's regional office in Costa Rica, which then moved to Mexico
- In the United States, MercyCorps's offices in Portland (headquarters) and in Washington, USAID/Washington, and Walmart's offices in Bentonville, Arkansas (headquarters), and Washington

Fortunately, the partners agreed that the decision-making would occur at the field level and only be escalated to a higher level if they could not find a solution. The partners try, as much as possible, to make joint visits to the field and regularly communicate, but this can be challenging with so many people and diverse schedules involved.[35]

The BPD water and sanitation cluster found that partners need to be able to enter and exit the partnership as their capacities, needs, and strategies dictate. Early discussion and agreement between partners on when and how individual and collective involvement begins and ends are essential because different skills are needed at the different stages of the partnership.[36]

NetMark experienced regular turnover of partners, joining and leaving the alliance, which required continual orientation and lots of communication to keep the partners on the same page. However, David McGuire, NetMark's director, commented, "the whole experience taught us how to make choices that capture partners who are hungry, committed and ready to stick with it for the long haul."[37]

Closure and Renewal

The Long-Arnold factors of success include:

- Evaluating results compared with the partnership goal
- Sharing credit among partners
- Identifying future value
- Developing institutional arrangements[38]

People

The Long-Arnold framework suggests that the aim of the people component of the closure and renewal phase is to share success. It is extremely important to acknowledge the contribution of the partners as well as other key stakeholders in the partnership's success. Both GiG and SSI have won awards for their innovative efforts and demonstrated success. Many of the partnerships have done joint press releases and other media events to share the success of the partnerships.

Goals

The Long-Arnold framework suggests that the aim of the goals component of the closure and renewal phase is to evaluate the results against stated goals. There are two aspects of this process: (1) the overall effect created by the partnership and the value created for each organization, and (2) the effectiveness and efficiency of the partnership approach.

It is interesting that for several of these partnerships, there were differing expectations about what constituted the partnership's success. For NetMark, public health advocates and companies had different measures of success. David McGuire, director of NetMark, commented,

> When you are trying to achieve a public health agenda, you want to save lives yesterday, not a year from now. A commercial partner that sees a 4–5 percent increase in its market share might consider that an astounding success while public health advocates need to impact 50–80 percent of the target population for a success.[39]

In addition, the belief was that developing a commercial relationship, rather than a philanthropic focus, would result in greater resources and corporate buy-in. However, in the NetMark case, the relationship was based on direct business interests. The partnership with SC Johnson failed when those business interests conflicted with the timeframe and expectations of the project. NetMark found that companies were more willing to rethink short-term profit and loss requirements associated with social programs than to rethink their business endeavors. NetMark and the ExxonMobil Foundation were able to agree on indicators that leveraged ExxonMobil's existing brand image and network of service stations in a manner that was not directly tied to their business growth.[40]

Incentives are key, but the BPD water and sanitation projects found that there was little analysis explicitly considering each partner's incentives with the aim of harnessing these into a collaborative plan with partnership goals. The relationships focused on improving service delivery, largely through coordination of activities rather than as part of an overall strategy. In addition, many indicators had not been agreed to at the outset of the partnership, making it difficult to evaluate progress and objectively review the benefits of being in a partnership.[41,42]

For the NGOs that participated in these partnerships, the key results achieved included:

- Increased community capacity
- Enhanced economic opportunities with resulting increased incomes
- Improved access to clean water
- Improved health benefits
- Improved working conditions for factory workers, with the workers leading the process
- Reduced greenhouse gases
- Conservation of key species
- Greater inclusion and empowerment of women

For the businesses that participated in these partnerships, the key results achieved included:

- Secured social license to operate
- Reduced costs through local sourcing
- Improved image and reputation by improving working conditions
- Improved access to quality EHS managers to meet government requirements
- Enhanced effectiveness of supply chains
- Increased sales in rural markets

For the governments that participated in these partnerships, the key results achieved included:

- Managed infrastructure project and successfully resettled villages
- Increased use of more effective strategies to support farmers to improve farming practices
- Improved environmental conditions
- Improved capacity of disadvantaged groups to participate in the formal sector
- Improved health conditions

Capacity Building

The Long-Arnold framework suggests that the aim of the capacity-building component of the closure and renewal phase is to sustain the results of the partnership by deepening relationships, obtaining commitments, and identifying resources to institutionalize the partnership arrangements

In the case of Global Alliance for Workers and Communities, the participatory process undertaken to develop the mission, objectives, and operating plan led to widespread ownership of the project, particularly at the factory level. In fact, some factory managers were willing to pay NGOs to continue to provide services, such as mobile clinics, because they recognized the benefit of these services to factory operations. The partnership also helped the capacity of local research institutions to conduct factory-based surveys. As a result, much of the work that had been undertaken by the partnership was incorporated into existing systems and taken on by other forums, such as the Fair Labor Association, so the partnership ended.[43] The partnership between ASHA and ICML also ended because it had a very specific goal that was achieved, after which there was no reason for the partnership.[44]

GiG and SSI created new organizations, so the focus was on improving their efficiency. Despite numerous successes, GiG had not achieved the commercial viability that they had anticipated with only two profitable months since their inception and a projected budget of £20,000 for 2009. Although their growing relationship with the tourism market holds potential, donor support is required to allow GiG to continue.[45]

Several of the partnerships were project based, so although the relationships continued, the specific partnership structures may have changed. For example, AED won a second project with USAID for the NetMark partnership. Although many of the partners who participated in the first phase continued, new partners were added and the scope was expanded to include 15 more countries. In the Angola example, USAID and ChevronTexaco continued to work together on other projects but with a different arrangement of NGOs.

GEP has gained many more partners and as a result expanded to another province and created a second EHS training school. The initial partners are still participating, but this is growing from a tri-sectoral partnership into a multi-stakeholder initiative.[46]

Several new organizations were created from these partnerships. The BPD water and sanitation cluster found significant benefits from the tri-party partnerships that they implemented. As result, a new British NGO, Building Partnerships for Development in Water and Sanitation, was established and continues to work on tri-party partnerships. Another example is the RSP program started in 2004 with support from the Canadian International Development Agency. Support from USAID/Bangladesh allowed CARE to further the development of the RSP model to a point at which it could be sustained by market mechanisms. In 2011 CARE Bangladesh will spin off the RSP into a for-profit social enterprise with an equity investment of $1 million from Danone Communities.[47]

Summary

The summary of the BPD projects found seven key lessons about tri-party partnerships that are consistent with the cases reviewed in this chapter.

1. *Maximize core competencies:* Utilizing the core complementary competencies of NGOs, businesses, and government can yield better results for all parties than alternative approaches. The closer the activities and benefits are aligned with the organization's core business, the more likely the partnership's overall chance of success.

2. *Analyze the context:* The environments that these partnerships operate in are complex and are influenced by economic, social, and political events. Partnerships thrive in conditions with stable economic and political environments, political support for the topic being addressed, and a willingness to build social capital.
3. *Understand partner incentives and conflicts:* It is important for each partner to understand one's own individual and institutional incentives, obstacles, and assets (including reputations). Partners need to find ways to share and understand each other's motivations, constraints, and definition of success.
4. *Manage differing timeframes:* Different stakeholder groups work within the bounds of different timeframes. Public sector officials are usually motivated by election and budget cycles, private sector firms are driven by shareholder and investor financial and reporting cycles, and NGOs need to meet donor and community requirements. This is an important point of negotiation, particularly in relation to measurements of success.
5. *Allow flexibility:* These partnerships are complex and take time to be built. They should be considered "flexible task forces." Partners need to be able to enter and leave as their capacities, needs, and strategies dictate. Early discussion and agreement between partners on when and how individual and collective involvement begins and ends are essential. Different skills are needed at the different stages of partnership.
6. *Build institutional capacity:* Organizations entering into a tri-party partnership often need to build their capacity to work with other sectors.
7. *Ensure personnel and institutional commitment:* Partnership champions play a critical role, particularly at the beginning of a partnership. However, partnerships must ensure that the commitment is also at the institutional level—if not, changes in personnel can destabilize the partnership.[48,49]

Notes

1. International Finance Corporation and World Resources Institute, *The Next 4 Billion: Market Size and Business Strategy for the Bottom of the Pyramid* (Washington, DC: International Finance Corporation and World Resources Institute).

2. Business Civic Leadership Center, Partnering for Global Development: *The Evolving Links Between Business and International Development Agencies* (Washington, DC: Business Civic Leadership Center, 2009).

3. Department for International Development (DFID), *Business Linkages Challenge Fund: Assessing Achievements and Future Directions* (London: Department for International Development, 2004).

4. Department for International Development (DFID), *DFID and the Private Sector: Working with the Private Sector to Eliminate Poverty* (London: Department for International Development, 2005).

5. "Business Innovation Facility" http://webarchive.nationalarchives.gov.uk/+/http://www.dfid.gov.uk/About-DFID/Who-we-work-with/Business/Business-Innovation-Facility/.

6. "Global Partnerships," *USAID,* http://idea.usaid.gov/organization/gp.

7. "NetMark Alliance," *USAID,* http://pdf.usaid.gov/pdf_docs/PDACL539.pdf.

8. Business Partners for Development, "1998–2001 Putting Partnerships to Work: Results and Recommendation for Bilateral and Multilateral Organizations," http://info.worldbank.org/etools/docs/library/57521/bmo3of5.pdf.

9. Fredrick Long and Matthew Arnold, *The Power of Environmental Partnerships* (Washington, DC: The Dryden Press Harcourt Brace College Publishers, 1995).

10. Dave Jones, *Conceiving and Management Partnership. A Guiding Framework* (London: Business Partners for Development: Water and Sanitation Cluster. Note Series: Cluster Practitioner, July 2001).

11. Personal interview with Mr. Saif-Al Rashid, RSP program manager of CARE Bangladesh, May 5, 2011.

12. Personal interview with Graham Craft, director of foundation and corporate partnerships of Mercy Corps, May 19, 2011.

13. "New US-China Initiative Promises to Transform Guangdong into Model for Green Development," *Institute for Sustainable Communities,* http://www.iscvt.org/news/press_releases/article/?id=45.

14. Zynia L. Rionda, *CSR Casebook* (Washington, DC: Catalyst Consortium and USAID, July 2002).

15. NetMark Alliance Brief, http://pdf.usaid.gov/pdf_docs/PDACL539.pdf.

16. Personal interview with Graham Craft.

17. NetMark Alliance Brief.

18. Rani Parker, Mark Schlagenhauf, and Gail Spence, *The Public-Private Alliances of USAID in Angola: An Assessment of Lessons Learned and Ways Forward* (USAID/Angola, September 2004).

19. Long and Arnold, *The Power of Environmental Partnerships.*

20. Rionda, *CSR Casebook.*

21. NetMark Alliance Brief.

22. Ibid.

23. Catherine Dolan and Linda Scott, *The Future of Retailing? The Aparajitas of Bangladesh* (Oxford, UK: CARE Bangladesh and Said Business School, Oxford University, 2008).

24. Personal interview with Mr. Saif-Al Rashid.

25. "New US-China Initiative Promises to Transform Guangdong into Model for Green Development," *Institute for Sustainable Communities,* http://www.iscvt.org/news/press_releases/article/?id=45.

26. Michael Warner and Rory Sullivan, eds., *Putting Partnership to Work: Strategic Alliances for Development between Government, the Private Sector, and Civil Society* (Sheffield, UK: GreenLeaf Publishing, 2004).

27. Long and Arnold, *The Power of Environmental Partnerships.*

28. Helen Wadham, "An Exploration of Business and NGO Perspectives on Corporate Social Responsibility, Sustainable Development and Partnership," Manchester Metropolitan University Business School. Submitted December 2007.

29. NetMark Alliance Brief.

30. Rionda, *CSR Casebook.*

31. Ibid.

32. Dolan and Scott, *The Future of Retailing?*

33. Personal interview with Mr. Saif-Al Rashid.

34. "Accomplishments," Wild Salmon Center, http://www.wildsalmoncenter.org/programs/sakhalin/accomplishments.php.

35. Personal interview with Graham Craft.

36. Ken Caplan, Simon Heap, Alan Nicol, Janelle Plummer, Susan Simpson, and John Weiser, *Flexibility by Design: Lessons from Multi-Sector Partnership in Water and Sanitation Projects* (London: Business Partners for Development: Water and Sanitation, Cluster Practitioner, 2001).

37. NetMark Alliance Brief.

38. Long and Arnold, *The Power of Environmental Partnerships.*

39. NetMark Alliance Brief.

40. Ibid.

41. Jones, *Conceiving and Management Partnership.*

42. Caplan, et al., *Flexibility by Design.*

43. Rionda, *CSR Casebook.*

44. Warner and Sullivan, eds., *Putting Partnership to Work.*

45. Wadham, "An Exploration of Business and NGO Perspectives on Corporate Social Responsibility, Sustainable Development and Partnership."

46. "New US-China Initiative Promises to Transform Guangdong into Model for Green Development," Institute for Sustainable Communities, http://www.iscvt.org/news/press_releases/article/?id=45.

47. Personal interview with Mr. Saif-Al Rashid.

48. Jones, *Conceiving and Management Partnership.*

49. Caplan, et al., *Flexibility by Design.*

8

Multi-Stakeholder Initiatives

What Are Multi-Stakeholder Initiatives?

This chapter explores multi-stakeholder initiatives (MSIs) that involve non-governmental organizations (NGOs), corporations, government agencies, academia, trade unions, and other stakeholders such as foundations. MSIs bring together diverse actors to tackle common problems such as human rights, labor standards, environmental standards, and governance.

MSIs can be categorized in at least three ways. First, some MSIs involve many stakeholder groups to garner support for general principles across many industries, such as the United Nations (UN) Global Compact. The second type of MSI focuses on specific industry issues. Many of the first-generation MSIs, such as Forest Stewardship Council (FSC), addressed industry-specific issues through standard setting and compliance, meaning they were implementing a certification system or code of conduct (CoC). The third type of MSI brings the core competencies of different sectors together to create new value and address development issues, such as Global Alliance for Improved Nutrition (GAIN). A review of 10 MSIs by the World Wildlife Fund (WWF) found that

> MSIs are an important tool in the toolbox but they are not a panacea. It is important to work with all relevant stakeholders to ensure that the necessary complementary mechanisms are in place to make MSIs work. However, without proper governance by governments and multi-lateral agencies, MSIs will continue to fight an uphill struggle.[1]

For review purposes, 11 cases were selected that represent the diversity of MSIs across issues and industries. Of these, the three represented in Table 8.1 fostered support for the general principles presented. Four MSIs focused on industry-specific issues as outlined in Table 8.2. Lastly, Table 8.3 presents four cases that were designed to create new value or address a development issue.

How Do MSIs Work?

As previously mentioned, the Long-Arnold framework identifies nine key success factors of NGO and corporate partnerships, presented in Table 6.2. This framework is used to review the selected MSI cases. The Long-Arnold framework is based on a Partnership Lifecycle, which starts with a seed phase that includes prepartnership activities. If organizations agree to develop a relationship, there are three partnership phases: initiation, execution, and closure and renewal. Within each phase, there are three key factors: people, goals, and capacity building.[2] Although the information provided explores all aspects of MSI cases, there is a specific focus on the role of NGOs within MSIs.

Partnership Lifecycle

Partnership Initiation

NGOs have played a key role in raising awareness about issues through research, advocacy, and protests against companies and countries that led to the creation of several MSIs. Significant public outrage was a key factor in the creation of the FSC, the Ethical Trading Initiative (ETI), the Kimberley Process Certification Scheme (KPCS), and the Sialkot Initiative. As a result of this public backlash, many MNCs developed their own voluntary CoCs but they were criticized by activists because they (1) didn't reference any of the international conventions, (2) rarely included freedom of association of workers, and (3) didn't include any implementation or monitoring mechanisms. NGOs and trade unions started to work on ways to improve the design, implementation, and monitoring of these CoCs. As result, the NGOs and unions started working with corporations.[3] An interviewee commented, "the willingness of NGOs to cooperate with the 'former enemy' grew out of the realization that confrontation cannot support firms to improve standards . . . you have to help companies make internal changes in order for them to embrace responsible business practices."[4]

Based on the cases in Tables 8.1–8.3, the role of NGOs was more varied in the MSIs that were created to develop new value or address a development issue. In some cases an NGO started the effort, whereas in others a business spearheaded the initiative. For example, the Foundation for Integrated Education and Development (FUNEDESIN), an Ecuadorian NGO, developed a

(*text continues on p. 201*)

Table 8.1
MSIs Adopting General Principles and Codes

	Ethical Trading Initiative (ETI)[a]	Global Road Safety Partnership (GRSP)[b]	UN Global Compact[c]
Goal	• Improve labor standards through the use of a basic ETI code.	• Improve road safety.	• Have businesses adopt the 10 economic, social, and governance (ESG) principles.
Partnership members	• Businesses, NGOs, and unions; businesses and NGOs pay fees.	• Businesses, NGOs, governments, and multilaterals	• Businesses, NGOs, and unions
Partnership structure	• Separate NGO created.	• Secretariat supported by the World Bank housed under International Federation of Red Cross and Red Crescent Societies (IFRC)	• Secretariat housed within UN, chaired by UN secretary-general
Use of logo	• No	• N/A	• Yes
Strength of the code or certification	• Medium. Company names are not published, no one has been excluded.	• N/A	• Have excluded 2,000 companies for not reporting on activities.
Stakeholder ownership	• High among members, but some external stakeholders question how rigorous the code is because no company has been excluded.	• High among stakeholders.	• High among members, seen as a credible initiative.

(*continues*)

Table 8.1 (*continued*)

	Ethical Trading Initiative (ETI)[a]	Global Road Safety Partnership (GRSP)[b]	UN Global Compact[c]
Strengths	• Continual improvement process; third-party evaluation of efforts. • Participatory decision-making.	• Raised awareness about the issue. • Created a policy framework.	• High level of participation and ownership.
Challenges	• Code does not adequately address responsible purchasing practices. • Many workers in developing countries are in the informal sector with limited representation.	• Weak objectives, difficult to measure overall results. • Different strategies in various countries.	• Addressing challenging issues.
Results	• Increased number of suppliers who were evaluated from 447 in 1998 to 9,529 in 2005. • Increased percentage of audited companies based on the code from 14% in 1999 to 64% in 2001.	• Vietnam reported that 1,577 fewer people died. • Programs in 10 target countries. • Developed UN Road Safety Resolution. • Global Road Safety Initiative in eight countries.	• 8,700 stakeholders from over 130 countries, the largest voluntary CSR initiative in the world.

a. "Resources," Ethical Trade Initiative, http://www.ethicaltrade.org/resources.

b. Tamara Bekefi, *The Global Road Safety Partnership and Lessons in Multi-Sectoral Collaboration* (Cambridge, Mass.: A Report of the Corporate Social Responsibly Initiative, Harvard University), http://www.hks.harvard.edu/mrcbg/CSRI/publications/report_6_Global%20Road%20Safety%20PartnershipFNL.pdf.

c. United Nations Global Compact, www.unglobalcompact.org.

Table 8.2
MSIs Addressing Industry-Specific Issues

	Forest Stewardship Council (FCS)[a,b]	Kimberley Process Certification Scheme (KPCS)[c]	Marine Stewardship Council (MSC)[d,e]	Sialkot Soccer Ball Initiative in Pakistan[f]
Goal	• Create sustainable forestry practices.	• Reduce the use of "blood diamonds."	• Create sustainable fisheries.	• Eliminate the use of child labor.
Partnership members	• NGOs and businesses that supply and purchase wood products	• Governments, mining and jewelry companies, NGOs	• NGOs and businesses that supply and purchase fish	• Global Brands, Fitness Associations Manufacturers, ILO, NGOs
Use of logo	• Yes, third-party certification of wood source, seal on product	• Yes, certificate for each diamond to ensure quality source	• Yes, third-party certification of fisheries, seal on product	• Yes, producers were certified, logo on product
Strength of certification	• Strong; seen as very credible.	• Strong or medium; website tracks imports and exports among countries, ensuring accuracy.	• Strong or medium.	• Medium; ILO was reluctant to sanction manufacturers that did not remove children from their factories.
Stakeholder ownership	• High; seen as credible.	• High; large-scale participation in KPCS by the diamond industry.	• Medium or low; stakeholders only consulted but not included in design. • Questions about Unilever's involvement.	• Medium; limited commitment by manufacturers to stop child labor.
Strengths	• Stakeholders determined FSC principles and concepts. • Able to address difficult problems and disputes.	• Strong monitoring structures. • Based on national legislation, rather than a UN treaty.	• Strong relationship with partners.	• High-level involvement.

(*continues*)

Table 8.2 (*continued*)

	Forest Stewardship Council (FCS)[a,b]	Kimberley Process Certification Scheme (KPCS)[c]	Marine Stewardship Council (MSC)[d,e]	Sialkot Soccer Ball Initiative in Pakistan[f]
Challenges	• Time consuming and expensive to involve all stakeholders. • Certification process expensive, limited consumer demand. • Performance standards don't allow for change over time. • Rotating membership requires constant training.	• Reluctant to sanction noncompliant members; breeches of enforcement. • Performance standards don't allow for change over time. • Political agendas and corruption affect process; limited resources.	• Certification process expensive, limited consumer demand. • Performance standards don't allow for change over time.	• Reluctant to sanction noncompliant members; breeches of enforcement. • Lack of resources in some developing countries to fully implement the program.
Results	• 125 million hectares are FSC-certified in over 80 countries (2009). • 5% of the world's productive forests are FSC certified (2009). • The value of FSC sales is estimated at over US$20 billion (2009).		• 97 fisheries are certified, 132 are being assessed (2009). • 7% of the marine fisheries were MSC certified (2009). • The value of MSC sales is estimated to be worth over US$1.5 billion (2009).	• 6,000 children removed; 10,400 received education, 5,000 received health care.

a. J. Bendel, *Terms of Endearment: Business, NGOs and Sustainable Development* (Sheffield, UK: GreenLeaf, 2003).
b. Forest Stewardship Council, http://fscus.org/.
c. "Kimberley Process Certification Scheme," *Wikipedia*, http://en.wikipedia.org/wiki/Kimberley_Process_Certification_Scheme.
d. Bendel, *Terms of Endearment*.
e. Marine Stewardship Council, http://www.msc.org/.
f. A. Ewing, "What Didn't Work: Dropping the Ball," *Stanford Social Innovation Review*, Fall 2008.

Table 8.3
MSIs: Creating New Value and Addressing Development Issues

	Amazon Cacao Alliance[a]	Global Alliance on Improved Nutrition (GAIN)[b]	River Blindness Program[c]	BridgeIt: Text2Teach[d]
Started	• 2003	• 2002	• 1987	• 2003
Goal	• Develop an international fairtrade market for chocolate products.	• Reduce malnutrition through access to fortified foods.	• Eliminate river blindness (1987), Merck; eliminate lymphatic filariasis (LF) (1998) GSK.	• Improve quality of teaching in elementary schools by providing access to interactive, multimedia packages.
Structure	• No separate structure	• Swiss foundation	• Secretariat at the Taskforce for Child Survival and Development	• SEAMEO-Innotech acts as the overall project coordinator.
Members	• NGOs, farmers, business, funding agencies, government	• 600 companies in 36 large-scale collaborations in 25 countries	• Merck, WHO, CDC, and over 20 NGOs	• Nokia, International Youth Foundation, Pearson Foundation, the UN Development Program (UNDP), USAID
Activities	• Trained farmers to lead the field production: buying, stocking, and processing.	• Delivered fortified foods to large populations through market-based approaches.	• Provided awareness, education, treatment, and aerial spraying to reduce incidence of the disease.	• Trained teachers to use cell phones to access interactive, educational videos in math, science, and English.
Strength	• Created market for cacao, ensuring that farmers could sell their product. • Improved intersectoral relationships.	• Created national and regional business alliances to bring high-quality, affordable fortified foods to poor populations.	• Strengthened overall health systems by combining river blindness and LF treatment with other key health interventions.	• Well accepted by teachers and students. • Easy for teachers to use.

(*continues*)

Table 8.3 (*continued*)

	Amazon Cacao Alliance[a]	Global Alliance on Improved Nutrition (GAIN)[b]	River Blindness Program[c]	BridgeIt: Text2Teach[d]
Challenge	• Unsupportive political and market conditions.	• Ways to deal with the multiple factors that affect nutrition.	• Long timeframe and competing priorities.	• Cost of the hardware (phones, TVs). • Modules were developed for American audience, needed local adaptation.
Results	• Yachana Gourmet recognized by the Fairtrade Federation as a responsible operator. • Tripled the income of families from $240 to $760 annually. • Earned premium price (30%) for cacao at fairtrade prices. • Created other cacao-related jobs, 17 village banks.	• Provided 400 million people with fortified food products; this included 205 million women and children. • Reduced neural tube defects by 30% in South Africa.	• Prevented 35 million people from getting river blindness. • Treated > 70 million people for river blindness and treated 80 million for LF each year. • Arial spraying allowed resettlement of 62 million acres that was previously abandoned.	• Provided access to the multimedia packages for more than 700,000 public elementary students in 203 schools. • Received 2005 Stockholm Challenge Award and the 2006 Asian Corporate Social Responsibility Awards.

a. Cynthia Goytia, *FUNEDESIN Case Study: Amazon Cacao Development Alliance, Partnering for Sustainable Agriculture and Rainforest Conservation* (The Partnership Initiative, November 2005).
b. GAIN: Global Alliance for Improved Nutrition, http://www.gainhealth.org/.
c. Jeffery Sturchio, "Business Engagement in Public Programs: The Pharmaceutical Industry's Contribution to Public Health and the Millennium Development Goals," *Corporate Governance* 8, no. 4 (2008):482–489.
d. "NOKIA and Pearson Bridge IT Partnership," *business.un.org*, http://www.business.un.org/en/documents/276.

for-profit company called Yachana Gourmet to develop a fairtrade chocolate business that would benefit local farmers. Once Yachana Gourmet was established, FUNEDESIN went to businesses and donors to support the development of an international market for fairtrade chocolate products.[5] In the case of the condition known as river blindness, Merck had the treatment but they needed partners to facilitate distribution and use of ivermectin (Mectizan) so they approached the World Health Organization and several NGOs.[6]

In many MSIs, governments, multilaterals, and foundations have played a key brokering and facilitation role, bringing various stakeholders together for a common cause. In addition, they have often provided valuable seed funding to start the MSIs as in the cases of the World Bank's support of Global Road Safety Partnership (GRSP) and Department for International Development's (DFID) support of ETI. Lastly, the participation of these stakeholders provided recognition and credibility to the MSIs.

Initiation Phase

The Long-Arnold framework factors of success include:

- Creating a well-defined partnership opportunity (value-proposition)
- Identifying key stakeholders
- Articulating a rationale for working together (mutual benefits)
- Sharing a common goal and vision.[7]

People

The Long-Arnold framework indicates that the key to the people component of the initiation phase is to identify all the internal and external stakeholders whose support is needed to ensure the partnership's success. Because MSIs involve so many different stakeholder groups, it is important for them to articulate their stakeholder engagement strategy. Key questions may include:

1. How many different stakeholder groups should be involved?
2. How should the stakeholders be selected (criteria) and who in the MSI will establish the criteria?
3. How should stakeholders be involved?
4. What level of decision-making should they be involved in, if any?

MSIs need to maintain a delicate balance between involving stakeholders and getting things done. For FSC, stakeholders were directly involved in determining the key principles and organizational concepts of FSC. This provided a great sense of ownership and credibility, but it was very time consuming and expensive, and resulted in an overly complex structure. Thus, when the WWF designed the Marine Stewardship Council (MSC), they used a consulting firm to conduct consultations with stakeholders, rather than direct stakeholder involvement. They also developed a more streamlined structure. This required much less time but stakeholders have questioned MSC's credibility and legitimacy because of this process.[8]

There are often issues about who represents various stakeholder groups such as indigenous communities. For example, ETI includes unions as a way to reach workers who are key stakeholders. However, union participation in some industries and countries is very low, particularly in less developed countries. Thus it begs the question of whether unions really represent the issues of workers if many do not belong to unions. If not, then ETI may need to develop another strategy to reach this important stakeholder group.[9]

In addition to key stakeholders, many MSIs—7 of the 11 cases reviewed in this chapter—are membership-based groups. This is most common among the MSIs that are focused on standard setting. Members are the key people who directly influence the partnership. Thus MSIs have to answer key questions about the members' roles and responsibilities in the partnership, including:

1. Who can be a member of the MSI?
2. How should members be selected?
3. What are the requirements to maintain memberships?
4. On what grounds can or should membership be terminated?

These requirements may vary by the type of member such as corporation, NGO, or entities from developing countries.

Most of the MSIs reviewed had selection criteria for their members and a committee that screens potential members. For example, the Kimberley Process has a participation committee as part of their Board that screens and makes recommendations about potential new members to the board chair. Table 8.4 provides some examples of how MSI members are selected and what is required to maintain their membership.

Partnership champions are important at this phase to sell the program internally, particularly if there is internal resistance. In the case of the MSC, there was considerable resistance within both the WWF and Unilever. The WWF fisheries staff was concerned how the partnership would affect its rela-

Table 8.4
MSI Member Requirements

Partnership	Members	Requirements
Ethical Trading Initiative	• Business, NGOs, and trade unions	• Businesses and NGOs pay annual fees. • Companies must monitor and verify compliance in their supply chains and inform their staff and suppliers about the code. Corporate members also have to report annually on their progress.
Forest Stewardship Council	• Business, NGOs	• Businesses commit to buying only from sustainable wood sources.
Global Alliance for Improved Nutrition	• Business, NGOs, government	• Businesses, NGOs, and governments commit to work toward addressing malnutrition.
Global Road Safety Partnership	• Business, NGOs, government	• Businesses and NGOs pay annual subscription fee. Donors and governments provide grants.
Kimberley Process	• Governments, business, NGOs	• Governments certify diamond sources and track exports and imports. • Government cannot export to banned countries. • Traders must present certificates of origin.
Marine Stewardship Council	• Business, NGOs	• Businesses commit to buying only from sustainable fisheries.
UN Global Compact	• UN, business, NGOs	• Business must communicate their progress on integration of the 10 ESG Global Compact principles.

tionships with government counterparts, other NGOs, and fish worker unions. Others were worried that the partnership would give the impression that WWF approved of all Unilever's practices, including its use of chemical and agricultural commodities, about which WWF might be in conflict with the company. For Unilever, their reward system focused on short-term profitability, which was not conducive to developing a creative marketing mechanism for environmental sustainability. Employees were only willing to make changes as long as there was no chance of jeopardizing their ability to meet their targets or get their bonus. Fortunately, Anthony Burgman, former Unilever chairman, recognized the importance of the WWF partnership to Unilever's long-term business strategies. He was a major champion for the project and was essential in getting employee buy-in for the partnership.[10]

Goals

The Long-Arnold framework indicates that the key to the goals component of the initiation phase is to define a shared agenda that embodies the vision and goals that they want to achieve through the partnership. This shared vision allows the partners to translate the goals into strategies and then actions that are crucial for a successful partnership. The goals of MSIs can be very broad, such as the UN Global Compact, in which businesses are encouraged to adhere to the following 10 principles:

Principle 1: Support and respect the protection of internationally proclaimed human rights.

Principle 2: Ensure that they are not complicit in human rights abuses.

Principle 3: Uphold the freedom of association and recognize the right to collective bargaining.

Principle 4: Eliminate all forms of forced and compulsory labor.

Principle 5: Abolish the use of child labor.

Principle 6: Eliminate discrimination with respect to employment and occupation.

Principle 7: Take a precautionary approach to environmental challenges.

Principle 8: Undertake initiatives to promote greater environmental responsibility.

Principle 9: Develop and diffuse environmentally friendly technologies.

Principle 10: Work against corruption in all its forms, including extortion and bribery.[11]

Other MSIs have very specific goals, as in the case of Sialkot Initiative, which aimed to eliminate child labor from the soccer ball industry in Pakistan. On the one hand, the more specific the goal, the more likely the initiative is to achieve its objective. This is due in part to the fact that it is easier to keep people focused on specific goals, and they are probably easier to measure. However, very specific goals may limit the MSI's ability to address the complex nature of many of these issues.

The more facets and greater complexity of an MSI's goals and objectives, the more challenging it can be to get agreement among a wide array of stakeholders on different issues. This implies that more time is required to involve a multitude of stakeholders at various levels and stages of the partnership to create and maintain a common understanding of the objectives, roles and responsibilities, and progress. In the long term, this process can produce a highly credible platform, but it is often more time consuming and challenging to implement.

A key task during this phase is to agree on indicators that will demonstrate the partnership's success, both in terms of the key deliverables and the effectiveness of the partnership. Partners need to ask four key questions when selecting metrics:

1. How will the outcomes be chosen?
2. How and by whom will the outcomes be achieved?
3. How will the outcomes be measured?
4. What is a fair measure of success for each organization and for the overall partnership?

A 2010 WWF review of 10 MSIs found that many of the MSCs did not design monitoring and evaluation (M&E) systems at the onset of the partnership.[12] In addition, reviews of FSCs and MSCs showed an important lag between the development of a standards system and the establishment of M&E systems and organizational capacity to measure effects.[13]

Capacity Building

The Long-Arnold framework indicates that the key to the capacity-building component of the initiation phase is threefold: (1) investing time and resources to develop relationships among the partners, (2) having or developing the requisite resources and skills to achieve the partnership goal, and (3) having adequate structures and systems in place to support the partnership. The size and complexity of MSIs often requires them to have specific partnership structures and governance bodies to develop a successful relationship and guide implementation. This is a major difference from the bilateral and tri-party partnerships previously discussed.

For example, for the GRSP there were several meetings to develop the MSI and establish relationships. In January 1999, roughly 70 road safety experts met at the Daimler-Chrysler headquarters to discuss the formation of a road safety partnership between business, civil society, and government. In February of the same year, 100 organizations gathered at the World Bank in Washington, DC, to officially create GRSP and establish a steering committee. In July 1999, 200 people attended the conference on road safety for low- and middle-income countries to determine the first priorities and projects.[14]

Decisions regarding an MSI's organizational structure are based on several key factors: (1) the purpose and size of the initiative, (2) the structures and capacities of existing organizations, (3) the need to establish a new brand or be independent, and (4) time and funding opportunities and constraints. Of the MSIs reviewed, three created new organizations and four decided to create a secretariat housed in an existing organization, as outlined in Table 8.5. This seemed to be the most common among standard-setting MSIs.

New organizations were created for FSC, MSC, and ETI, largely to create a new identity with a level playing field for the various stakeholders. In the cases of FSC and MSC, corporations provided funding to support the certification process. For ETI, businesses and NGOs pay membership fees that supplement the support provided by the DFID. A new organization provides the opportunity to (1) clearly define roles, responsibilities, and communication channels among the organizations; (2) focus staff on key objectives without competing missions; and (3) facilitate diverse revenue streams. A key challenge for these organizations is ensuring financial sustainability.

Four of the MSIs—GRSP, the Merck Mectizan Donation Program to Eradicate River Blindness, GAIN, and the UN Global Compact—created secretariats that are housed in an existing organization. This structure provided the MSIs with a communication and coordination focus without having to start a new organization, which can be time consuming and costly. These MSIs gained economies of scale because they are housed in existing organizations that already have infrastructure and networks in place. The drawback is that the secretariat is not an independent or legal entity. This means that they are reliant on the host organization for financial management, legal status, and information and communication systems, which may or may not be a challenge. Although the Sialkot Initiative did not have an overall partnership structure, it did develop a separate monitoring body to take over the certification process from the International Labour Organization (ILO).

Table 8.5
MSI Organizational and Governance Structures

Partnership	Structure	Governance
Ethical Trading Initiative[a]	• New NGO	• Board: business and NGO voting power, unions and DFID observers, three working groups
Forest Stewardship Council[b]	• New NGO	• Board: business and NGOs
Global Alliance for Improved Nutrition[c]	• Secretariat at a Swiss Foundation	• Board composed of leaders from the donor, UN, development, research, business, and civil society communities.
Global Road Safety Partnership[d]	• Secretariat at the International Federation of Red Crescent	• Steering Committee, governed by Executive Committee
Kimberley Process Certification Scheme[e,f]	• No	• Board with representatives of a variety of countries and companies; chair rotates annually; working groups monitor progress of diamond exports.
Marine Stewardship Council[g]	• New NGO	• 10-member board of directors with advisory committee
River Blindness (Mectizan) Program[h]	• Secretariat at the Taskforce for Child Survival and Development	• Expert committee
Sialkot Initiative[i]	• Independent monitoring body	• No

(*continues*)

Six of the eleven MSIs had a board structure as outlined in Table 8.5. Each of the MSIs has clearly outlined the board's functions. In addition, most of the MSIs also have working groups on specific topics to support the board in monitoring activities and addressing key issues. It is interesting to note

Table 8.5 (*continued*)

Partnership	Structure	Governance
UN Global Compact[j]	• Secretariat housed at the UN	• Board is appointed and chaired by the UN secretary-general. It includes representative UN bodies, businesses, NGOs, and trade unions There are also several working groups.

a. "Resources," Ethical Trading Initiative, http://www.ethicaltrade.org/resources.
b. Jem Bendell, *Terms of Endearment: Business, NGOs and Sustainable Development* (Sheffield, UK: GreenLeaf Publishing, 2003).
c. GAIN: Global Alliance for Improved Nutrition, http://www.gainhealth.org/.
d. Tamara Bekefi, *The Global Road Safety Partnership and Lessons in Multi-Sectoral Collaboration* (Cambridge, Mass.: A Report of the Corporate Social Responsibly Initiative, Harvard University), http://www.hks.harvard.edu/mrcbg/CSRI/publications/report_6_Global%20Road%20Safety%20PartnershipFNL.pdf.
e. "Kimberley Process Certification Scheme," *Wikipedia,* http://www.en.wikipedia.org/wiki/Kimberley_Process_Certification_Scheme.
f. Holger Meyer, *Business, Boycott & Bureaucracy: The Kimberley Process Certification Scheme and the Global Quest for Conflict-Free Diamonds* (Paper presented at the 7th Pan European Conference on International Relations, Stockholm, Sweden, September 9–11, 2010).
g. Bendell, *Terms of Endearment.*
h. Jeffrey Sturchio, "Business Engagement in Public Programs: The Pharmaceutical Industry's Contribution to Public Health and the Millennium Development Goals," *Corporate Governance* 8, no. 4 (2008):482–489.
i. Andrew Ewing, "What Didn't Work: Dropping the Ball," *Stanford Social Innovation Review,* Fall 2008.
j. United Nations Global Compact, http://www.unglobalcompact.org.

that even though the Kimberley Process did not have a specific partnership structure, it has a board. Two MSIs—GRSP and the Mectizan Donation Program—did not have a board, but they had an advisory committee to guide implementation.

Execution

The Long-Arnold factors of success include:

- Establishing ground rules to guide the partnership
- Ensuring a clear process for managing disputes (outlined in the initial phase)
- Securing adequate financing
- Regularly reviewing work plans, addressing issues, and making revisions based on discussions among the partners

- Continuing to build the relationship throughout the organizations (partnership).[15]

People

The Long-Arnold framework suggests that the aim of the people component of the execution phase is that it is important to listen to key stakeholders whose participation is required to have a successful outcome. Although it is important to listen to external stakeholders, partnerships have greater challenges when questions come from internal stakeholders.

In both the Kimberley Process and the Sialkot Initiative, internal stakeholders raised concerns about the monitoring entities' unwillingness to sanction violators. These differences in stakeholder perceptions can weaken the certification process and challenge the effectiveness of the MSI. In the case of Sialkot Initiative, Nike stopped sourcing from Pakistan because their supplier was not able to adequately demonstrate a childfree workplace. This was a major blow to the Sialkot Initiative, even though Nike began sourcing from another Pakistani supplier less than a year later.[16]

The Amazon Cacao Development Alliance found that they needed to work with lead agencies that had strong business and marketing skills, because the farmers did not have these skills. The Alliance found that it was more efficient to develop relationships with these businesses and for them to link with the small farmers, rather than train farmers to undertake these efforts directly. This stakeholder group was not identified at the onset of the partnership but was included as the program was implemented.[17]

Goals

The Long-Arnold framework suggests that the aim of the goals phase of the execution phase is to get agreement on implementation approaches and detailed efforts to deliver on the overall objectives. Groups can agree on the general principles and the overall objective of the partnership, but, as they say, "the devil is in the details." This is often where the main differences about the causes, solutions, and ways to achieve the objectives arise among the partners.

Compromises are required from all stakeholders to make MSIs work. NGOs may be at odds with other MSI stakeholders because they want to see greater reforms in a shorter timeframe. To participate in an MSI, NGOs need to understand the limitations of the overall MSI goal, if any, and decide whether it is worthwhile for them to participate. Several reports indicate that a key component for NGOs working in an MSI is to have an open mind. In some cases it has been difficult for NGOs to transition from attacking companies to working with them. For example, some stakeholders in the Kimberley Process reported, "[T]he inability of NGOs to accept the diamond industry as an ally is distasteful. They want to increase the scope of the Kimberley Process and then portray the diamond industry as slackers."[18] Although NGOs can always voice their concerns about the operations of an MSI, they also need to be respectful of their partner's efforts toward the achievement of the MSI's agreed-upon goal. NGOs may not fully understand the complexities of a company's value chain and what is required to make the desired changes. This is where investments in relationship building—communication between the partners to understand each other's differing points of view—can pay big dividends.

As presented in Table 8.5, most of the MSIs (8 of the 11) had a specific partnership structure and dedicated staff who monitored work plans and coordinated the partners' efforts. One of the major cited weaknesses of the Kimberley Process was the lack of a centralized structure, staff, and budget. For the Kimberley Process, efforts were left to the working groups and individuals (volunteers) who were already busy with other full-time responsibilities, which greatly limited the effectiveness of the overall effort.[19]

It is important that the people participating in the partnership have the authority to make decisions. If people attending the partnership meetings are not able to make decisions, it can lead to delays and frustration among the partners. A key component of the UN Global Compact is high-level chief executive officer (CEO) support for the initiative, which is chaired by the UN secretary-general. This greatly enhances its credibility within the UN and member corporations as well as among external stakeholders. It also increases the partners' commitment to follow through on their agreed-upon actions. If the CEO supports an action, things usually get done.[20]

Capacity Building

The Long-Arnold framework indicates that the key in the capacity-building component of the execution phase is to develop adequate systems and skills to translate the vision into results. MSIs face three key challenges in terms of capacity building: (1) strength and credibility of the CoC and certification process; (2) skills, capacity, and resources of individuals and organizations to implement requirements; and (3) adequate structures and systems in place to support the partnership.

Many of the standard-setting MSIs utilize a continuous improvement process, meaning that as long as a company reports on its progress, it is considered to be in good standing. As CoCs and certifications are refined and certification bodies mature, greater expectations are placed on corporations. As a result, companies must provide continual training to their employees and ensure that their suppliers meet these evolving requirements to effectively implement the CoCs or certifications.

Another key issue for standard-setting MSIs is the willingness and ability of the monitoring organization to sanction violators to ensure creditability of the process. For example, there was some concern in the Sialkot Initiative that the ILO and later the independent monitoring body were reluctant to sanction manufacturers for not removing children from their premises.[21] Members of the Kimberley Process raised similar questions. For example, in 2004 Zaire was removed from the KPCS for not fulfilling its membership requirements. However, they rejoined KPCS in 2007 on what many believed was faulty data.[22] This reluctance on the part of the monitoring bodies to fully enforce the certification process calls into question the legitimacy of the entire process. In contrast, the UN Global Compact has removed over 2,000 companies from the initiative for not reporting on their progress toward the 10 environmental, social, and governance (ESG) principles, which is seen as a strength of the effort. The UN reports, "[W]e are driving a strict enforcement of corporate integrity measures while introducing a platform that provides incentives and recognition for businesses to make meaningful progress towards a comprehensive implementation of the principles in their strategy and operations."[23]

To implement the CoCs or certifications, the changes need to start on the farm, in the mine, or on the factory floor. These efforts may include eliminating harmful practices; introducing new practices; or redesigning processes, products, and approaches. This all takes time and resources, because it requires participation of each level of the supply chain to (1) fully understand the implications of these changes, (2) design strategies to implement the new approaches, and (3) train staff and suppliers on new expectations. In addition, monitors need to be trained to understand the acceptable application of the CoC in different settings.

The costs of implementing and verification of the CoCs or certifications can be high. Most of these costs are born by the local suppliers, who are often small or medium entities (SMEs) that have greatly limited resources and personnel. Suppliers need to train their employees on new practices, implement changes in management and operational practices, and still deliver the product on time per their buyers' specifications. A study of 439 small-scale export vegetable producers in Kenya found that the initial and recurrent cost of certifications was 30% of their annual income. For most certifications, small businesses face more problems in getting certifications because of higher production costs, infrastructure requirements, and the need to implement control and management systems. In the FSC certification process the majority of costs have to be borne by forest owners and certifications can become a "critical cost barrier" for individual forest owners.[24]

Some buyers provide training and other support for their suppliers, but this varies greatly by industry and company. The main costs for buyers are monitoring their suppliers' progress in implementing the CoCs and certification requirements, and addressing issues as they arise. This enables the buyers to report their progress to stakeholders and the MSIs.

Initial investments can be cost prohibitive to the success of the partnerships. There needs to be sufficient funding over an adequate period to ensure that new organizations and systems can sustain the partnership's results. For example, in the Text2Teach partnership, the hardware costs (TV media equipment, cell phones, and airtime) are about $2,500 per school. In the pilot phase Nokia and Globe Telecom covered these costs. Even though the program was well received by school administrators, teachers, and students, expansion of these efforts was limited because of the upfront costs. Fortunately, the program secured USAID funding to expand into other schools, but the partnership will need to establish a more sustainable approach to scale up the program countrywide.[25]

Lack of resources can also be a major constraint to building the capacity of the members to implement the partnership. For the Kimberley Process, each government was responsible for training their officials about the KPCS. However, in many developing countries, where most of the diamonds are mined, these funds were very limited. As a result, some government officials did not understand the data that they received from the mining companies to certify the diamonds. This variation among countries limits the effectiveness of the overall KPCS process.[26]

Building capacity also includes communication with key stakeholders. It is important that this communication occurs both internally within each of the organizations, involving different departments and locations, as well as externally with the organization's network. In the case of the Amazon Cacao Alliance, each partner perceived time in a different way. The FUNEDESIN had a long-term vision of development, whereas the local farmer groups were more concerned with the day-to-day issues. This mix of differences in timescales and perspectives could have become an obstacle, but it was overcome by "improving communication and transparency, both crucially important factors that improved over time."[27]

Many, if not all, stakeholders underestimate the amount of work that MSIs represent.[28] Although this is also true in the bilateral and tri-party partnerships, this is particularly important for MSIs because there is a greater requirement for coordination and communication among a larger number of members and stakeholders. This is compounded by operations in many different cultures, languages, and locations. It appears that MSI staff, working groups, and steering committees undertake coordination of activities. Most of the MSIs implement their activities through a variety of regional, national, and local networks. For example, the UN Global Compact has 80 local networks that work individually and collectively to advance understanding and implementation of human rights, labor, environment, and anticorruption in business practices.[29] In addition, several of the MSIs have subinitiatives that give greater attention to a specific topic that their members have helped establish. For example, GAIN works with specific micronutrient initiatives, including the Flour Fortification Initiative and the Iodine Network. In addition, GAIN's Business Alliance members helped launch the Amsterdam Initiative on Malnutrition, which aims to eliminate malnutrition for 100 million people in Africa by 2015.[30] Another example is the Global Road Safety Partnership (GRSP), in which seven energy and transport companies, GRSP members, established the Global Road Safety Initiative, a five-year, $10 million initiative that implements pilot projects in Brazil, China, and several other Asian countries through GRSP.[31]

MSIs often manage and monitor their efforts differently. A key issue for standard-setting MSIs is the strength of the organizations that conduct the certification or monitoring efforts. For example, FSC does not conduct certifications. Instead, it accredits third-party organizations to conduct the certifications. Thus the credibility of the FSC certification relies on the rigor of the accreditation process and the abilities of the accredited third-party organization to conduct the certifications.[32] In contrast, the Kimberley Process is led by governments. As a result, the government of each KPCS country is required to have an assessment of its diamond mining conditions every three years. The monitoring teams consist of volunteers, who can pay their own way, from other governments, NGOs, and diamond mining companies that do not work in the country being reviewed. Unfortunately, it is often difficult for NGO representatives and government officials to pay to participate on these review teams, which limits the expertise of these review teams. As a result, only a small group of people who can pay to participate have conducted these reviews, which has led to questions about the strength of the overall certification process.[33]

Closure and Renewal

The Long-Arnold factors of success include:

- Evaluating results compared with the partnership goal
- Sharing credit among partners
- Identifying future value
- Developing institutional arrangements[34]

People

The Long-Arnold framework suggests that the aim of the people component of the closure and renewal phase is to share success. NGOs played a prominent role in some of the MSIs, such as the FSC and MSC. MSIs with CoCs or certifications provided information to consumers and the general public about a company's responsible operating practices and the source of its products. Many of these MSIs are highly regarded and recognized. For example, Text2Teach won the 2005 Stockholm Challenge Award and the 2006 Asian Corporate Social Responsibility Award for Support and Improvement of Education.[35]

Goals

The Long-Arnold framework suggests that the aim of the goals component of the closure and renewal phase is to evaluate the results against stated goals. There are two aspects of this process: (1) the overall effect created by the partnership and the value created for each organization, and (2) the effectiveness and efficiency of the partnership approach.

As previously mentioned, the more complex an MSI's goals, the more challenging it is to measure progress. For standard-setting MSIs, company reports on their progress are a key indicator of success and are required for continued membership. For example, the UN Global Compact expects all companies to report annually on their progress toward integrating the 10 ESG principles. A company's membership is terminated if it does not report on its progress. For the Kimberley Process, each country has to (1) certify every diamond's source of origin, (2) track exports and imports, and (3) only trade with countries participating in the KPCS. In addition, each country is expected to be reviewed every three years. Although the process is clearly defined, there are many implementation challenges that limit the effectiveness of the review process.[36]

As previously mentioned, many of the MSIs did not have monitoring or evaluation systems at the onset of the partnership. With that said, most of the MSIs' defined metrics for the results of specific activities that the partners had implemented.

The *NGOs* that participated in these MSIs achieved the following results:

- Improved working conditions across several industries, including significant reduction in the use of child labor in the soccer ball industry
- Reduced road accidents and resulting deaths
- Increased use of sustainable forestry and fishery practices
- Reduced use of diamond revenues to fund conflicts
- Improved economic opportunities for local farmers and other businesses
- Improved access to effective treatment for river blindness
- Improved nutrition through access to fortified foods
- Enhanced educational approaches and engagement
- Increased community involvement and engagement

For companies, the standard-setting MSIs' endorsement enhanced their reputation as a good company with investors, consumers, employees, NGOs, and local communities. For many companies the MSIs also helped them develop stronger relationships with their suppliers and created supply-chain efficiencies.

Specific results for the *businesses* that participated in these partnerships included:

- Secured social license to operate
- Reduced costs through local sourcing
- Improved image and reputation by improving working conditions
- Enhanced effectiveness of supply chains
- Development of new products and technologies
- Increased competitive advantage through certification of forest products, fish, and diamonds

It should be noted that mostly larger companies experienced these results. As previously mentioned, the results on small producers are less understood. In some cases, the producers saw a rise in economic effect, but the costs of certification often dwarfed the profits.

For the *governments* that participated in these partnerships the key results included:

- Improved accountability and transparency in several industries
- Increased adoption of ESG principles by companies
- More effective strategies to improve farming, forestry, and fishing practices

- Enhanced data to enforce government policies, such as child labor
- Improved health and safety for their populations

In 2010, WWF conducted a review of 10 MSIs in different industries. The summary of these results is presented in Table 8.6.

Some of the MSIs have reviewed their overall partnership approach. This seems to be more common among MSIs than bilateral or tri-party partnerships, probably because MSIs require more complex and somewhat more formal relationships. For example, the UN Global Compact had a leadership summit to review its progress, both programmatic and managerial, over its first 10 years. The ETI also has conducted several organizational reviews. These studies provided valuable information to the MSIs in terms of the need for greater engagement with stakeholders, changes in processes to improve efficiency, and new areas to be explored.

After reviewing the partnership's performance, from both an effect and partnership efficiency perspective, the members and stakeholders need to decide if the partnership can provide additional value. If not, then it is time for the partnership mechanism to end. This does not mean that the relationship has to end per se.

Creating value can be defined in many different ways. It may mean that more time is needed to achieve the original objectives, particularly when establishing global standards. This was the case with the FSC. The initial target that all wood would be sourced from sustainable forests by 1995 was not met, so the deadline was extended. By 2010, there were over 90 FSC members and almost 125 million hectares of forest had been certified worldwide; however, this only represents 5% of all forests so the initiative is continuing.[37,38]

In some cases, there were significant achievements toward the initial objective, but conditions changed, requiring different or additional approaches. For example, although the Sialkot Initiative was quite successful in removing children from the soccer ball supply chain in Pakistan, manufacturing shifted to northern India and China, making the initiative ineffective for these new conditions.[39] Similarly, the initial issues in diamond mining were with large companies, which KPCS addressed. As KPCS became successful, the problems with individual miners became the most pressing, but KPCS was not designed to manage these issues. KPCS members will have to determine if the scope of the initial KPCS should be expanded or if another approach would be more effective in dealing with the current issues.[40]

Another change in conditions is increasing stakeholder expectations. For instance, the Sialkot Initiative's sole aim was to eliminate child labor in the soc-

Table 8.6
Summary of MSI Results

MSI Strengths	MSI Weaknesses
Economic	
• Improved market access. • Created a competitive advantage; secured a price premium on some products. • Improved working conditions for employees. • Created employment opportunities for local people.	• Favored large producers who can afford to implement the CoC. • Limited participation of SMEs in the CoCs or certification because of high costs of implementation. • Shifts toward more scientifically rigorous models of management may be at the expense of valid local customs.
Environmental	
• Improved forest planning, biodiversity protection (FSC). • Improved fishery management leading to reduced by-catch mortalities (MSC).	• Limited environmental and social effects because of small market share of certified products.
Social	
• Created mechanisms to solve disputes. • Involved the community to manage forests (FSC). • Increased acceptance of community representatives in policy forums.	• CoC and certification have inadequate expertise on social issues and limited ability to address complex social issues. • Limited community involvement in designing and implementing MSIs.
Overall	
	• Lacked M&E metrics at the outset of the MSI. M&E systems and indicators need to be strengthened. • Stakeholders underestimated the amount of work that MSIs represent; time and commitment are crucial to success.

Source. World Wildlife Fund, *Certification and Roundtables: Do They Work? World Wildlife Fund Review of Multi-stakeholder Sustainability Initiatives* (Washington, DC: World Wildlife Fund, September 2010).

cer ball supply chain in Pakistan. This is an admirable and challenging effort and, as previously mentioned, was quite successful. However, some stakeholders criticized the Initiative for not addressing other labor abuses, such as forced overtime and the rights of workers, which the Initiative was never designed to tackle. Thus the Sialkot Initiative would have to decide if expanding its scope or bringing in additional partners with new skills makes sense for them or if another approach would be more successful.[41]

Capacity Building

The Long-Arnold framework suggests that the aim of the capacity-building component of the closure and renewal phase is to sustain the results of the partnership by deepening relationships, obtaining commitment, and identifying resources to institutionalize the partnership arrangements. Of the MSIs reviewed, six—ETI, GRSP, UN Global Compact, FSC, MSC, and the Merck Mectizan Donation Program—have lasted for over 10 years, implying that they have been able to sustain value through these partnerships. This also highlights that significant time is required to see substantial changes when addressing complex social and environmental issues.

The standard-setting MSIs face continual challenges to maintain the credibility and legitimacy of their certification processes to ensure that violators are removed from the MSIs and that they remain relevant to their stakeholders. For example, for MSIs such as FSC and MSC, the challenge is how to reduce the barriers to participation of SMEs, particularly in developing countries.

Despite increases in awareness of CSR practices, the relationship between business and society has not improved markedly in the last decade, as evidenced by spiraling inequality, steeply rising carbon emissions, commodity inflation, and global financial crises, all suggesting ineffective economic governance. There has been some criticism of the UN Global Compact and ETI for focusing on increasing membership and being a safe place for corporations. This has been a useful approach to gain participation, but some argue that more challenging issues such as trade, investment policy, and economic governance have been sidestepped or sidelined. The UN Global Compact is struggling to decide if it wants to continue to focus on a membership goal—the current goal is reaching 20,000 members in 10 years—or if it wants to see more "systemic changes" articulated by its vision. This is an important issue to settle as it shapes a future role with corporations.[42]

Some MSIs need to determine if their approach is appropriately designed to address emerging issues. For example, although the GRSP has been quite effective, it is still too small to have a significant effect on the global crisis. As Andrew Pearce, GRSP's CEO commented, "[W]e're a $6 million a year operation up against a $65-billion a year problem. While GRSP has undergone significant change in the last few years, it still remains to be seen if a multi-stakeholder partnership approach is the most effective and efficient way to address the issue of road safety."[43]

Unlike bilateral partnerships, most of the MSIs had some structure to at least facilitate coordination, communication, and monitoring. Therefore, the focus of the MSIs is moving forward to improve the efficiency and effectiveness of these bodies. The Kimberley Process did not have a centralized structure or dedicated staff. This was identified as a limitation of the partnership and it is something they are considering for the future.[44]

Summary

Although there have been positive effects from standard-setting MSIs' efforts, the data are contradictory and there is little understanding about under which conditions standard setting is an effective tool to foster sustainable development and improve livelihoods. A 2010 WWF review of standard-setting MSIs provided three key recommendations:

1. *Greater collaboration:* MSIs need to engage more with a variety of different types of stakeholders. Three key groups were identified: (1) community representatives, (2) experts in addressing complex social problems, and (3) SMEs. First, although many of the MSIs increased the participation of local communities, their levels are still low and more work is needed to ensure local problem solving, buy-in, and ownership. Second, existing standard-setting systems are very limited in how they address complex social issues. Thus partnering with individuals and organizations that have an in-depth understanding of the issues and solutions could greatly benefit these MSIs. Third, SMEs are the backbone of many supply chains, but they often lack the capacity and resources to engage in standard-setting processes. To address these issues, some MSIs are creating pilot projects to build the capacity of SMEs. These innovations appear to be useful ways to ensure that these entities can maximize the market benefits that standards may provide. SMEs need to be able to understand the key elements of the standards and have the tools to assess whether one or more of these standards represents an opportunity to increase their income and improve well being.[45]
2. *Better understanding of the problem:* Supply chains function with local economic, social, political, and cultural systems that can

support or hinder implementation of the standards setting system. Thus it is important for MSIs to understand how these factors affect their work.[46]

3. *Increased partnership efficiencies:* As previously mentioned, most of the stakeholders underestimated the amount of work that MSIs represent. Thus it is essential that MSI partnership structures develop effective decision-making processes, clear systems of "checks and balances," and complaint- and dispute-resolution systems to make efficient use of member and stakeholder time. In addition, MSIs need to work more collaboratively to address crosscutting issues such as climate and water, streamline processes such as improved coordination of technical assistance programs, and reduce stakeholder fatigue.[47]

The MSI cases reviewed provide an overview of a diverse group of MSIs, ranging in terms of size, topic, location, and types of organizations. Some MSIs are struggling to remain relevant as stakeholders are questioning programs over the scope of their mandates, participation levels, and credibility and governance mechanisms. Analysis of these case studies identified six key insights that can help participants understand the benefits and challenges of MSIs as described here.

1. *Balance stakeholder engagement with credibility:* Stakeholder involvement is key for MSIs. Stakeholders can be very involved, but this can be time consuming and expensive. However if the right stakeholders are not adequately involved, the legitimacy of the MSI may be questioned.
2. *Be aligned on MSI goals and objectives:* All members of MSIs should be aligned around the overall agreed-upon goal, which may require significant compromise. NGOs need to decide if the overall goal is an acceptable level of change for them to participate in the MSI.
3. *Be patient:* MSIs are complicated and involve a lot of people, requiring a significant amount of time and effort to build relationships. In the beginning of the partnership it may seem like progress is very slow, but investments in the relationship can have major payoffs in the long run if people are willing to put in the time.

4. *Support dedicated staff and budget:* Because of the complexity of MSIs, it is beneficial to have a few dedicated staff to fully focus on the initiative. A centralized budget for activities that support all partners can make the process more efficient and transparent.
5. *Clearly define members' roles and responsibilities:* In many of the MSIs, membership is granted based on demonstrated implementation of the CoC or certification. Because membership can be terminated because of lack of performance or reporting, the membership requirements and expectation need to be clearly articulated.
6. *Secure adequate funding for equal participation:* The resource base of MSI stakeholders varies greatly. Often, NGOs, SMEs, and governments in developing countries have fewer resources, which may exclude or greatly reduce their participation in the MSI. MSIs need to develop strategies to minimize this issue.

Notes

1. World Wildlife Fund, *Certification and Roundtables: Do They Work? World Wildlife Fund Review of Multi-stakeholder Sustainability Initiatives* (Washington, DC: World Wildlife Fund Review, September 2010).

2. Fredrick Long and Matthew Arnold, *The Power of Environmental Partnerships* (Washington, DC: The Dryden Press, Harcourt Brace College Publishers, 1995).

3. "Resources," Ethical Trading Initiative, http://www.ethicaltrade.org/resources.

4. World Wildlife Fund, *Certification and Roundtables.*

5. Cynthia Goytia, *FUNEDESIN Case Study: Amazon Cacao Development Alliance, Partnering for Sustainable Agriculture and Rainforest Conservation* (The Partnership Initiative, November 2005).

6. Jeffrey Sturchio, "Business Engagement in Public Programs: The Pharmaceutical Industry's Contribution to Public Health and the Millennium Development Goals," *Corporate Governance* 8, no. 4 (2008):482–489.

7. Long and Arnold, *The Power of Environmental Partnerships.*

8. Marine Stewardship Council, http://www.msc.org.

9. "Resources," Ethical Trading Initiative.

10. Jem Bendell, *Terms of Endearment: Business, NGOs and Sustainable Development* (Sheffield, UK: GreenLeaf Publishing, 2003).

11. United Nations Global Compact, http://www.unglobalcompact.org.

12. World Wildlife Fund, *Certification and Roundtables.*

13. Ibid.

14. Tamara Bekefi, *The Global Road Safety Partnership and Lessons in Multi-Sectoral Collaboration* (Cambridge, Mass.: A Report of the Corporate Social Responsibly Initiative, Harvard University), http://www.hks.harvard.edu/mrcbg/CSRI/publications/report_6_Global%20Road%20Safety%20PartnershipFNL.pdf.

15. Long and Arnold, *The Power of Environmental Partnerships.*

16. "Kimberley Process Certification Scheme," *Wikipedia,* http://www.en.wikipedia.org/wiki/Kimberley_Process_Certification_Scheme.

17. Goytia, *FUNEDESIN Case Study.*

18. Holger Meyer, *Business, Boycott & Bureaucracy: The Kimberley Process Certification Scheme and the Global Quest for Conflict-Free Diamonds* (Paper presented at the 7th Pan European Conference on International Relations, Stockholm, Sweden, September 9–11, 2010).

19. Ibid.

20. United Nations Global Compact.

21. Andrew Ewing, "What Didn't Work: Dropping the Ball," *Stanford Social Innovation Review,* Fall 2008.

22. Meyer, *Business, Boycott & Bureaucracy.*

23. "Number of Expelled Companies Reaches 2,000 as Global Compact Strengthens Disclosure Framework," United Nations Global Compact, http://www.unglobalcompact.org/news/95-01-20-2011.

24. International Trade Center, "Market Access, Transparency and Fairness in Global Trade. Chapter IV: Voluntary Standards: Boom or Bust for Developing Countries," International Trade Center, http://www.standardsmap.org/documents/flagship/files/738/Publications%20-%20Chapter%20IV%20-%20Voluntary%20Standards.pdf.

25. "NOKIA and Pearson Bridge IT Partnership," *business.un.org,* http://www.business.un.org/en/documents/276.

26. Meyer, *Business, Boycott & Bureaucracy.*

27. Goytia, *FUNEDESIN Case Study.*

28. World Wildlife Fund, *Certification and Roundtables.*

29. UN Global Compact.

30. GAIN: Global Alliance for Improved Nutrition, http://www.gainhealth.org/.

31. Bekefi, *The Global Road Safety Partnership.*

32. Bendell, *Terms of Endearment.*

33. Meyer, *Business, Boycott & Bureaucracy.*

34. Long and Arnold, *The Power of Environmental Partnerships.*

35. "NOKIA and Pearson Bridge IT Partnership."

36. Meyer, *Business, Boycott & Bureaucracy.*

37. Bendell, *Terms of Endearment.*

38. Forest Stewardship Council, http://www.fscus.org/.

39. Ewing, "What Didn't Work."

40. Meyer, *Business, Boycott & Bureaucracy.*

41. Ewing, "What Didn't Work."

42. "Number of Expelled Companies Reaches 2,000."
43. Bekefi, *The Global Road Safety Partnership.*
44. Meyer, *Business, Boycott & Bureaucracy.*
45. World Wildlife Fund, *Certification and Roundtables.*
46. Ibid.
47. Ibid.

9

Partnership Decision-Making Framework

Overview

As shown in the previous chapters, there are many facets and decisions that influence a partnership's success. The cases in Chapter 6 indicated that many non-governmental organizations (NGOs) do not have a systematic approach to guide how they engage or partner with corporations. This chapter presents a framework to assist managers in designing, implementing, and evaluating successful partnerships. In addition to this text, I recommend the following excellent resources:

1. *The Partnering Toolkit* was developed jointly by the Global Alliance for Improved Nutrition, the United Nations Development Program, the International Atomic Energy Agency, and the International Business Leaders Forum. Key topics include (1) the phases of a partnership, (2) how to build a resource map, (3) examples of partnership agreements, (4) approaches to manage the partnership, and (5) ways to build institutional capacity within existing organizations or create a new organization.[1]
2. *Meeting the Collaboration Challenge Workbook: Developing Strategic Alliances Between Nonprofit Organizations and Business* was published by the Drucker Foundation and Jossey-Bass. This workbook provides many sample tools to help guide managers in designing, structuring, implementing, and evaluating NGO-corporate partnerships.[2]
3. *Guide to Successful Corporate-NGO Partnerships* was jointly developed by the Global Environmental Management Initiative and the Environmental Defense Fund (EDF). This guide uses several

> environmental case studies to provide best practices to design, implement, and evaluate effective NGO-corporate partnerships.[3]

Different partnership models vary in the number of phases; however, the general concepts are similar. For example, the Long-Arnold framework has three partnership phases—initiation, execution, and closure and renewal, whereas *The Partnering Toolkit* expands these 3 phases into 12 phases.

Partnership Decision-Making Framework

Capitalizing on the best of the literature and interviews with over 100 NGO and business managers, I have developed an eight-step decision-making framework to guide managers in asking the right questions to effectively design, execute, and evaluate successful partnerships. Although this framework focuses on partnerships between NGOs and corporations, it can also be used with other types of partnerships.

Each of the eight steps in the framework provides key questions for consideration and tools to assist managers in making partnership decisions. Table 9.1 outlines the eight steps and the key task to be accomplished in each step.

This decision-making framework embraces a partnership lifecycle approach based on continuous value creation. This means that if the partnership is not providing value for all partners, then other mechanisms should be explored, because partnerships are not easy and they may not be the best solution for every problem. Figure 9.1 depicts the cyclical nature of the framework and identifies where the NGO needs to make key decisions.

Step 1: Conduct an Internal Assessment

It is important for an organization to understand the rationale and value of a collaborative effort as well as its capacity to make the effort a success. A manager must consider four questions during this step, including:

1. Why do we want to partner?
2. What is the best partnership arrangement to achieve our objectives?
3. Do we have the capacity to start a new partnership?
4. What assets can we bring to the partnership?

Why Partner?

Studies have found that 75% of NGO respondents have a written policy about whom they would work with, but only 32% share these policies with busi-

Table 9.1
Steps in the Partnership Decision-Making Framework

Steps	Task
Step 1: Conduct an internal assessment.	• Determine rationale for the partnership. • Determine type of partnership desired. • Assess organizational capacity to support partnership. • Identify assets partners can contribute.
Step 2: Identify, research, and short-list potential partners.	• Develop selection criteria. • Research potential partners.
Step 3: Approach potential partners and make the business case.	• Leverage key contacts. • Identify key decision-makers. • Organize the initial meeting. • Make the business case.
Step 4: Conduct a due-diligence process to select an appropriate partner.	• Create a due-diligence process. • Use a due-diligence matrix. • Select partners.
Step 5: Negotiate the partnership agreement, structures, and systems.	• Determine the elements of partnership agreement. • Decide on partnership structures. • Decide on partnership systems.
Step 6: Initiate the partnership.	• Create plan to launch the partnership.
Step 7: Execute and implement the partnership.	• Execute work plans. • Communicate; hold regular partner meetings. • Redesign strategies as needed.
Step 8: Evaluate and reassess the partnership.	• Assess indicators to measure partnership effect and value created. • Assess indicators to measure partnership efficiency.

nesses.[4] The case studies reviewed in the previous chapters demonstrated that many of the environmental and human rights NGOs had a specific corporate engagement strategy that governed their behavior and partnerships. For example, several NGOs, such as EDF and Greenpeace, do not accept any corporate

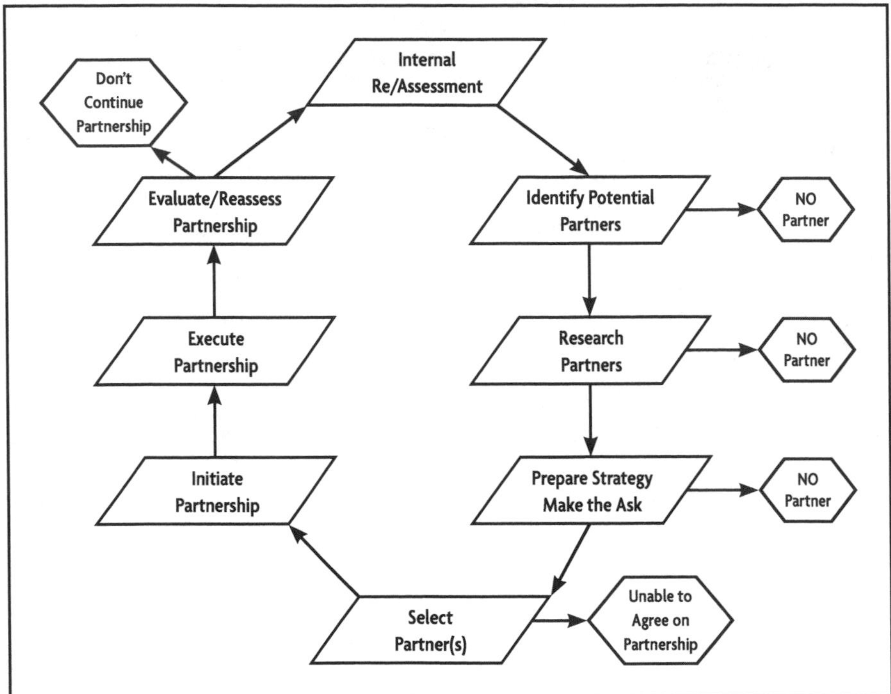

Figure 9.1 Partnership decision-making framework.

funding, whereas World Wildlife Fund will not accept any funding from companies remotely linked to any of their active campaigns. Other NGOs avoid working with specific industries because of their poor practices such as support of gambling, or their products such as weapons.

NGOs without a corporate engagement strategy are often at a disadvantage because they lack a framework to guide them in decision-making. Thus each case has to be evaluated separately. For philanthropic activities, it is easy to see how the funding will contribute to the NGO's objectives. However, for joint programming or integrative partnership efforts that require more negotiation and a strategic fit with core competencies, the lack of a framework can greatly delay the process, frustrating potential corporate partners. Without an overall guiding framework, it also means that an NGO may have a "hit or miss" approach, yielding mixed results from their partnerships. For example, an NGO corporate sponsorship officer said, "[W]e don't have a written policy but life would be much easier if we did. The only unwritten rule we have is around not accepting sponsorship from oil and nuclear fuel companies."[5]

Several barriers seem to inhibit NGOs from making a commitment to how they will engage with corporations. First, it takes time for an organization to develop a strategy with widespread support. In addition, NGO staff may have differing views about working with certain industries or companies, which may take time to change. Second, even when there is a framework, it may be difficult for financially strapped NGOs to say no to potential funding opportunities, even if they are less than ideal. Third, as previously mentioned, units within an NGO may have different incentives for developing partnerships. For example, marketing departments may be rewarded by the amount of funds they raise, whereas technical units often focus on innovation. These differences can cause conflicts within an NGO and they can lead to delays and missed partnership opportunities.

What Type of Partnership Is Desired?

As presented in Chapter 5, there are many ways that NGOs can partner with corporations, ranging from in-kind donations to joint ventures. Thus an NGO needs to determine how it wants to engage with a company to achieve its objectives. Identifying the type of partnership enables the NGO to conduct more targeted research on potential corporate partners. It also helps the NGO identify the skills and resources it will need to support the partnership. For example, if an NGO would like to do a cause-related marketing campaign, then the point of contact within the company will probably be the marketing department rather than the foundation. In addition, the NGO should assess its own capacity to support a marketing campaign.

Partnerships are developed based on negotiation and compromise. The final partnership may be different from the NGO's original thinking, based on discussions with the partner, but this planning phase is very important.

Table 9.2 outlines the different ways that an NGO may engage with a company. It also identifies which departments are most likely to be involved in the partnership as well as the main outcomes. The key factors influencing the type of partnership desired include (1) the required level of resources and organizational commitment, (2) timeframe, (3) operational strategies, and (4) expected outcomes.

What Is Our Internal Capacity to Implement the Partnership?

Once partnership with a business has been deemed beneficial, an NGO needs to ensure that it can make the commitment in terms of funds, human resources,

Table 9.2
Types of NGO-Corporate Engagement

Type of Engagement	Relationship Mechanisms	Involvement of Key Departments: NGO	Involvement of Key Departments: Business	Results
Engagement Without Exchange of Resources				
Consumerism	• Purchasing power	• Procurement	• Sales	• Reward positive behaviors with buying practices.
Consultation		• Technical units	• Technical units	• Provide key information to each stakeholder.
Shareholder resolution			• Board, CEO, senior management	• Adoption of shareholder resolution.
Campaigning				• Change corporate practices.
Engagement With Exchange of Resources				
Resource exchanges	• Grants, in-kind donations, volunteers	• Project and finance staff, some management	• Community affairs, volunteer coordinators, foundation, some senior management involvement	• Project outcomes successful. • Corporate visibility increased.
Transactional	• Subcontracts	• Project and finance staff, some senior management involvement	• Unit that needs the service and finance	• NGO provides a service to a business or vice-versa.
Joint programming	• Cause-related marketing, licensing	• Marketing, legal, finance • Greater senior management involvement, including some CEO involvement	• Marketing, legal, finance • Greater senior management involvement, including some CEO involvement	• Project outcomes successful. • NGO and corporate visibility increased, funds for NGO increased. • Increased corporate sales.

(*continues*)

Table 9.2 (*continued*)

Type of Engagement	Relationship Mechanisms	Involvement of Key Departments: NGO	Involvement of Key Departments: Business	Results
Integrative	• Series of agreements, joint venture	• Significant CEO and senior management involvement, including the board • Variety of departments involved in different efforts throughout the organization	• Significant CEO and senior management involvement, including the board • Variety of departments involved in different efforts throughout the organization	• Project outcomes successful. • NGO and corporate visibility increased, joint ownership increased. • Increased value creation.

and organizational support required to make the partnership a success. The NGO may have to strengthen its capacity in key areas or develop new capacities to participate in some partnerships.

As previously discussed, most NGO and corporate managers grossly underestimated the time required to develop and implement partnerships. Many corporate managers felt frustrated because the process took much longer than they thought it should, based on their corporate experience. The biggest challenge for NGOs is the staff time required to develop potential partnerships. Because the lead-time to agree on a partnership can be quite long, NGOs often have to tap staff, who may be paid by other projects, to develop the relationship until a partnership agreement is in place and funds are available to hire more staff. For example, the partnership between Denny's and Save the Children took eight months of discussions before an agreement was signed. Kurt Ackermann, chief marketing officer of the Boys and Girls Club, reported that the relationship between the Boys and Girls Club and Major League Baseball took four years to develop. He goes on to say, "[W]hen you do come up with a plan, patience will be rewarded with a stronger, longer-lasting relationship—because your partner helped create it."[6]

Interviews with NGO managers, particularly large NGOs, indicate that there can be a limited understanding within an NGO about the breadth and depth of the entire portfolio of the NGO's partnerships. This is because different people and departments manage several projects, but only a few people have the overall view from an organizational perspective.

In my discussions with NGO managers, many reported that they have 10 to 15 strategic alliances. Most people agree that strategic alliances require a significant level of investment in time and resources, particularly by senior management, to be successful. However, many of these NGOs did not have any specific criteria that could classify a partnership as a "strategic alliance" as opposed to other types of partnerships. Managers often do not understand that an important relationship does not automatically provide strategic value.

To help managers classify and manage their partnerships, I developed the Partnership Portfolio Map presented in Table 9.3. This tool provides a framework for organizations to map the status of all their current partnerships and objectively classify their partnerships against specific criteria to understand how they are currently managing their portfolio. This process also allows the organization to (1) better understand how much personnel time is required to manage different types of partnerships, (2) identify best practices and lessons learned about managing partnerships, and (3) assess the value of its current partnership in terms of the organization's growth potential. (Note that this process can be conducted for all partnerships or only for private-sector partners.)

When I have conducted this exercise with NGOs, using index cards for each partnership, most participants classified their partnerships in the far-right-hand columns as "joint programming" or "integrative partnerships." As people discussed the partnerships and compared them with the criteria, the cards shifted to the left, and partnerships were reclassified as "transactional" or "resource exchange" partnerships. By the end, only a few partnerships remained as joint programming or integrative relationships and the majority were reclassified as resource exchanges or transactional relationships. For example, one NGO had a subcontract with a trucking company to distribute food. Initially, this relationship was identified as a joint programming effort because the distribution system was vital to the project's success. However, after much discussion, the staff admitted that the trucking company was not bringing any added value, such as new skills or ideas to the partnership, and there was no senior management involvement required. Thus the partnership was reclassified as a transactional relationship in which the NGO pays the trucking company to move food from the port to a clinic. That is not to say that this is not an important relationship—it provided vital input for the project. However, it does not produce the same value as other types of partnerships such as a joint programming effort.

It should be noted that the Partnership Portfolio Map can change over time as the partnerships themselves change. For example, the early years of the City Year and Timberland partnership, during which Timberland donated

Table 9.3
Partnership Portfolio Map

Type of Organization	Resource Exchange	Transactional	Joint Programming	Integrative
Other NGOs				
Corporation				
Foundation				
Government				
University				

boots to the City Year volunteers, would have been classified as a resource exchange. Today, City Year is located in Timberland's headquarters and they have many joint initiatives, so the relationship is classified as an integrative partnership.

It is very powerful for an NGO to know its partnership capacity, because this enables it to make decisions. It may decide that newer opportunities provide more value than an existing partnership, so it may need to develop exit strategies or restructure the way it manages these relationships. Or the NGO may decide that additional skills and resources are needed to take on new partnerships. Whatever decision is reached, this information allows an NGO to develop strategies to effectively manage its partnership portfolio and ensure that it has adequate organizational capacity to implement successful partnerships.

What Assets Can We Bring to the Partnership?

Many NGOs do not fully understand or go through the process to value their assets, particularly in quantitative and monetary terms. Key NGO assets include (1) brand and reputation; (2) their field presence, such as country office infrastructure; (3) expert understanding about local context, conditions, and relationships with local communities that can provide useful information and greatly expedite implementation; (4) ability to pilot new innovations; and (5) policy advocacy and mobilization skills. NGOs need to articulate these assets to their partners so that they can understand the important contributions NGOs can offer a corporate partner.

Brand is a vital asset for NGOs. This is why NGOs are so concerned that working with a corporation will tarnish their brand, which is a reflection of their credibility within society. The authors of *The New Global Brands: Managing NGOs in the 21st Century* acknowledge that NGOs have missions and constituencies that add to the complexity of brand valuation and management. Some NGOs are only now realizing the strength and credibility of their brand, and they are exploring how best to capitalize on it.[7] Although businesses are more familiar with the concept of brand value, many are unclear how to apply these values to partnerships. It is important for any organization to know the value of its brand, so that it can allocate adequate resources to nurturing, building, and protecting it.

The idea of valuing an NGO brand is still quite a new concept. Interbrand's valuation of an NGO's brand considers factors such as (1) the public's level of trust that a donation will be used effectively, (2) the public's perception of an NGO's financial stability, (3) the public's experience with the cause, (4) the NGO's relationship with its donors, and (5) the ease of donations for the donor.[8] In 2001, Habitat for Humanity International's brand was valued at nearly $2 billion by Interbrand, which was about the same brand value as Starbucks.[9]

If NGOs are unaware of the value of their brand, they run the risk of not extracting the full financial value from these partnerships and cobranding opportunities that they deserve.

Step 2: Identify, Research and Short-List Potential Partners

As a result of step 1, the NGO should have a clear idea of (1) why it wants to partner, (2) who it wants to partner with and in what manner, (3) if it has the capacity to engage in a new partnership, and (4) what assets it can bring to the partnership. If the NGO decides that it wants to pursue a partnership with a corporation, whether it is a bilateral, tri-party, or a multi-stakeholder initiative (MSI), the next step is to research potential partners.

At this point, the NGO needs to do a preliminary review of potential corporate partners' operations and practices. Once the pool of partners has been narrowed down, then an NGO can conduct a due-diligence process, which is an in-depth review of the company's operations described in step 4. There are two key tasks to this step: (1) Identify specific selection criteria for a suitable partner and (2) perform a preliminary review of potential partners to develop a shortlist of possible corporate partners.

Develop Selection Criteria

Based on the NGO's corporate engagement strategy, if one exists, and the rationale of the partnership, an NGO can establish a list of selection criteria that will help it evaluate the potential partners. NGOs may have different types of selection criteria. For example, they may screen out companies from specific industries, such as tobacco, alcohol, weapons, gambling, or pornography. Some NGOs may want to target companies that are the largest violators or have the greatest market share as a way to have the greatest effect. On a more positive note, some NGOs may want to work with companies that are interested in working with the poor through inclusive business models or base-of-the-pyramid mechanisms. Other NGOs may want to work with companies that have new technologies that they can adapt for their target populations. Other selection criteria may include (1) where the company works; (2) if the company works with the same target population as the NGO, such as women or children; or (3) the company's CSR and community engagement efforts.

Research Potential Partners

Researching potential partners can be an overwhelming task for NGOs and businesses because information on potential partners may not be readily available. In addition, information sources may provide a biased view of the company, either positive or negative, so it is important to gather information from multiple sources.

Many websites provide information on multinational corporations (MNCs) and large publicly traded companies such as FTSE4Good Index, Dow Jones Sustainability Index, or CorpWatch, as well as the company's own website. In addition, users can see if a company is a member of any of the MSIs, such as UN Global Compact or an industry-specific MSI, such as the Forest Stewardship Council.

It is much harder to find information about smaller or local companies, particularly in developing countries. In this case, it might be useful to look at newspaper stories about the company for either awards or scandals, and speak with people from the local Chambers of Commerce or the U.S. Embassy Commerce Officer.

A key aspect of general company research is to begin to learn how the corporation manages its operations—employee policies, environmental practices, supply chain sourcing—and its relationship with stakeholders and community engagement efforts. First, it is important to understand who owns the company. As discussed in Chapter 4, mergers and acquisitions are a key driver of corporate growth. Many NGOs do not want to work with companies in certain industries, such as tobacco, but looks can be deceiving. For example, many nutrition-related NGOs would probably be interested in working with Kraft Foods. However, they may not know that from 1998 until 2007 Philip

Morris, the largest tobacco company in the world, owned Kraft Foods. So the question is, if you work with Kraft, are you also working with Philip Morris?[10]

Second, examine the company's reputation and track record in environmental, social, and governance (ESG) issues. It might be useful to understand the drivers behind the company's actions. For example, is the company making ESG changes because it is required to do so through regulations or negative public views? Or does the company view these changes as an opportunity to gain a competitive advantage? The difference in these perspectives between seeing these changes as part of risk mitigation or a business opportunity influences the company's approach and commitment to these efforts.

Third, determine basic information on where the company works; the nature of its products, services, and technology; and specific skills it has that would complement the NGO's work such as distribution systems, marketing campaigns, or other assets such as its networks. Some key questions to ask when researching a company may include:

1. Who owns the company? Do they have subsidiaries?
2. Does the company include corporate social responsibility (CSR) in its strategic plan?
3. What is the company's reputation in terms of ESG issues?
4. Does the company produce a CSR report?
5. Which department is responsible for CSR, community engagement, or other stakeholder engagement efforts?
6. Does the company have a foundation? What is the relationship between the foundation and the company?
7. Does the company currently work with NGOs? If yes, on what topics and what types of relationships?

Step 3: How to Approach Potential Partners and Make the Business Case

Once a company is identified as a potential partnership candidate, three tasks need to be completed, including (1) leveraging key contacts to identify and contact people within the company, (2) identifying the key company decision-makers, and (3) making the initial contact and presenting the business case for the potential partnership.

Leverage Key Contacts

NGOs have a broad network of contacts who can help them identify potential corporate partners. It is important that NGOs leverage their networks—board members, donors, volunteers, employees' contacts, and other stakeholders—to facilitate introductions. Initially the NGO will want to collect as many contacts as possible. Then, based on the selection criteria, the pool should be narrowed down to a limited set of potential partners, depending on the type of partnership and resources available.

It is best to have a direct introduction to someone at the company. Even if the corporate contact is not in the right department, the fact that the organization has some relationship with the corporation can help identify the right decision-makers, which is a major challenge.

Identify the Right Decision-Makers

Companies vary greatly in how they manage their community engagement and social responsibility efforts, including which units are involved in decision-making and implementation, as outlined in Table 9.4. Thus it is important for NGOs to research how different corporations manage these efforts to identify

Table 9.4
Involvement of Business Units in Key Engagement Efforts

Type of Engagement	Possible Business Unit Involved
• Grants	• Community affairs, corporate foundation
• Sponsorship	• Foundation, sales, marketing
• In-kind donations	• Pharmaceutical and ICT companies often have a specific unit to deal with this such as government or community relations.
• Pro bono services	• Either the specific unit that offers the service, such as marketing, or human resources
• Volunteers, matching grants, health and wellness policy, employee training	• Human resources
• Improving working conditions	• Procurement and ethical sourcing, supplier relations, human resources, corporate foundation
• Certification, change in environmental practices, climate change efforts	• Environment and engineering, procurement and sourcing, supplier relations

people who can make partnership decisions. Initially, this can be done through a website search, followed by discussions with the key contacts or calls to the corporation.

Organize Initial Meeting

As demonstrated by the cases reviewed in the previous chapters, the initial meeting can occur in a variety of ways. Sometimes NGOs come with a proposal in hand. Business people like to be involved in creating solutions, so a proposal that already defines the problem and the solution limits the potential of the partnership from the beginning. A more useful approach may be to explain the problem you are trying to address (e.g., creating jobs for women, improving health care, or reducing greenhouse gases) and ask how the company might be able to help. This allows the corporation to be an active participant, which is highly desired, and it may expand the conversation to include other departments and efforts that the NGO may not even know exist. Kurt Aschermann, of the Boys and Girls Club, has noted,

> Some of our best proposals happen without paper. Bringing a written proposal, an actual document, to the first meeting gives your potential partner the option of saying "no." At Boys & Girls Clubs, we practice "proposal-less fundraising," listening to our partners and identifying their needs. Then, we draft a proposal with the partner. This gives the partner a sense of ownership in the project—something to feel good about. We do bring public relations and other information along on the calls; we don't burden potential partners with too much reading material. At the same time, we make sure our partner knows what Boys & Girls Clubs can offer.[11]

How to Make the Business Case for Your Cause

Many NGOs fail to address the need to make the case for their causes. Businesses are very different from foundations and government agencies, which are often the main relationships for many NGOs. As a result, some NGOs approach businesses with the same strategy they use with existing donors, which usually isn't very successful. Although NGO managers understand what objectives their efforts are designed to reach, business people don't understand these linkages. Thus NGOs need to explain their work and any potential collaboration in a way that business managers can understand—in other words, making the business case for the partnership.

Business managers usually have 10 to 15 minutes to listen to your idea. They do not have time to go through lengthy reports or studies to learn about your organization's great work. They need to hear how the collaboration will help them in terms of cost savings, increased sales, improved productivity, or greater visibility. If they are not able to glean this information quickly, it will be difficult to pique their interest. In addition, they will not be able to sell the idea to their senior management, who often need to approve the engagement effort.

What is a business case? It is a way to explain the rationale of the partnership in relevant business objectives and results. For example, let's say that a health NGO would like to get funding from a garment factory to provide services for its female workers. One approach would be to explain to the factory manager that health is an important human right and improving the workers' health would be beneficial for the workers and the company. Another approach would be to explain that many of these women have low iron levels (anemia), which makes them tired and less productive. In addition, programs in other factories have shown that for every 1% increase in hemoglobin levels, there is a 1% increase in productivity. Thus if these women were treated with a low-cost intervention, the company could see increases in worker productivity and a reduction in sick days. Both of these versions are true. However, the second version presents the information in terms that a garment factory manager understands; the manager can see how the benefits directly relate to the bottom line. This effort provides benefits for all: The women get better health outcomes, the NGO receives funding to work with the women, and the business reaps cost savings and potentially greater profits.

After the initial meeting between the NGO and company, each organization will need to have further internal discussions about the potential partnership. In addition, more information between the entities may need to be exchanged and additional follow-up meetings conducted to determine if a partnership makes sense. This phase can take several months to a few years, depending on people's schedules, the type of the partnership, and the capacity of all the organizations, as well as the existing external environment.

Step 4: Conduct a Due-Diligence Process to Select an Appropriate Partner

Based on the selection criteria outlined in step 2 and discussion with potential partners, the NGO can determine which business might be the best fit. Some interesting trends affect partner selection. Studies have found that 79% of NGOs and 69% of businesses say that the media are more interested in partner selection than five years ago. Similar levels of NGOs and businesses,

56% and 54% respectively, say supporters and shareholders are more interested in the organization's partners.[12] Thus selecting a partner is an important decision for each organization.

Reputational risk from partnerships is openly recognized by both businesses and NGOs. Part of this has to do with how NGOs perceive their missions. NGOs have three key concerns regarding how working with corporations can affect their reputation, including (1) being "used" by corporations to gain credibility without supporting the NGO's efforts, (2) guilt by association, and (3) the loss of independence.

NGOs are fearful that companies only want to work with them to gain credibility within society, but they may not be serious about supporting the NGO's efforts. One author argues,

> While most businesses want some visibility of their efforts, this should not be the main objective of the partnership. For business, it's undeniable that partnering with NGOs has positive effects on their image. However, if this benefit is misused and not underscored by a willingness to actually work with an NGO towards shared goals, it will quickly lose its value, as the NGO's credibility diminishes, along with that of the business.[13]

NGOs are concerned that working with a corporation will result in "guilt by association," tarnishing their credibility with stakeholders and jeopardizing their ability to raise funds. After the recent Gulf oil spill, The Nature Conservancy (TNC) was bombarded with complaints from their members who were horrified by the discovery that TNC had received about $10 million in cash and land from British Petroleum (BP) over the last decade. To make matters worse in the minds of the members, TNC had given the oil giant a seat on its International Leadership Council. It should be noted that all this information was readily available on TNC's website, so they were not hiding it from their members. From TNC's perspective, BP was a good partner, but it seemed that many of their members were not aware of the relationship.[14] This example shows how a scandal with an existing organization can greatly affect a partner's reputation, even when the actual partnership is considered a success. It also demonstrates the balancing act that NGOs have to play in terms of managing different stakeholder expectations.

It is important for NGOs to be able to maintain their independence. NGOs are afraid that they will be labeled as a "sell-out" if they are seen as being too close to business. Part of this concern stems from disagreements about whether NGOs should accept money from corporations. Some argue that if an NGO accepts corporate money, it may compromise the NGO's objectivity and loyalty to its mission. For NGOs such as TNC that protect ecologically sensitive spots by buying them or persuading others to set them aside, businesses are a big source of income. Other NGOs do not take any corporate money to maintain their independence and ensure that there are no misperceptions about their actions. For example, the Greenpeace website is full of reminders that it never accepts money from companies. Ironically, this policy prompted grumbles from some of Greenpeace's large individual members, who asked why firms as rich as Walmart should be the recipients of their charity.[15]

Designing a Due-Diligence Process

To address these concerns, NGOS need to conduct an in-depth assessment of their potential partners to understand the potential risk and develop mitigation strategies as well as identify synergies to maximize the benefits of the partnership. NGOs need to share their approach with the potential partners so they understand the NGO's process and timeframe for making a final decision. In addition, NGOs should be open to corporations conducting a similar process to understand the NGO's operations. These assessments are a key part of building the relationship and learning about each other's strengths and weaknesses.

Organizations need to establish a management system that outlines how they will undertake a due-diligence process. There are four key issues to be considered. First, the process should identify the types of partners that require a review and how often they should conduct the process. Some NGOs conduct a due-diligence process on an entire sector, such as the extractive industry, to determine if they want to engage with that sector at all. These reviews can also highlight the preferred companies that an NGO may want to partner with if it decides to work with that sector.

Second, the process needs to identify who will be responsible to ensure that the process is completed, in terms of both individuals and departments. For example, is this the responsibility of the marketing unit or the technical staff? This can become very complex in a large organization that works in many locations. For example, let's say that an MNC headquartered in the United States wants to develop a partnership with the NGO's Kenya office. Who is responsible for the due-diligence process?

- Does the NGO's country office lead the process? If so, which department?

- Does the NGO's headquarter office lead the process? If so, which department?
- Or do both offices have to conduct the due-diligence process? How are discrepancies managed?

Third, the NGO needs to decide on the criteria and tools that will be used to conduct the due-diligence process, which is further discussed in the next section on the due-diligence matrix. The NGO should develop a core set of questions that it wants to ask of each potential partner. These responses should have some rating system to evaluate the partner. The preferred rating system is a numeric scoring system with scores that can be plotted on the matrix. This helps reduce subjectivity and facilitates decision-making, but it may be that the NGO has to start with a simple system to begin this process.

Fourth, the NGO needs to articulate its decision-making process. Some NGOs have a multi-sectoral committee that represents the entire organization, in which the potential partners are presented and reviewed, and decisions are made. Other NGOs base decision-making on the size or type of partnership. For example, if a partnership represents a certain dollar amount, then a department director or country director can approve the partnership, whereas larger dollar-value partnerships need to be approved by a senior executive or a board committee. In addition, the NGO must determine how it will manage the discrepancies that may occur among different departments or with contrasting data about its partners. The goal of the due-diligence process is to learn as much as possible about the potential partner to reduce risk and maximize benefits.

Due-Diligence Matrix

There are many different types of criteria that can be utilized in a due-diligence process. I have consolidated these into two broad categories that include (1) the strategic alignment of objectives between the partners and (2) the potential value created by the potential partnership. Both of these elements can include risks and opportunities.

> *Partnership alignment (risk):* These elements can be tailored to meet specific organizational requirements, but general areas include (1) the fit between the two organizations' mission and objectives, (2) the organization's reputation, (3) if the organization incorporates ESG issues into its operating practices, (4) CSR reporting, and (5) the organization's current stakeholder- and community-engagement

efforts. The lower the alignment between the potential partners, the greater the risk.

Potential value creation (reward): Potential value creation relates to how much value can be created by the proposed partnership for all the stakeholders. Thus, as with the engagement framework, a single sponsorship effort creates less value than a cause-related marketing campaign or value chain initiative that enhances an NGO's effect and increases a company's sales. Table 9.5 presents a due-diligence matrix to help both NGO and corporate managers maximize value creation and minimize risks.

Quadrant 1: High alignment (low risk) and low value: (Philanthropy) This relationship has good alignment between the partners, but the proposed partnership creates limited value. These are philanthropic efforts that can provide some value, although they could be made more effective by incorporating other approaches, thus moving them to Quadrant 2.

Quadrant 2: High alignment (low risk) and high value: (Highly Successful Partnerships) This relationship is ideal. There is a high degree of alignment between the partners and the proposed partnership creates significant value for each partner. These are joint programming and integrative partnerships, such as the City Year and Timberland relationship or the Rural Sales Program.

Table 9.5
Due Diligence Matrix

		Partnership Value	
		Low	**High**
Partnership Alignment	**High**	Quadrant 1 High Alignment/Low Value (Philanthropy)	Quadrant 2 High Alignment/High Value (Highly Successful Partnerships)
	Low	Quadrant 3 Low Alignment/Low Value (No Engagement)	Quadrant 4 Low Alignment/High Value (Careful Consideration)

Quadrant 3: Low alignment (high risk) and low value: (No Engagement) This relationship is the least likely to develop into a successful partnership. The alignment between the organizations may be low for three reasons. First, the industry may be considered harmful, such as weapons or gambling, and is not likely to change over time. Second, one partner may have a bad reputation, because of the way it manages its business as evidenced by recent scandals, unsafe work conditions, or harmful environmental practices, which may change over time. Third, there may not be a good match between the two organizations. In addition, the value created by these partnerships is low. Thus organizations should probably not engage in these relationships.

Quadrant 4: Low alignment (high risk) and high value: (Careful Consideration) This relationship provides high-value opportunities, but there is a low level of alignment. This may be due to a partner's bad reputation as evidenced by recent scandals, unsafe work conditions, or harmful environmental practices. This may be why the potential opportunity can create so much value. NGOs need to carefully manage the risks of this relationship if they decide to engage in these types of partnerships. An example of this type of relationship is the Global Alliance for Workers and Communities, which is further discussed in the next section.

Based on this process, managers can develop a strategy for each potential partner and identify the companies, if any, with which they want to negotiate a specific partnership agreement.

Due-Diligence Analysis and Decision-Making

A due-diligence process is more of an art than a science, because it needs to balance conflicting information in an ever-changing environment. Organizations are dynamic and continually evolving to respond to a changing environment. Thus the dynamics for any organization can shift over time, which may negatively affect the partnership. For example, when TNC began its partnership with BP over 10 years ago, the oil giant had a good reputation. However, BP's reputation quickly changed as a result of their response to the Gulf oil spill.

In contrast, there was significant public outcry against Nike for poor working conditions in its supplier factories at the onset of their partnership with the International Youth Foundation (IYF). IYF could have viewed working with Nike as a risk, because of its negative image. However, they saw this as an opportunity to dramatically improve the workers' conditions (value-added) because Nike had to address these issues and there were few systems in place to intervene. Today, most footwear and apparel companies have developed systems to monitor workplace issues and address them. In addition, several MSIs, such as the Fair Labor Association, also work on these topics. Thus a similar partnership undertaken today may have less effect because many other stakeholders work on this topic.

Although organizations have general policies that guide their practices, they are not monolithic. There can be many differences in how a company or an NGO operates in different settings or with different stakeholders. It is often a challenge for managers to weigh the positive and negative actions of their potential partners. For example, if we review the past experience of BP, we would find the following events:

- In 1997, BP was the first major oil company to publicly acknowledge the need to take steps against climate change, and it established a company-wide target to reduce its emissions of greenhouse gases.
- BP Solar is a leading producer of solar panels with its purchase of Lucas Energy Systems (1980) and Solarex (2000).
- In 2005, BP launched its alternative energy division and planned to invest $8 billion in the sector over 10 years.
- In 2005 and 2006, BP ranked among the Global Corporate Knights 100 Index that identifies the most sustainable companies based on their track record.
- In 2005, BP was named by *Mother Jones* magazine, an investigative journal that "exposes the evils of the corporate world, the government, and the mainstream media," as having one of the 10 worst corporation-based environmental and human rights records.
- In April 2010, an offshore drilling rig (called Deepwater Horizon, leased to BP by owner Transocean Ltd.) exploded after a blowout, killing 11 people and resulting in a massive oil spill that damaged the environment and livelihoods of the people who live along the whole Gulf coast. The rig sank two days later. BP has claimed responsibility for the spill and has established at the government's request a $20 billion fund to help those affected by the spill.[16]

It is interesting that a company can be praised for its practices (Global Corporate Knights 100) and be classified as one of the 10 worst companies in the same year. This is the dilemma that managers face in conducting due-diligence processes and why it is so important to have selection criteria. More research and discussion with the company is needed for the NGO to have a better understanding of the company's practices. For example, it would be useful for the NGO to know how the company plans to change its practices in light of the safety issues raised. In addition, the NGO should consider how these events have affected the company's brand. Thus, depending on the NGO's selection criteria, the positives might outweigh the negatives or vice versa.

As a result of this decision-making process the NGO might decide to (1) develop a partnership with a company, (2) redesign the proposed partnership to reduce risks or create more value, (3) wait for a while to see if the company changes any of its practices and conduct another due-diligence process sometime in the future, (4) continue to dialogue with the company but not develop a partnership, or (5) refrain from developing a relationship or partnership with the company at this point in time. It is important for NGOs to document their decision-making process so that when future questions or opportunities arise, the NGO knows the history it has had with a specific company.

Step 5: Negotiate a Partnership Agreement With Appropriate Partnership Structure and Systems

In most cases, NGOs are much smaller than their corporate partners and they may be less skilled at negotiating. If NGOs have not completed the tasks in step 1, particularly identifying what they want to get out of the partnership and the value that they bring to the relationship, it may be difficult to negotiate the terms of the agreements or know when to walk away.

A negotiation process can be limited if any of the parties view the outcome as a fixed pie. This limited view often reinforces competition and a win-lose attitude. This makes their actions focus on winning rather than on creating value that can expand the entire pie. Some NGOs view relationships with corporations solely as the exchange of financial resources, which limits the NGO's engagement opportunities with a business. One example is between an agribusiness that was courting an NGO that worked with local farmers in many developing countries. There was great concern within the NGO about accepting corporate funding. After many months of heated internal debate, the NGO decided not to take any money from the corporation. The focus on whether to take the money limited the partnership options. Unfortunately, the NGO was not able to develop any alternative mechanisms to continue their engagement or discussions with the business. As a result, the corporation never got to hear the local farmers' issues and the NGO lost its opportunity to influence the company's practices. It is important for partners to be willing to think outside the box and develop low-risk alternatives that can still achieve their overall objectives.

As previously described, partnership agreements can vary greatly in terms of type and level of formality. Each agreement must be tailored to the specific needs of the partners. However, based on the literature and interviews with managers, 10 general principles that are useful to consider in designing a partnership agreement are presented in Table 9.6.

As identified in the Long-Arnold framework, building capacity among the partners is a key factor of a partnership's success. NGOs need to clearly articulate what capacities they have and what areas they need support to develop to participate in the partnership.

Part of this effort is learning about each other and developing a common purpose. To achieve this objective, the organizations need to agree on a partnership structure, which can range from informal relationships to formal structures, and systems that support the partnerships. The previous chapters show that these structures can range from being very informal to creating completely new complex structures. Michael Prideau, British American Tobacco's director of corporate and regulatory affairs, has stated,

> It depends on how the partnership is set up, its governance, clarity of purpose and objectives and the commitment of the partners to the program of activities. The extent to which partnerships are able to deliver real and measurable conservation benefits is inextricably linked to their design and operation, and to the safeguards put in place by both partners.[17]

As discussed in the previous chapters, a key component to designing effective partnerships is understanding how the partners make decisions (centralized versus decentralized), and communicate internally and externally. In Chapter 7, the case between USAID/Angola and ChevronTexaco highlighted the limited understanding between the organizations because one made decisions in the field, whereas the other made decisions from its corporate headquarters, thousands of miles away from where the partnership was being implemented.[18]

People are the key to partnerships: They are the drivers and champions for these efforts. Partnerships are more effective if they have some level of

Table 9.6
Elements of Partnership Agreement

Partnership Area	Key Questions	Key Considerations
Formality of the agreement	• How formal or informal should the partnership be?	• Memorandum of understanding (MOU) may or may not be legally binding.
Vision	• What is the vision of the partnership? • What is the effective timeframe of the partnership?	• Does it benefit everyone? Has everyone "bought into" the vision?
Partnership objectives	• What are the objectives of the partnership? • How does each organization contribute to the objectives?	• Objectives should be SMART: specific, measurable, achievable, realistic, and time-bound. • Agreement on key indicators is essential, as well as how they will be measured. For example, will the partners use third party auditors or independent evaluators?
Roles and responsibilities of each organization	• What are the assets and resources each partner will provide, including financial, human resources, skills, products, office space, intellectual property, and networks?	• A specific scope of work can be included in the body of the agreement or provided as an attachment.
Exchange of resources	• What agreements need to be in place for the exchange of resources? • What are the reporting requirements?	• If either partner is going to provide specific resources to the other partner, such as a grant, then the funding amounts and activities should be clearly articulated as well as payment agreements, schedules, and reimbursement policies.
Partnership management	• How will the partnership be managed? • Is a specific structure required? • What systems are needed to support the partnership? • Which departments or staff will be the key liaisons for the partnership?	• This may be as simple as agreeing to a monthly or quarterly meeting to approve activities and monitor progress. It should include who should be represented at the meetings, and responsibilities for note taking and communication among the partners.

(*continues*)

Table 9.6 (*continued*)

Partnership Area	Key Questions	Key Considerations
Partnership decision-making	• How will decisions be made between the partners?	
Partnership communication	• How will partners communicate within their organizations? • How will the partners communicate with each other? • How will the partners communicate externally? • What permissions are needed from each organization to allow their partner organization to use their logos or to cobrand? • Who owns the data about the partnership? With whom can the data be shared?	• Use an intranet, newsletters. • Distribute updates from partner meetings. • What information can be put on each other's websites? • What is the approval process for each organization discussing the partnership with external parties?
Grievance and dispute resolution process	• What are the levels of grievances? • How will each level be settled? • Who will represent the organization in a dispute process? • What makes a fair grievance?	• Mediation versus arbitration
Termination parameters	• Under what conditions can either organization terminate the relationship?	• What type of notification is required to terminate the partnership?

support, which could be a part-time manager or a committee that meets on a regular basis. The *Guide to Successful Corporate-NGO Partnerships* suggests that a cross-functional team provides organization-wide accountability and taps varied expertise within partner organizations. It also educates more people about the partnership and its goals, while minimizing the challenges of bringing new people on board once the project is underway.[19]

Step 6: Initiate the Partnership

Depending on the size and nature of the partnership, starting a partnership may be a small step or a major effort. For example, it may be as basic as sharing information with relevant departments about the partnership, through staff meetings and other communication forums, or hiring a few staff. For other partnerships, such as a cause-related marketing campaign, there may be a press release or specific launch activities to publicly announce the partnership. The latter requires more support and coordination among the partners.

Step 7: Execute and Implement the Partnership

In general, there is nothing different about implementing a project in a partnership with a corporation. Good programming principles dictate participatory planning processes with key stakeholders, baseline assessments, well-articulated monitoring and evaluation plans, annual work plans, and regular review of progress with readjustments as required.

What may be different is your partner's understanding and approach to addressing the agreed-upon objective. This can be both a strength and a challenge for the partnership. As previously discussed in Chapter 3, NGOs and businesses have differing timeframes, technical languages, and measures of success. Hopefully, most of these issues were addressed during the development of the partnership agreement. However, often it is not until the partners become fully engaged in the process that they can fully understand what issues they have to overcome to make the partnership a success.

Step 8: Evaluate the Partnership

As the Long-Arnold framework indicates, it is important to evaluate performance against stated goals. Partnerships require assessment at two levels: (1) the overall effect created by the partnership and the value created for each organization and (2) the effectiveness and efficiency of the partnership approach.

Partnership Effects

Most partnerships measure the first level of the partnership fairly well. Some indicators that demonstrate *NGO results* include:

- Improved incomes of farmers, workers, or other groups
- Improved worker conditions in several industries
- Increased sustainable forestry, farming, and fisheries practices
- Reduced greenhouse gas emissions and improved biodiversity
- Improved health benefits and nutrition
- Increased community capacity
- Improved access to clean water
- Greater inclusion and empowerment of women

Indicators that demonstrate *business results* include:

- Secured social license to operate
- Enhanced supply-chain efficiencies
- Increased access to key markets resulting in increased sales
- Reduced labor disputes
- Improved image and reputation by improving working conditions
- Reduced costs through local sourcing and improved energy efficiency

Indicators that demonstrate *governments' results* include

- Managed infrastructure projects and successfully resettled villages
- Increased use of effective strategies to support farmers to improve farming practices
- Improved environmental conditions
- Improved capacity of disadvantaged groups to participate in the formal sector
- Improved health conditions

Partnership Approach

As previously mentioned, less attention has been directed toward measuring the partnership's efficiency, which includes the partnership structures and systems as well as quantification of the costs or value added through a partnership approach as compared with other strategies. For example, relatively few partnerships track rate of return on investments, which would be useful for all partners. The MSIs reviewed in Chapter 8 appeared to have more structure and specific personnel and systems to support their efforts than the bilateral or tri-party partnerships. This is probably because of the size and complexity of MSIs that are composed of many different individual and organizational members and a wide array of stakeholder groups.

Because partnerships vary so much it is difficult to develop indicators that capture their diverse nature. There is a lot of work underway to develop more meaningful indicators that can be adapted to accurately reflect the various aspects of different types of partnerships. The International Business Leadership Forum conducted an 18-month action research program that involved more than 100 partnership practitioners from around the world. This effort identified potential indicators in three key partnership areas, including (1) greater efficiency, (2) improved effectiveness, and (3) increased equity, as described here.[20]

Indicators to demonstrate *greater efficiency* include:

- Pooling resources and optimizing "division of labor"
- Decreasing costs associated with conflict resolution and societal disagreement on policies and priorities
- Creating economies of scale
- Promoting technological cooperation
- Facilitating the sharing of information
- Overcoming institutional rigidities and bottlenecks[21]

Indicators to demonstrate *improved effectiveness* include:

- Leveraging greater amounts and a wider variety of skills and resources than can be achieved by acting alone
- Accommodating broader perspectives and more creative approaches to problem-solving
- Obtaining the "buy-in" of recipients and local "ownership" of proposed solutions, thereby ensuring greater sustainability of outcomes
- Speeding the development and implementation of solutions
- Acting as a catalyst for policy innovation[22]

Indicators to demonstrate *increased equity* include:

- Improving the level and quality of consultation with other stakeholders in society
- Facilitating broader participation in goal setting and problem solving
- Building the trust needed to work toward shared responsibilities and mutual benefit
- Building community-level institutional structures, networks, and capacities to enable local control and ownership[23]

Thus, based on the quantitative and qualitative information as well as the partners' experience and reflection on their relationship, they will have to decide if they want the partnership to continue. This decision should be based on the partners' ability to continue to create value. This may require the partnership to (1) stay in its current form but extend the timeframe, (2) add more partners; or (3) take on new topics or work in different locations. All these questions need to be addressed as the partnership cycle continues.

It is important to note that relationships do not necessarily end when specific partnership arrangements cease. It may be that the objective of the partnership was achieved, thus ending the partnership mechanism. There may be a lapse in time before another opportunity that would truly create value arises.

Notes

1. Ros Tennyson, International Business Leaders Forum, Global Alliance for Improved Nutrition, United Nations Development Program, and International Atomic Energy Agency, *The Partnering Toolkit* (London: International Business Leaders Forum, Global Alliance for Improved Nutrition, United Nations Development Program, and International Atomic Energy Agency, 2003).

2. The Drucker Foundation, *Meeting the Collaboration Challenge Workbook: Developing Strategic Alliances Between Nonprofit Organizations and Business* (San Francisco: Jossey-Bass, 2001).

3. The Global Environmental Management Initiative and the Environmental Defense Fund. *Guide to Successful Corporate-NGO Partnerships* (Washington, DC: The Global Environmental Management Initiative and the Environmental Defense Fund, 2008).

4. Amanda Powell-Smith, "Finding the Right Corporate NGO Partnership," *Corporate Responsibility Management,* August 1, 2005.

5. Ibid.

6. Kurt Aschermann, "The Ten Commandments of Cause-Related Marketing," http://www.causemarketingforum.com/site/apps/nlnet/content2.aspx?c=bkLUKcOTLkK4E&b=6415417&ct=8971401.

7. John Quelch and Anthalie Laidler-Kylander, *The New Global Brands: Managing Non-Government Organizations in the 21st Century* (Mason, Ohio: Thompson South Western, 2006).

8. Interbrand: Creating and Managing Value, http://www.interbrand.com/en/Default.aspx.

9. Ibid.

10. "Kraft Foods," *Wikipedia,* http://en.wikipedia.org/wiki/Kraft_Foods.

11. Aschermann, "The Ten Commandments of Cause-Related Marketing."

12. Powell-Smith, "Finding the Right Corporate NGO Partnership."

13. Ibid.

14. "Reaching for the Longer Spoon: The Disaster in the Gulf of Mexico Is Straining Ties Between Companies and Activists," *The Economist,* June 3, 2010, http://www.economist.com/node/16274145.

15. Ibid.

16. "BP: Environmental Record," *Wikipedia,* http://en.wikipedia.org/wiki/BP#Environmental_record.

17. "British American Tobacco plc," EarthWatch Institute, http://www.earthwatch.org/europe/our_work/corporate/corporate_partners/bat/.

18. Rani Parker, Mark Schlagenhauf, and Gail Spence, *The Public-Private Alliances of USAID in Angola: An Assessment of Lessons Learned and Ways Forward* (USAID/Angola, September 2004).

19. The Global Environmental Management Initiative and the Environmental Defense Fund, *Guide to Successful Corporate-NGO Partnerships.*

20. International Business Leaders Forum, *Measure of Success* (London: International Business Leaders Forum).

21. Ibid.

22. Ibid.

23. Ibid.

Bibliography

Aburdene, Patricia. *Mega Trends 2010: The Rise of Conscious Capitalism.* Charlottesville, Va.: Hampton Road, 2005.

Akintoye, Akintola, Matthias Beck, and Cliff Hardcastle. *Public-Private Partnerships: Managing Risks and Opportunities.* London, UK: Blackwell Publishing, 2003.

Alsop, Ronald. *A Good Corporate Reputation Draws Consumers and Investors.* New York, NY: The Wall Street Journal Books, 2004.

American Enterprise Institute. *Dictating Norms: Who Decides What is Right for the World? The Inauguration of Global Governance Watch.* Washington, DC: American Enterprise Institute, April 14, 2008.

Amis, Lucy, Peter Brew, and Caroline Ersmarker. *Human Rights: It Is Your Business: The Case for Corporate Engagement.* London, UK: International Business Leader's Forum, 2005.

Anderson, Lisa. "Child Sponsorship Programs—Idea of Saving One Child Is Marketing Myth." *The Chicago Tribune,* March 16, 1998.

Anheier, Helmut, Marlies Glasius, and Mary Kaldor, eds. *Global Civil Society.* Oxford, UK: Oxford University Press, 2001.

"Anybody Who's Anybody Is an NGO These Days." *The Economist,* January 29, 2000.

Associated Press. "American Medical Association to Pay Sunbeam $9.9Million." *Washington Post,* August 2, 1998.

Austin, James. *The Collaboration Challenge: How Nonprofits and Business Succeed Through Strategic Alliances.* San Francisco, Calif.: Jossey-Bass, 2000.

Bamford, James, and Benjamin Gomes-Casseres. *Mastering Alliance Strategy: A Comprehensive Guide to Design Management and Organization.* San Francisco, Calif.: Jossey-Bass, 2003.

Barstone, David. *Saving the Corporate Soul and Who Knows Maybe Your Own.* San Francisco, Calif.: Jossey-Bass, 2003.

Barton, Noelle, and Caroline Preston. "America's Biggest Businesses Set Flat Giving Budgets." *The Chronicle of Philanthropy,* August 7, 2010.

Bekefi, Tamara. *The Global Road Safety Partnership and Lessons in Multi-Sectoral Collaboration.* Cambridge, Mass.: A Report of the Corporate Social Responsibly Initiative, Harvard University.

Bendell, Jem. *Debating NGO Accountability. NGLS Development Dossier.* New York: United Nations, 2006.

Bendell, Jem. *Terms of Endearment. Business, NGOs and Sustainable Development.* Sheffield, UK: GreenLeaf, 2003.

Benioff, Marc. *The Business of Changing the World: Twenty Great Leaders on Strategic Corporate Philanthropy.* New York: McGraw Hill, 2004.

Bloom, Paul, and Gregory Dees. "Cultivate Your Ecosystem." *Stanford Social Innovation Review* (Winter 2008):47–53.

Boccalandro, Bea. *A Helping Hand or a Hijacking: How Non-Profits Can Respond to Ever-Increasing Corporate Involvement in the Community.* Germany: Centrum fur Corporate Citizenship Deutschland, 2005.

Bovaird, Tony. "Public-Private Partnerships: From Contested Concepts to Prevalent Practice." *International Review of Administrative Sciences* 70, no. 2 (2004):199–215.

Bromberger, Allen. "A New Type of Hybrid." *Stanford Social Innovation Review* (Spring 2011): 49–53.

Buse, Kent, and Andrew Harmer. "Seven Habits of Effective Global Public-Private Health Partnerships: Practice and Potential." *Social Science and Medicine* 62 (2007):259–271.

Business Civic Leadership Center. *Partnering for Global Development: The Evolving Links Between Business and International Development Agencies.* Washington, DC: Business Civic Leadership Center, 2009.

Business Leadership Forum Monograph 2005: Senior Executives at Award-Winning Companies Share Keys for Successful Employee Volunteer Programs. Washington, DC: Points of Light Foundation, 2005.

Cairns, Ben, and Margaret Harris. *Bridge Over Troubled Water: Collaboration to Improve Collaboration Across Nonprofit/Sectoral Divide.* London: Institute for Voluntary Action Research, Seminars Series, 2007.

Caplan, Ken, Simon Heap, Alan Nicol, Janelle Plummer, Susan Simpson, and John Weiser. *Flexibility by Design: Lessons From Multi-Sector Partnerships in Water and Sanitation Projects.* Washington, DC: Business Partners for Development: Water and Sanitation Cluster, 2001.

Carr, D.L., and Emma Norman. "Global Civil Society? The Johannesburg World Summit on Sustainable Development." *Geoforum* 39 (2008):358–371.

Center for Corporate Citizenship at Boston College. *What Do Surveys Say About Corporate Citizenship?* Chestnut Hill, Mass.: Center for Corporate Citizenship at Boston College, 2007.

Center for Corporate Citizenship at Boston College. *The 2010 Profile of the Practice.* Chestnut Hill, Mass.: Center for Corporate Citizenship at Boston College, 2010.

Center for Corporate Citizenship at Boston College. *Community Involvement Index 2003.* Chestnut Hill, Mass.: Center for Corporate Citizenship at Boston College, 2003.

Center for Corporate Citizenship at Boston College, *Teaming Up to Brand and Bond: Timberland Partners With City Year, SOS and Skills USA. In Practice: A Series About Integrating Business and Community Development.* Chestnut Hill, Mass.: Center for Corporate Citizenship at Boston College, no. 5, March 2004.

Chowdhury, Shyamal. *Attaining Universal Access: Public-Private Partnership and Business-NGO Partnership.* Bonn, Germany: ZEF Bonn, Discussion Papers on Development Policy, July 2002.

Clarke, Thomas. "Balancing the Triple Bottom Line: Financial Social and Environmental Performance," *Journal of General Management* 26, no. 4 (2001):16–27.

Cohen, Jonathan. "State of the Union: NGO-Business Partnerships Stakeholders." *AccountAbility* 2003.

Collins, James. *Good to Great and the Social Sectors: A Monograph to Accompany Good to Great.* Boulder, Colo.: Self-published by Jim Collins, 2005.

Committee Encouraging Corporate Philanthropy. *Giving in Numbers: 2008.* Washington, DC: Committee Encouraging Corporate Philanthropy, 2008.

Contreras, Manuel, ed. *Corporate Social Responsibility in the Promotion of Social Development.* Washington, DC: Inter-American Development Bank, 2004.

"Corporate Power Flexes Its Muscles." *Foreign Direct Investment Magazine,* August 1, 2002.

Corporation for National and Community Service, Office of Research and Policy Development. *Volunteering in America 2010: National, State, and City Information.* Washington, DC: Corporation for National and Community Service, June 2010.

Cowe, Roger. *Business-NGO Partnerships—What's the Payback?* London: Ethical Corporation, April 2004.

Das, T.K., and B.S. Teng. "Between Trust and Control: Developing Confidence in Pattern Cooperation in Alliances." *Academy of Management Review* 23 (1998):491–512.

Das, T.K., and B.S. Teng. "Relational Risk and Its Personal Correlates in Strategic Alliances." *Journal of Business and Psychology* 15, no. 3 (Spring 2001):445–461.

Department for International Development (DFID). *Achievements and Future Directions.* London, UK: Department for International Development, 2004.

Department for International Development (DFID). *Business Linkages Challenge Fund.* London, UK: Department for International Development, 2004.

Department for International Development (DFID). *DFID and the Private Sector: Working With the Private Sector to Eliminate Poverty.* London, UK: Department for International Development, 2005.

Diller, Janelle. "A Social Conscience in the Global Marketplace? Labour Dimensions of Codes of Conduct, Social Labeling and Investor Initiatives."*International Labor Review* 138, no. 2 (1999):99–129.

Dolan, Catherine, and Linda Scott. *The Future of Retailing? The Aparajitas of Bangladesh.* Oxford, UK: CARE Bangladesh and Said Business School, Oxford University, 2008.

Drayton, Bill, and Valerie Budinich. "A New Alliance for Global Change." *Harvard Business Review* (September 2010):1–8.

Drucker Foundation. *Meeting the Collaboration Challenge Workbook: Developing Strategic Alliances Between Nonprofit Organizations and Business.* San Francisco, Calif.: Jossey-Bass, 2001.

Drumwright, Minette, Peggy Cunningham, and Ida Berger. "Social Alliances: Company and Non-profit Collaboration." *Social Marketing Quarterly* 5, no. 3 (1999):43–47.

Eade, Deborah, and Alan Leather, eds. *Terms Of Engagement.* Bloomfield, Conn.: Kumarian, July 2005.

Edwards, Michael. *Small Change: Why Business Won't Change the World.* San Francisco, Calif.: Berrett-Koehler, 2010.

Eisner, David, Robert T. Grimm, Jr., Shannon Maynard, and Susannah Washburn. "New Volunteer Workforce," *Stanford Social Innovation Review* (Winter 2009):32–37.

Elliot, Stuart. "When a Corporate Donation Raises Protests." *New York Times,* March 12, 2008.

Emerson, Jeb. "The Blended Value Proposition: Integrating Social and Financial Returns." *California Review Management* 45, no. 4 (Summer 2003):35–51.

Ewing, Andrew. "What Didn't Work: Dropping the Ball." *Stanford Social Innovation Review* (Fall 2008):73–75.

Foroohar, Rana. "Where the Money Is: The $1.6 Trillion Non-profit Sector Behaves (or Misbehaves) More and More Like Big Business." *Newsweek International,* September 5, 2005.

Friedman, Thomas L. *The World Is Flat.* New York: Farrar, Straus, and Giroux, 2005.

Gammal, Denise, Caroline Simard, Hokyu Hwang, and Walter Powell. *Managing Through Challenges: A Profile of San Francisco Bay Area Non-Profits by Stanford.* Palo Alto, Calif.: Stanford Business School, August 2005.

Gardyn, Rebecca. "Handling the Ethical Dilemmas that Corporate Partners Can Bring to a Charity," *The Chronicle of Philanthropy,* February 13, 2003.

Global Environmental Management Initiative and the Environmental Defense Fund. *Guide to Successful Corporate-NGO Partnerships.* Washington, DC: Global Environmental Management Initiative and the Environmental Defense Fund, 2008.

"Global Survey of Business Executives." *McKinsey Quarterly,* January 2006.

Googins, Bradley, and Steven Rochlin. "Creating the Partnership Society: Understanding the Rhetoric and Reality of Cross-Sectoral Partnerships." *Business and Society Review* 105, no. 1 (Spring 2000):127–144.

Goytia, Cynthia. *FUNEDESIN Case Study: Amazon Cacao Development Alliance, Partnering for Sustainable Agriculture and Rainforest Conservation.* London: The Partnership Initiative, November 2005.

Gramsci, Antonio. *Prison Notebooks.* Vol I, J.A. Buttingigieg, ed., J.A. Buttingigieg and A. Callari (trans), in A. Gramsci. *NGOs Can Be Part of Government, Business Sector or Civil Society.* New York: Columbia University, 1992.

Grimsey, Darrin, and Mervyn Lewis. *Public Private Partnerships: The Worldwide Revolution in Infrastructure Provision and Project Finance.* Cheltenham, UK: Edward Elgar Publishing Limited, 2005/2006.

Hamann, Ralph, and Nicola Acutt. "How Should Civil Society (and Government) Respond to Corporate Social Responsibility? A Critique of Business Motivations and the Potential for Partnerships." *Development Southern Africa* 20, no. 2 (June 2003):255–270.

Hart, Stuart. *Capitalism at the Crossroads: The Unlimited Business Opportunities in Solving the World's Most Difficult Problems.* Upper Saddle River, NJ: Wharton School Publishing, 2005.

Harvard Business School Social Enterprise Summit. *Summary Report.* Cambridge, Mass.: Harvard Business School, 2008.

Heap, Simon. *NGOs Engaging With Business: A World of Difference and a Difference in the World.* Oxford, UK: INTRAC, 2000.

Helsin, Peter, and Jenn Ochoa. "Understanding and Developing Corporate Social Responsibility." *Organizational Dynamic* 37, no. 2 (2008):124–144.

Hertz, Norma. *The Silent Takeover: Global Capitalism and The Death of Democracy.* London: Arrow Books, 2001.

Herz, Steven, Jon Sohn, and Antonio La Vina. *Development Without Conflict: The Business Case for Community Consent.* Washington, DC: World Resources Institute, May 2007.

Hutchinson, Moira. *NGO Engagement With the Private Sector on a Global Agenda to End Poverty: A Review of the Issues: A Background Paper for the Learning Circle on NGO Engagement with the Private Sector.* Canadian Council for International Cooperation Policy Team, January 2000.

International Business Leaders Forum. *Measure of Success.* London: International Business Leaders Forum.

International Finance Corporation. *Investing in People: Sustaining Communities Through Improved Business Practice: A Community Development Resources Guide for Companies.* Washington, DC: International Finance Corporation, 2000.

International Finance Corporation and World Resources Institute. *The Next 4 Billion: Market Size and Business Strategy for the Bottom of the Pyramid.* Washington, DC: International Finance Corporation and World Resources Institute.

International Labour Organization. *The Financial and Economic Crisis: A Decent Work Response.* Washington, DC: International Labour Organization, 2009.

Iyer, E. "Theory of Alliances: Partnership and Partnerships Characteristics." *Journal of Nonprofit and Public Sector Marketing* 11, no. 1 (2003):41.

Jackson, Ira, and Jane Nelson. *Profits With Principles: Seven Strategies for Delivering Profits With Principles.* New York: Currency Doubleday, 2004.

Johnson-Xanhon, Kay. "Selling to the Poor." *Time,* May 29, 2005.

Johnson, Lauren. "Understanding the Role of Cross-Sector Strategic Alliances in the Age of Corporate Social Responsibility." PhD Diss., Tufts University Fletcher School, April 12, 2005.

Johnston, David Cay. "The Gap Between Rich and Poor Grows in the United States." *New York Times,* March 29, 2007.

Jones, David. *Conceiving and Managing Partnership: A Guiding Framework. Business Partners for Development: Water and Sanitation.* Washington, DC: World Bank Business Partners for Development. Note Series: Cluster Practitioner, July 2001.

Jorg, Andriof, Sandra Waddacok, Bryan Husted, and Sandra Sutherland-Raham, eds. *Unfolding Stakeholder Thinking, Vol 1: Theory, Responsibility, and Engagement.* Sheffield, UK: GreenLeaf, 2003.

Jorg, Andriof, Sandra Waddacok, Bryan Husted, and Sandra Sutherland-Raham, eds. *Unfolding Stakeholder Thinking, Vol 2: Relationships, Communication, Reporting and Performance.* Sheffield, UK: GreenLeaf, 2003.

Kay, Andrea. "Nonprofit Groups Pay Competitive Salaries." *Hartford Business Journal,* November 1, 2007.

Kerlin, Janelle. "Social Enterprise in the United States and Abroad: Learning From Our Differences." Washington, DC: Paper Presented for the Emerging Issues in Social Entrepreneurship Research Colloquy, *34th Annual ARNOVA Conference,* November 17–19, 2005.

Key Facts About Corporation Foundations. New York: Foundation Center, 2010.

Kinkade, Sheila, and Katrin Verclas. *Wireless Technology for Social Change.* Washington, DC, and Berkshire, UK: UN Foundation and Vodafone Group Foundation, 2008.

Korngold, Alice. *Leveraging Good Will: Strengthening Non-Profits by Engaging With Business.* San Francisco: Jossey-Bass, 2005.

Korten, David. *Getting to the 21st Century: Voluntary Action and the Global Agenda.* Bloomfield, Conn.: Kumarian, 1990.

Korten, David. *When Corporations Rule the World,* 2nd ed. Bloomfield, Conn., and San Francisco: Kumarian and Berrett-Koehler, 2001.

Kotler, Philip, and Nancy Lee. *Corporate Social Responsibility: Doing the Most Good for Your Company and Cause.* Hoboken, NJ: John Wiley and Sons, 2005.

Kuglin, Fred, and Jeff Hook. *Building, Leading and Managing Strategic Alliances: How to Work Effectively and Profitably With Partner Companies.* Washington, DC: American Management Association, 2002.

Lafferty, Barbara, Ronald E. Goldsmith, Tomas M. Hult. "The Impact of the Alliance on the Partner: A Look at Cause Brand Alliances." *Psychology and Marketing* 21, no. 7 (2004): 509–531.

Leipzer, Deborah. *Canadian Companies on the Cutting Edge: Bata Promotes Development Research Report.* Council on Economic Priorities, July/August 1996.

Linden, Russ. *Working Across Boundaries: Making Collaboration Work in Government and NGOs.* San Francisco: Jossey-Bass, 2002.

Lewicki, Roy, et al. *Essentials of Negotiation.* Boston, Mass.: McGraw Hill, 1997.

London, Ted, Dennis Rondinelli, and Hugh O'Neill. "Strange Bedfellows: Alliances Between Corporations and Non-profits." In *Handbook of Strategic Alliances,* edited by Oded Shenkar and Jeffrey Reuer. Thousand Oaks, Calif.: Sage, 2005.

Long, Frederick, and Matthew Arnold. *The Power of Environmental Partnerships.* Washington, DC: The Dryden Press: Harcourt Brace College Publishers, 1995.

Macy, Christy. *Workable: Tackling Youth Unemployment Crisis.* Baltimore, Md.: International Youth Foundation Spotlight, Spring 2009.

Martin, Roger, and Sally Osberg. "Social Entrepreneurship: The Case for Definition." *Stanford Social Innovation Review* (Spring 2007):29–39.

Mason, Kenneth. "Responsibility for What's on the Tube." *Businessweek,* August 13, 1979.

McCambridge, Ruth. "Merger Fever in San Francisco." *Nonprofit Quarterly,* January 7, 2011.

McIntosh, Malcolm, Deborah Leipziger, Keith Jones, and Gill Coleman. *Corporate Citizenship: Successful Strategies for Responsible Companies.* London: Financial Times Management, Pitman Publishing, 1998.

"Mergers and Acquisitions." *Businessweek,* November 23, 2009.

Meyer, Holger. "Business, Boycott & Bureaucracy: The Kimberley Process Certification Scheme and the Global Quest for Conflict-Free Diamonds." Prepared for presentation at the 7th Pan European Conference on International Relations, Stockholm, Sweden, September 9–11, 2010.

Morrison, John, and Luke Wilde. *The Effectiveness of Multi-Stakeholder Initiatives in the Oil and Gas Sector: Summary Report.* London: TwentyFifty Ltd., March 2007.

National Council on Workplace Volunteerism Achieves Important Milestone. Washington, DC: Points of Light Foundation, March 29, 2007.

Nelson, Jane, and Simon Zadek. *Partnership Alchemy: New Social Partnership in Europe.* Copenhagen, Norway: The Copenhagen Center, March 2002.

Nelson, Jane, and David Prescott. *Partnering for Success: Business Perspectives on Multi-Stakeholder Partnerships.* World Economic Forum Global Corporate Citizen Initiative, January 2005.

"Nongovernmental Organizations Show Their Growing Power." *New York Times,* March 22, 2002.

"Norms on the Responsibilities of Transnational Corporations and Other Business Enterprises with Regard to Human Rights." U.N. Doc. E/CN.4/Sub.2/2003/12/Rev.2 2003.

Organization for Economic Cooperation and Development (OECD). "Growing Unequal? Income Distribution and Poverty in OECD Countries." Organization for Economic Cooperation and Development, October 2008, http://www.oecd.org/document/53/0,3746,en_2649_33933_41460917_1_1_1_1,00.html.

Otting, Laura. *Transitioning to the Nonprofit Sector.* New York: Kaplan, 2007.

Panel on the Nonprofit Sector. *Principles of Good Governance and Ethical Practices: A Guide for Charities and Foundations.* Panel on the Nonprofit Sector, October 2007.

Parker, Rani, Mark Schlagenhauf, and Gail Spence. *The Public-Private Alliances of USAID in Angola: An Assessment of Lessons Learned and Ways Forward.* USAID/Angola, September 2004.

Patterson, Kerry, et al. *Influencer: The Power to Change Anything.* New York: McGraw Hill, 2008.

Peizer, Jonathan. "Cross Sector Information and Communications Technology Funding for Development: What Works, What Doesn't and Why." *Massachusetts Institute of Technology Information Technologies and International Development* 1, no. 2 (Winter 2003):83–90.

Pellicelli, Anna Claudia. "Strategic Alliance: Clusters and Global Value Chains in the North and Third World." Presented at EADI Workshop, Nova, Italy, October 2003.

"Performance Bonds: Who Succeeds and Gets Paid. Barack Obama Imports a Big Idea from Britain." *The Economist,* February 17, 2011.

Porter, Michael, and Mark Kramer. "Creating Shared Value: How to Reinvent Capitalism and Unleash a Wave of Innovation and Growth." *Harvard Business Review* (January–February 2011):2–17.

Powell-Smith, Amanda. "Finding the Right Corporate NGO Partnership." *Corporate Responsibility Management.* August 1, 2005.

Prahalad, C.K., and Stuart Hart. *The Fortune at the Bottom of the Pyramid: Eradicating Poverty Through Profits.* Princeton, NJ: Wharton School Publishing, 2005.

Quelch, John, and Anthalie Laidler-Kylander. *The New Global Brands: Managing Non-Government Organizations in the 21st Century.* Mason, Ohio: Thompson South Western, 2006.

Rionda, Zynia. *CSR Casebook.* Washington, DC: Catalyst Consortium and USAID, July 2002.

Rondinelli, Dennis, and Ted London. "How Corporations and Environmental Groups Cooperate: Assessing Cross-sectoral Alliances and Collaborations."*Academy of Management Executives* 17, no. 1 (2003):61–74.

Rosso, Henry. *Corporate Philanthropy: Achieving Excellence in Fund Raising,* 2nd ed. San Francisco: Jossey-Bass, 2003.

Ruggie, John, Charles Kolb, Dara O'Rourke, and Andrew Kuper. *The Impact of Corporations on Global Governance.* New York: Center for International Cooperation and Carnegie Council on Ethics and International Affairs, 2004.

Sagawa, Shirley, and Eli Segal. *Common Interest: Common Good: Creating Value Through Business and Social Sector Partnerships.* Boston, Mass.: Harvard Business School Press, 2000.

Salomon, Lester, et al. *Global Civil Society Comparison: An Overview.* Baltimore, Md.: Johns Hopkins University Press, 2003.

Schiller, Ben. *Business-NGO Partnerships.* London: Ethical Corporation, December 2005.

Segil, Lorraine. *Measuring the Value of Partnering: How to Use Metrics to Plan, Develop and Implement Successful Alliances.* New York: American Management Association, 2004.

Selsky, John, and Barbara Parker. "Cross-Sector Partnerships to Address Social Issues: Challenges to Theory and Practice." *Journal of Management* 31, no. 6 (2005):849–873.

Sharp, Paine. *Value Shift: Why Companies Must Merge Social and Financial Imperatives to Achieve Superior Performance.* New York: McGraw Hill, 2003.

Smith, Craig. "New Corporate Philanthropy." *Harvard Business Review* (May–June 1994):1–12.

Stancich, Rikki. "Pension Funds See Potential in Climate Investment." *Climate Change Corp,* September 22, 2008.

Stiglitz, Joseph. *Globalization and Its Discontents.* New York: WW Norton and Company, 2003.

Stiglitz, Joseph. *Making Globalization Work.* New York: WW Norton and Company, 2006.

Strom, Stephanie. "The Philanthropreneurs." *New York Times,* November 13, 2006.

Sturchio, Jeffrey. "Business Engagement in Public Programs: The Pharmaceutical Industry's Contribution to Public Health and the Millennium Development Goals." *Corporate Governance* 8, no. 4 (2008):482–489.

SustainAbility. *The 21st Century NGO: In the Market for Change.* London: SustainAbility, 2003.

Svenserson, Ann. *The Stakeholder Engagement Theory.* San Francisco: Berrett-Koehler Publishers, 1998.

Taylor, Gary J., and Patricia Scharlin. *Smart Alliance: How a Global Corporation and Environmental Activists Transformed a Tarnished Brand.* New Haven, Conn.: Yale University Press, 2004.

Tennyson, Ros, International Business Leaders Forum, Global Alliance for Improved Nutrition, United Nations Development Program, and International Atomic Energy Agency. *The Partnering Toolkit.* London: International Business Leaders Forum, Global Alliance for Improved Nutrition, United Nations Development Program, and International Atomic Energy Agency, 2003.

The Corporate Citizen. *Interview With Daniel Runde, Outlook for Public-Private Global Development Initiatives.* Washington, DC: US Chamber of Commerce, March 2007.

Tierney, Thomas, *The Nonprofit Sector's Leadership Deficit.* Boston, Mass.: Bridgespan, 2009.

United Nations. *Human Development Report 2007–2008.* New York: United Nations, 2008.

UN Environmental Program, UN Global Compact, Utopies and Dupré Standislas, eds. *Talk the Walk: Advancing Sustainable Lifestyles Through Marketing and Communications.* New York: UN Environmental Program, UN Global Compact and Utopies, 2005.

UN Global Compact. *Who Cares Win: Connecting Financial Markets to a Changing World.* New York: UN Global Compact, 2004.

Uphoff, Norman. "Why Are NGOs Not a Third Sector: A Sectoral Analysis With Some Thoughts on Accountability, Sustainability and Evaluation." In *Beyond the Magic Bullet: NGO Performance and Accountability in the Post-Cold War World,* edited by Michael Edwards and David Hulme. Bloomfield, Conn.: Kumarian, 1996.

Utting, Peter. *UN-Business Partnerships Whose Agenda Counts*? Paper presented at seminar on Partnerships for Development or Privatization of the Multilateral System, Oslo, Norway December 8, 2000.

Urban Institute. *The Nonprofit Sector in Brief: Public Charities, Giving and Volunteering.* Washington, DC: Urban Institute, 2010.

Wadham, Helen. "An Exploration of Business and NGO Perspectives on Corporate Social Responsibility, Sustainable Development and Partnership." Manchester, UK: Manchester Metropolitan University Business School, December 2007.

Wadham, Helen. "How Can Partnerships Between NGOs and Business Add Value to Corporate Social Responsibility Programmes in Developing Countries?" PhD diss., Cass Business School, November 2005.

Warner, Michael, and Rory Sullivan, eds. *Putting Partnership to Work: Strategic Alliances for Development Between Government, the Private Sector and Civil Society.* Sheffield, UK: GreenLeaf, 2004.

Werther, William, and David Chandler. *Strategic Corporate Social Responsibility: Stakeholders in a Global Environment.* Thousand Oaks, Calif.: Sage, January 2006.

World Bank Group. *Addressing the Challenges of Globalization: An Independent Evaluation of the World Bank's Approach to Global Programs.* Washington, DC: Operations Evaluation Studies Unit, the World Bank Group, 2005.

World Commission on Economic Development. *Our Common Future.* Oxford, UK: World Commission on Economic Development, 1987.

World Wildlife Fund. "Certification and Roundtables: Do They Work?" London: World Wildlife Fund Review, September 2010.

Wymer, Walter, et al. *Dimensions of Business and Nonprofit Collaborative Relationships in Nonprofit and Business Sector Collaboration.* New York: Hawthorne Press, 2003.

Yamamoto, Tadashi, Kim Gould, and K.G. Ashizawa. *Corporate-NGO Partnerships.* Tokyo, Japan: Japanese Center for International Exchange, 1999.

Appendix

Name of Organization	Website
Academy of Educational Development	http://www.aed.org
American Red Cross	http://www.redcross.org
American Medical Association	http://www.ama-assn.org
Association of Social Health and Advancement	http://www.ashaodisha.org
CARE	http://www.care.org
City Year	http://www.cityyear.org
Concern Universal	http://www.concernuniversal.org
Dana Mitra Lingkunga	http://www.dml.or.id/dml5/
Delancey Street	http://delanceystreetfoundation.org
Endangered Wildlife Trust	https://www.ewt.org.za
Environmental Defense Fund	http://www.edf.org
EarthWatch Institute	http://www.earthwatch.org
Fauna & Flora International	http://www.fauna-flora.org
First Responder Institute	http://www.firstresponder.org
Foundation for Integrated Education and Development	http://www.funedesin.org
Food for the Hungry	http://www.fh.org
Girl's, Inc.	http://www.girlsinc.org

(*continues*)

Appendix (*continued*)

Name of Organization	Website
Goodwill Industries	http://www.goodwill.org/
GreenPeace	http://www.greenpeace.org
Grameen Bank	http://www.grameen.com/
Haygrove Development (not-for-profit company)	http://www.haygrove.co.uk/haygrove-development
International Youth Foundation	http://www.iyfnet.org
Institute for Sustainable Communities	http://www.iscvt.org
Juma Ventures	http://www.jumaventures.org
Jumpstart	http://www.jstart.org
Kaboom	http://kaboom.org
MedShare	http://www.medshare.org
Mercy Corps	http://www.mercycorps.org
PCI Global	http://www.pciglobal.org
Rainforest Alliance	http://www.rainforest-alliance.org
Rubicon	http://www.rubiconprograms.org/
Save the Children	http://www.savethechildren.org
Share our Strength	http://www.strength.org
Population and Community Development Association	http://www.pda.or.th/eng/background.asp
The Nature Conservancy	http://www.nature.org
Universal Giving	http://www.universalgiving.org
Wild Salmon Center	http://www.wildsalmoncenter.org
World Vision	http://www.worldvision.org

Index

Abercrombie & Fitch, 111
Academy of Educational Development (AED). *See* NetMark
accountability
  advocacy and, 66–67
  business, 7, 37
  as business trend, 91–93, 94
  due diligence and, 71–72
  Gulf Coast oil spill and, 91, 92
  improving, 215
  MNCs and, 92, 235, 241
  NGO, 13, 48–49, 56, 65–68, 71–72
  providing, 180, 247, 249
  regulation and, 66
  standards for, 104, 141
acquired immune deficiency syndrome (AIDS), 34, 47, 92, 106–7, 122
advice
  accepting money for, 112
  advisory boards and committees, 148–49, 207–8
  community advisory councils, 56–57
  donor-advised funds, 44–45
  NGOs offering, 38, 90
  as partnership engagement, 17, 116, 118
advocacy
  accountability and, 66–67
  as asset, 101, 233
  joint, 8, 62
  as NGO role, 14, 36
  NGOs oriented toward, 6, 55, 57, 59
  raising awareness through, 196
  shareholder, 77–78
AED (Academy of Educational Development). *See* NetMark
age. *See also* children
  in community service, 45
  in labor pool, 33–34, 84, 89, 182
  LOHAS and, 79
  in philanthropy, 40, 49
AGM. *See* Aqua Gold Mississippi
AIDS. *See* acquired immune deficiency syndrome
alliance
  project, 100
  strategic, 15, 18, 117, 232
alternative organizational structures. *See* hybrid models
AMA. *See* American Medical Association
American Council for Voluntary International Action (InterAction), 56, 59, 62, 67
American Medical Association (AMA), 56, 123, 145
Annan, Kofi, 46, 92
anticorruption. *See* corruption
Aparajitas, 128, 173, 183
approaching partners. *See* partners, approaching
Aqua Gold Mississippi (AGM), 135–36, 154, 156, 160
ASHA. *See* Association for Social and Health Advancement
Asian Corporate Social Responsibility Award, 200, 214

assessment, internal, 18, 20, 144
  of assets, 233–34
  of desired partnership type, 229
  of internal capacity, 229–33
  of partnership purpose, 226–29
assessment, of partnership
  approach, 251–52
  effects, 250–51
  value creation, 110, 114, 227, 250
Association for Social and Health Advancement (ASHA), 170, 176, 180, 187
Austin, James, 111, 117

banking crisis. *See* economic crisis
BAT. *See* British American Tobacco
B Corporations, 39, 49
benefit corporations, 39, 49
bilateral partnerships. *See also* Partnership Lifecycle
  definition, 17, 115
  difficulty implementing, 144
  examples, 134–43
  joint programming as, 121–28
  key elements, 133, 144
  resource exchange as, 119–20
  transactional services as, 120
biodiversity, 6, 113–14, 136, 151, 156. *See also* environmental, social, and governance issues
blended value proposition, 9–10
boom-bust cycle, 29, 31
bottom of the pyramid, 107
boycott
  as confrontational, 16, 99, 110
  efficacy of, 78
  as engagement, 17, 57, 116
  willingness to, 80
Boys & Girls Clubs of America, 238
  Coca-Cola and, 124
  Major League Baseball and, 126, 231
  Reader's Digest and, 88
BP. *See* British Petroleum
BPD. *See* Business Partners for Development
BP oil spill. *See* Gulf Coast oil spill
Brecher, Jeremy, 91–92
Brent Spar protest, 8, 11
BridgeIt. *See* Text2Teach
British American Tobacco (BAT), 143, 148, 247
British Petroleum (BP), 16, 247. *See also* Gulf Coast oil spill
Bruntland Commission, 5, 6, 11
BSR. *See* Business for Social Responsibility
business. *See also* specific topics
  accountability, 7, 37, 91–93, 94
  classification of, 75, 245–46
  conflict within, 113
  consolidation of, 29, 30, 76, 93
  CSR and, 75, 83, 89–91, 94
  definition of, 14
  inconsistency within, 113
  networks, 69–70, 104, 140
  practices, negative, 7, 57, 77, 80
  procurement, 82, 90, 122, 147, 237
  public trusting, 48–49, 79, 91, 94, 105
  research by, 90, 120, 122
  role of, 36–37, 81, 107
  sector overview, 75
  stakeholders, 7, 15, 37, 91–93
  trends in, 75–94
  trust between NGOs and, 108–11, 114, 133
  visibility benefitting, 110, 112, 230, 239, 240
  women-owned, 75, 121, 140–41
Business for Social Responsibility (BSR), 11
Business Partners for Development (BPD)
  as case study, 170, 176, 188
  creation of, 12, 169, 176
  on water and sanitation, 169, 184, 186, 188

Calphalon, 142, 146, 150
campaigning
  case studies of, 138, 140–41
  as confrontational, 16, 71, 99, 150–51
  efficacy of, 118, 159
  as engagement, 6, 17, 57, 116, 230
  ICT and, 61–62
  shareholder advocacy and, 78
cause-related marketing (CRM)
  as advertising and public relations, 90, 104, 122–24, 156–57, 229

as engagement, 17, 116
ethics of, 124
examples of, 127, 134, 137, 140–42
forms of, 124
funding through, 63, 125, 159
goals in, 150, 159
history of, 11, 124–25
initiating collaboration, 160
initiation of, 146–47, 249
as joint program, 121–26, 230
key lessons about, 126, 161
legal considerations in, 125–26
by Save the Children, 126
value creation by, 243
CBOs. *See* constituency-based organizations
Center for Women's Business Research, 75
Centre on Transnational Corporations, 92
CEO. *See* chief executive officer
charity. *See* non-profit organization (NPO)
chief executive officer (CEO)
attitude of, 7, 83, 86
awards to, 132, 141, 159
corruption, 65
involvement of, 130, 152, 210, 230–31
on NGO board, 135, 138
Child and Youth Health, 127
child labor
as issue, 7, 12, 80, 150
preventing, 105, 197–198, 204, 205, 215
sanctions, 209, 211, 216–18
children. *See also* Save the Children
Child and Youth Health, 127
child mortality, 47
education for, 138, 148–49, 198
marketing to, 111–12, 124
in poverty, 32–33, 129, 141, 170, 200
Social Accountability International's Child Survival Code of Conduct, 67
City Year. *See* Timberland
classification
business, 75, 245–46
of engagement, 16–17, 115–16, 230–31, 237
of ETI, 59
mistaken, 232
NGO, 55–57, 59
partnership, 2, 122, 130, 232–33
of philanthropy, 40–42
climate change. *See also* environmental, social, and governance issues
companies addressing, 61, 80, 148, 245
difficulty of, 34, 99
at Earth Summit, 6–7, 11
economic freedom and, 29
in engagement, 90, 237
urgency of, 1–2
at World Summit, 8
closure and renewal phase
capacity building in, 159–60, 187–88, 218–19
goals in, 159, 185–87, 214–18
overview, 158, 185, 213–14
people in, 159, 185, 214
Coca-Cola, 124
code of conduct (CoC)
communication of, 221
developing, 12, 71–72, 100
inadequacy of, 177–78, 196, 217
MSIs and, 193, 210–11, 214, 217, 221
SMEs and, 211–12, 217
Social Accountability International's Child Survival Code of Conduct, 67
supplier, 12, 90, 155
training on, 211
Code of Conduct for International Funding Agencies Working in South Africa, 67
Commonwealth Foundation, 12, 67
community investment, 77–78
companies, domestic, 75
competition, international
benefits of, 23–25, 30
drawbacks of, 26–30, 92
complexity. *See* problems, complexity of
confidentiality, 114
consolidation
of businesses, 29, 30, 76, 93
of NGOs, 45, 59–60
constituency-based organizations (CBOs), 56–57
consulting
as engagement, 17, 106, 116, 118, 230
as NGO role, 57–58, 59

rather than inclusion, 197, 202
of unconventional sources, 154
consumerism, 17, 116, 117–18, 230
contacts. *See* networks
contribution, in-kind. *See* in-kind contribution
core competency
building on, 100, 193, 230
maximizing, 94, 100, 153, 188
of specific sectors, 57–58, 93, 121, 168
corporate citizenship, 13, 104
growth of, 37, 47
percentage of, 85–86
corporate philanthropy, 43–44, 86–88, 127
corporate social responsibility (CSR)
activities, 86–87, 90
Asian Corporate Social Responsibility Award, 200, 214
awareness of, 218
business case for, 83
Business for Social Responsibility, 11
as business trend, 75, 80–91, 94
business unit engagement and, 89–91
community engagement and, 89
corporate reputation and, 84–85
as criterion, 236
definitions of, 5
drivers of, 83
examples of, 195
inconsistency and, 113
license to operate and, 84–85
limitations in, 81–82
as management imperative, 8–9
nature of efforts in, 121
overview, 80–83
poverty and, 5
recruitment and, 85
reporting on, 91, 236, 242
researching, 236
retention through, 106
strategies, 85–86
structures, 86
types of, 122
UN Global Compact and, 94
volunteerism and, 88–89
corporations. *See* business
CorpWatch, 92, 235
corruption, 65–67, 81, 200
UN Global Compact against, 8, 9, 13, 204, 213
cotton, 27, 79
Creating Shared Value (Porter & Kramer), 10
credibility. *See also* legitimacy
brand, 101, 233–34
CARE and, 155, 179–80
costs of building, 149–50, 201–2, 205, 220
CSR and, 84–85
of FSC, 197
general lack of, 48–49
as NGO asset, 102, 105, 110, 125
NGOs lacking, 66, 68, 114, 157
partnerships damaging, 60–61, 106, 111, 112, 240
protecting, 182
of regulation, 25, 35, 210, 213, 218
stakeholder engagement and, 194, 201, 210, 220
CRM. *See* cause-related marketing
crowdsourcing, 62
CSR. *See* corporate social responsibility

Daly, Herman, 29
Dana Mitra Lingkungan (DML), 135–36, 154–55, 156
decision-making framework, 19–20, 225–26, 227, 228. *See also* specific steps
Denny's, 105, 147. *See also* Save the Children
Department for International Development (DFID), 167–68
ETI and, 12, 201, 206, 207
GiG and, 171, 176
grants from, 63, 206
developed and less developed countries
assistance to, 36–37, 46, 47
capital access and, 6, 25, 26
direct integration in, 89–91, 115, 218, 246–47
distribution to, 107, 140
emerging markets in, 107
globalization and, 11, 24, 26, 28
ICT in, 61, 70

income gap between, 32
MNCs in, 75–76, 92
poverty in, 27, 32, 167–68
research in, 235
resource limitations in, 298, 212, 221
subsidies and, 11, 25–26
tariffs and, 25, 26
workers in, 197, 202
development assistance, 36–37, 46–47, 50
DFID. *See* Department for International Development
distrust. *See* trust
DML. *See* Dana Mitra Lingkungan
Doha Trade Talks, 13, 25–26
domestic companies, 75
donation, in-kind. *See* in-kind contribution
Donors' Rights Charter, 67
dot-com bubble, 31
due diligence
accountability and, 71–72
decision-making and, 227, 244–46
designing process of, 241–42
internal conflict and, 60–61
and joint programming, 243
matrix, 227, 242–44
in philanthropy, 243
in research, 234, 239–41

Earth Summit, 6–7, 11
economic crisis
consequences of, 34, 40, 157
globalization and, 26–27
governments and, 48–49, 92–93
economic efficiency, 23–24, 26–27, 82
economic freedom, 23–25, 27, 29, 92
economic strata, 165–67
Edelman Trust Barometer, 85
EDF. *See* Environmental Defense Fund
education
approaches, 217
funding for, 29, 40, 44, 123
for literacy, 32
loans for, 78–79
ministry of, 104, 108
as mission, 13–14, 43, 47, 91, 105
sector, 7, 57, 58
of staff, 60, 90–91
as value, 15
via Internet, 46
for women, 153
youth, 138, 148–49, 198
EHS. *See* environmental, health, and safety
Emerson, Jeb, 9
employee protection, 28
Enron, 81, 92–93
entrepreneurs, social, 14–15, 65
environmental, health, and safety (EHS)
EHS Academy, 171, 180, 188
managers, 171, 175, 187
environmental, social, and governance (ESG) issues, 101, 105. *See also* climate change; sustainable development
increased adoption of, 37, 215
investing priorities and, 93–94
natural resources, 26–27, 29, 168, 170, 176
in NGO role, 36
pension funds and, 77–78
track records in, 236, 242
UN and, 11, 12, 79–80, 106
UN Global Compact and, 37, 92, 194, 203, 211, 214
ways to address, 106
Who Cares Wins and, 9, 13
Environmental Defense Fund (EDF)
BP and, 112
Climate Corps, 120
funding of, 148, 227–28
Guide to Successful NGO-Corporate Partnerships, 225–26
McDonald's and, 106–7, 137, 150–51, 159
targeting specific corporations, 148
Ethical Trading Initiative (ETI)
classification of, 59
creation of, 12, 196
criticism of, 218
DFID and, 12, 201, 206, 207
governance structure of, 207
longevity of, 218
in MSI, 18, 194–95, 206
requirements of, 203

- reviews by, 216
- unions and, 202

evaluation. *See* assessment, internal; assessment, of partnership

execution phase
- capacity building in, 158, 183–85, 210–13
- goals and objectives in, 156–57, 182, 209–10
- overview, 153, 181, 208–9
- people in, 153–56, 181–82, 209

expectations, 79–80, 94, 109–10

fair-trade
- chocolate, 38, 79, 100, 196–201
- coffee, 11, 79

financial crisis. *See* economic crisis

Fiorina, Carly, 87

flexibility
- of organizations, 37–38, 110, 114
- of partnerships, 63–64, 130, 189

Forest Stewardship Council (FSC)
- certification through, 211–12, 213
- creation of, 11, 196, 206
- credibility of, 197
- CSR trends and, 121
- governance structure of, 207
- history, 11–13
- longevity of, 218
- M&E and, 205
- as MSI, 193, 197–198, 214, 235
- requirements by, 203
- results of, 216, 217
- stakeholder involvement in, 197, 201–2

for-profit corporations. *See* business

40/4 gap, 79–80

Foundation for Integrated Education and Development (FUNEDESIN)
- funding of, 38, 196, 201
- time perception by, 212

foundations. *See* philanthropy

framework. *See* decision-making framework; Long-Arnold framework

freedom, economic, 23–25, 27, 29, 92

Friedman, Milton, 15, 81

Friedman, Thomas, 32
- *The World Is Flat*, 30

FSC. *See* Forest Stewardship Council

funding
- annual and multi-year, 63–64, 103
- corporate, refusing, 148, 227–28, 240–41
- through CRM, 63, 125, 159
- donor requirements and, 63
- for education, 29, 40, 44, 123
- efficiency, 196, 218–19
- in hybrid models, 37–40, 187, 196, 201
- independence and, 111–13
- investment access, NGO, 64
- patient capital, 64
- proposal-less fundraising, 238
- sources of, 62–65, 69–70
- stewardship of, 66–67
- unrestricted, 63–64

FUNEDESIN. *See* Foundation for Integrated Education and Development

GAIN. *See* Global Alliance for Improved Nutrition

Gambia is Good (GiG)
- DFID and, 171, 176
- funding of, 187
- governance structure of, 180
- initiation of, 169
- people and, 181, 185
- training by, 183
- as tri-party partnership, 171, 176

GATT. *See* General Agreement on Tariffs and Trade

GB. *See* Grameen Bank

GDA (Global Development Alliance). *See* United States Agency for International Development

GDP. *See* gross domestic product

General Agreement on Tariffs and Trade (GATT), 25, 26

generation
- future, 5, 7–8, 49
- lost, 33–34
- Y, 84

Georgia Pacific (GP), 106–7, 140

GEP. *See* Guangdong Environmental Partnership

GiG. *See* Gambia is Good

Gilding, Paul, 108
girls. *See* children; women
Girls Clubs. *See* Boys & Girls Clubs of America
Global Alliance for Improved Nutrition (GAIN)
governance structure of, 206, 207
as MSI, 193, 199–200
The Partnering Toolkit and, 225–26
requirements by, 203
subinitiatives of, 213
Global Alliance for Workers and Communities
due diligence and, 244–45
goals and, 182
initiation of, 176
people and, 177–78
as tri-party partnership, 171, 174
widespread ownership of, 187
Global Development Alliance (GDA). *See* United States Agency for International Development
Global Forum, 6
globalization
definition of, 23–25
in developed and less developed countries, 11, 24, 26, 28
disparate benefits of, 27, 29–30, 32, 48
economic crisis and, 26–27
key events in, 26
managed, 29, 35
origins of, 25–26
results of, 28
UN and, 65–66
Global Reporting Initiative (GRI), 12, 91
Global Road Safety Partnership (GRSP)
funding of, 201, 218–19
governance structure of, 207–8
history of, 206, 218
as MSI, 194–95, 203, 207, 213
GlobalScan, 80, 85
global warming. *See* climate change
Goodland, Robert, 29
Goodwill, 37–38
governance
corporate, 9, 81
global, 9
structure, 206–8, 212–13, 216
government
economic crisis and, 48–49, 92–93
role of, 35
GP. *See* Georgia Pacific; Grameen Phone
Grameen Bank (GB), 39, 138, 155
Grameen Danone Foods Limited, 129
Grameen Foundation, 155, 156
Grameen Phone (GP), 39, 138, 155, 156
Grameen Telecom, 39
Green and Black, 100
Greenpeace, 108, 138
as advocacy organization, 55, 59
Foron and, 138, 156, 160
funding of, 112, 148, 227–28, 240–41
at Partnership Summit, 8
protests by, 8, 11
GRI. *See* Global Reporting Initiative
gross domestic product (GDP)
growth measured by, 26–27
NGOs contributing to, 13–14
private wealth and, 32–33, 36
trade in, 24–25
GRSP. *See* Global Road Safety Partnership
Guangdong Environmental Partnership (GEP), 171, 176, 180, 188
Guide to Successful NGO-Corporate Partnerships (EDF), 225–26
guilt by association, 111, 240
Gulf Coast oil spill
accountability and, 91, 92
due-diligence and, 240, 244, 245
partnerships and, 105, 112

human immunodeficiency virus (HIV), 34, 47, 92, 106–7, 122
hybrid models, 70–71
B Corporations, 39, 49
benefit corporations, 39, 49
examples of, 37–39
low-profit limited liability corporations, 39–40, 49
United States law and, 37

ICCR. *See* Interfaith Center on Corporate Responsibility

ICML. *See* Integrated Coal Mining Limited
ICT. *See* information, communication, and technology
IFRC. *See* International Federation of Red Cross and Red Crescent Societies
ILO. *See* International Labour Organization
IMARE. *See* Inclusive Marketplace Alliance Rural Enterprises
IMF. *See* International Monetary Fund
Inclusive Marketplace Alliance Rural Enterprises (IMARE), 172, 176, 177, 184
income gap
  between countries, 32
  within countries, 32–33, 48
  increasing, 33, 34, 48, 99
independence, loss of, 111–13
informal sector, 6, 28, 29–30
information, communication, and technology (ICT)
  advances in, 48, 61–62, 69, 70
  campaigning and, 61–62
  in developed and less developed countries, 61, 70
  flatteners of, 30–32
  ICT companies, 83, 119
  tariffs on, 28
INGOs. *See* international NGOs
initiation phase
  capacity building in, 151–53, 179–80, 205–7
  goals and objectives in, 150–51, 178–9, 204–5
  overview, 149, 177, 201
  people in, 149–50, 177–8, 201–4
in-kind contribution
  as engagement, 17, 116, 229, 230, 237
  in Kaboom, 139
  as philanthropy, 40, 86–87, 119
insecticide-treated bednets (ITNs), 172, 178–9, 181
insourcing, 32
Institute of Sustainable Communities (ISC), 169, 175, 176
Integrated Coal Mining Limited (ICML), 170, 176, 180, 187
integrated programming, 17, 116, 117
integrity acts, 68, 71
intellectual property, 25, 28, 121–23, 248
InterAction. *See* American Council for Voluntary International Action
Interfaith Center on Corporate Responsibility (ICCR), 78, 118, 157
Internal Revenue Service (IRS), 59
international competition. *See* competition, international
International Federation of Red Cross and Red Crescent Societies (IFRC), 194
International Labour Organization (ILO), 12, 33–34, 197, 206, 211
International Monetary Fund (IMF), 25–26
international NGOs (INGOs), 58–59
International Youth Foundation (IYF), 199. *See also* Global Alliance for Workers and Communities
Internet, 31
  commerce via, 37–38, 124
  education via, 46
  philanthropy via, 40, 124
  research via, 235, 237–8
intra-firm trade, 76
IRS. *See* Internal Revenue Service
ISC. *See* Institute of Sustainable Communities
ITNs. *See* insecticide-treated bednets
IYF. *See* International Youth Foundation

joint programming, 228–30
  advocacy in, 8, 62
  bilateral partnerships as, 121–28
  buy-in to, 123
  CRM in, 121–26, 230
  due diligence and, 243
  examples of, 127
  inclusive business models in, 128
  legal considerations in, 123, 125–26
  licensing in, 121–23
  misclassification as, 232
  overview of, 17, 116, 130, 230
  questions for, 121, 123
  value creation in, 82

Jumpstart, 138–39
just-in-time inventories, 31

Kaboom, 139
Katrina, Hurricane, 105, 134
Kimberly Process Certification Scheme (KPCS)
  accreditation under, 211–13
  as addressing industry-specific issues, 197–200
  goals of, 214, 216
  governance structure of, 207
  initiation of, 13, 196
  requirements by, 203
Kramer, Mark, 81–82
  Creating Shared Value, 10

L3Cs. *See* low-profit limited liability corporations
leadership vacuum, 35, 58, 68–69, 72
legitimacy. *See also* credibility
  corruption and, 66
  effectiveness and, 67
  stakeholders and, 149, 177, 220
  standards and, 68, 201–2, 211, 218
less developed countries. *See* developed and less developed countries
license to operate, 84–85
Lifecycle, Partnership. *See* Partnership Lifecycle
lifestyles of health and sustainability (LOHAS), 79
literacy, 32, 155
LOHAS. *See* lifestyles of health and sustainability
Long-Arnold framework, 18–19, 144–45. *See also* specific phases
low-profit limited liability corporations (L3Cs), 39–40, 49

M&A. *See* mergers and acquisitions
Major League Baseball, 126, 231
Marine Stewardship Council (MSC)
  as addressing industry-specific issues, 197–200
  certification by, 176, 200, 205
  governance structure of, 207
  initiation of, 12, 201–4, 206
  people and, 201–4, 214
  results of, 217, 218
market, free, 23–25, 27, 29, 92
MBOs. *See* membership-based organizations
McDonald's, 148
  Child and Youth Health, 127
  in Los Angeles uprising, 84
  Ronald McDonald Houses, 12, 84, 124, 127
  solid waste and, 106–7, 137, 150–51, 159
MDGs. *See* Millennium Development Goals
M&E. *See* monitoring and evaluation
membership-based organizations (MBOs), 56–57, 58
memorandum of understanding (MOU), 149, 176, 177, 180, 248
mergers and acquisitions (M&A), 60, 76, 93, 160, 235–36
Millennium Development Goals (MDGs), 7–8, 37, 47, 50
misconduct. *See* corruption
mistrust. *See* trust
MNCs. *See* multi-national corporations
monitoring and evaluation (M&E), 57, 63, 205, 217, 250
morale, 85–86, 88, 102, 106, 110, 147
mortgage crisis. *See* economic crisis
MOU. *See* memorandum of understanding
MSC. *See* Marine Stewardship Council
MSIs. *See* multi-stakeholder initiatives
multi-national corporations (MNCs), 14
  accountability and, 92, 235, 241
  CoCs and, 196
  consolidation of, 29
  growth of, 75–76
  in NetMark partnership, 175, 181–82
  wealth of, 36–37
multi-sector response, 34–35, 46, 48, 94, 116–17
multi-stakeholder initiatives (MSIs). *See also* Partnership Lifecycle
  addressing industry-specific issues, 197–200
  adopting general principles, 194–95

categories of, 193, 196
CoC and, 193, 210–11, 214, 217, 221
definition of, 115–17
framework discussing, 5, 18–19, 144
growing into, 188
networks, 206
researching, 234–35
results of, 217
SMEs and, 218, 219, 221
structure in, 251
summary of, 219–21

natural resources, 26–27, 29, 168, 170, 176
The Nature Conservancy (TNC)
BP and, 112, 240, 244
Georgia Pacific and, 106–7, 140
MBNA and, 140
negative-screen methodology, 9, 77–78
negotiation, 248–49, 249
timeframe, 120, 181, 241
Nestlé, 57, 84
NetMark
as competitive, 175
expansion of, 188
goals and timeframes in, 178–79, 185–86
partner turnover in, 184–85
SMEs and, 181–82
as tri-party partnership, 172, 176
networks
access to, 16–17, 100–102, 168, 248
business, 69–70, 104, 140
champions', 155
creating, 170, 252
CRM and, 125
for donors, 40
external, 180, 212
informal, 6
of investors, 64
Jumpstart, 138–39, 152
local, 126, 129, 155, 165
MSI, 208, 215
NGO, 68, 108, 236–37
New Partnerships Initiative, 47, 168
NGO Accountability Charter, 13, 68
NGO-corporate engagement
confrontational, 16, 71, 99, 110, 150–51
with exchange (partnerships), 16–17, 115
without exchange, 16, 115
philanthropic, 99–100, 110, 116
NGO-corporate partnerships. *See also* specific topics
benefits of, 101–8
bilateral, 17, 115
business-NGO and, 1
challenges of, 108–14
cross-sectoral, 100
elements of, 248–49
as engagement, 16–17, 115
as financial only, 109
initiation, 249
multi-stakeholder, 5, 18, 193, 196
sector and, 99
tri-party, 18, 165–68
types of, 2
NGO Guidelines for Good Policy and Practice, 12, 67
NGOs. *See* non-governmental organizations
Nike. *See also* Global Alliance for Workers and Communities
in Asia, 83
criticism of, 12, 37, 84, 182
in Niger Delta, 7
in Pakistan, 13, 209
in Vietnam, 92
working with NGOs, 105, 179–80
non-governmental organizations (NGOs). *See also* specific topics
definition of, 13–14
quantity, 58–60
registration, 62–63, 126
size of, 59–60
non-profit organization (NPO), 6, 13–14, 14–15, 55. *See also* specific topics

OECD. *See* Organisation for Economic Co-operation and Development
operations and service provision, 58
Organisation for Economic Co-operation and Development (OECD), 32–33
Our Common Future (WCED), 5

outsourcing, 26, 31, 62
overhead, 62, 64

Partnering for Global Development, 47, 167
The Partnering Toolkit, 225–26
partners, approaching, 20, 227
business case in, 238–39
through decision-makers, 237–38
initial meeting in, 238
through networks, 236–37
Partnership Lifecycle, 18, 144, 168–69, 196. *See also* specific phases
partnerships. *See also* NGO-corporate partnerships; specific topics
business-NGO, 1
need for working, 1–2
public-private, 18, 117, 165, 177
Partnership Summit, 7–8
patient capital, 64
PET. *See* polyethylene terephthalate
phase. *See* closure and renewal phase; execution phase; initiation phase; seed phase
philanthrocapitalism, 41–42, 50, 64, 103
philanthropy
age in, 40, 49
classification of, 40–42
by community (public) foundations, 44–45
community service as, 45–46
corporate, 43–44, 86–88, 127
in due diligence, 243
as engagement, 99–100, 110, 116
by family foundations, 42–43, 49–50
individual, 40
in-kind, 40, 86–87, 119
institutional, 40–41
resource exchange as, 17, 116
through Social Impact Bonds, 42
venture, 41–42, 50, 64, 103
via Internet, 40, 124
by women, 40, 45, 49
polyethylene terephthalate (PET), 135, 154–55, 156
Porter, Michael, 81–82
Creating Shared Value, 10
poverty
children in, 32–33, 129, 141, 170, 200
credit access, 29–30, 32, 78, 139, 173
CSR and, 5
in developed and less developed countries, 27, 32, 167–68
economic strata, 165–67
marketing to, 107
pro-poor value chains, 91, 121, 128, 171
unemployment and, 25, 26, 33–34, 48
PPP. *See* public-private partnership
Prahala, C.K., 107
problems, complexity of
addressing, 168, 205, 217, 218, 219
increase in, 23, 48, 167
recognition of, 46, 50, 100
requiring multi-sector response, 34–35, 46, 48, 94, 116–17
procurement
business, 82, 90, 122, 147, 237
donor, 47
as engagement, 17, 116, 117–18, 230
project alliance, 100
Pro-Planalto, 173, 176
public-private partnership (PPP), 18, 117, 165, 177

Rainforest Action Groups (RAGs), 11
Reader's Digest, 88
reputation. *See* credibility; legitimacy
Reputation Institute, 80, 85
research
by business, 90, 120, 122
CSR, 236
in developed and less developed countries, 235
due diligence in, 234, 239–41
by NGOs, 26–27, 36, 57–59
of potential partners, 227–29, 234, 235–36, 237–38
selection criteria in, 234–35
resource exchange, 17, 116, 119–20, 130, 230
risk and reward, 100–101, 115, 151, 179
risk management, 7, 15–16, 81
role
of business, 36–37, 81, 107

changes in, 48–49
of government, 35
of NGOs, 14, 36, 57–58, 59, 67
Ronald McDonald Houses, 12, 84, 124, 127
Rouse, James, 81
Rural Sales Program (RSP)
development of, 169, 173, 179–80, 188
empowering women, 128, 183
partnership structure of, 173, 176, 243

Sakhalin Salmon Initiative (SSI), 174, 176, 180, 185, 187
Sarbanes-Oxley Act, 66, 68, 92–93
Save the Children, 141
CRM by, 126
funding by, 63
initiating partnership, 147, 231
partnership agreement and, 148
partnership champions and, 149–50, 156, 159
in Pro-Planalto, 173, 176
structure of, 59
Say, Jean-Baptiste, 15
Schmidheiny, Stephan, 6–7
SdE. *See* Senegalese des Eaux
sector
business, 75
classification, of NGOs, 55–56
core competencies, 57–58, 93, 121, 168
education, 7, 57, 58
informal, 6, 28, 29–30
multi-sector response, 34–35, 46, 48, 94, 116–17
NGO, growth of, 58–60, 69
partnerships and, 99–100
private, growth of, 75–76, 93
seed phase
overview, 145, 169
partnership agreement in, 148–49, 173, 177, 246–49
partnership initiation in, 146–47, 169, 173, 196, 201
partnership strategy in, 147–48
sell-out, 111–12, 240–41
Senegalese des Eaux (SdE), 170, 176
shadow assembly, 6
shared value, 81–83, 91, 94, 160
Creating Shared Value (Porter & Kramer), 10
shareholder advocacy, 77–78
shareholder resolutions, 17, 78, 116, 118, 230
shareholder value, maximizing
aims other than, 9–10, 15, 85
as main aim, 14, 15, 36, 81
TBL and, 5
Share our Strength (SOS)
Calphalon and, 142, 146, 150
Timberland and, 153
Shell, 7, 8, 11, 37, 84
small and medium enterprises (SMEs), 14, 121
CoCs and, 211–12, 217
MSIs and, 218, 219, 221
NetMark and, 181–82
SoCap. *See* social capital
Social Accountability International's Child Survival Code of Conduct, 67
social capital (SoCap), 64–65, 83, 188–89
social enterprise, 14–15
business practices in, 9–10
Goodwill as, 37–38
hybrid models and, 39
investment access by, 64–65
RSP as, 188
Social Impact Bonds, 41, 42, 64, 70–71, 103
socially responsible investing (SRI)
community investment in, 77–78
growth of, 93–94
investor priority change and, 76–79
negative-screen methodology in, 9, 77–78
shareholder advocacy in, 77–78
shareholder resolutions and, 118
solid waste, 106–7, 137, 150–51, 159
SOS. *See* Share our Strength
SRI. *See* socially responsible investing
SSI. *See* Sakhalin Salmon Initiative
stakeholders. *See also* multi-stakeholder initiatives
business, 7, 15, 37, 91–93
credibility and, 194, 201, 210, 220
engagement with, 15–16, 115

framework for engagement with, 16–17, 114–16
management of, 15
NGO, 48–49, 56, 65–68, 71–72
participation by, 8–9
passing risk to, 16
trust by, 84, 93
Statue of Liberty restoration, 11, 124
status quo interventions, 1–2
stewardship, 66–67, 70, 144
strata, economic, 165–67
strategic alliance, 15, 18, 117, 232
subsidies, 11, 25–28, 166, 178–79
success. *See also* Long-Arnold framework
factors for partnership, 18–19, 144–45
measures of, 110
so-called, 118
Supreme Court, 87
sustainable development, 29, 80. *See also* environmental, social, and governance issues
communities fostering, 168
contribution and attribution, 113–14
focus of, 7
standard-setting and, 219
timeline of, 11–13
as trend, 121
Swartz, Jeff, 7–8, 111, 152, 158
sweatshops. *See* child labor

tariffs, 25, 26, 28, 170–71, 179
TBL. *See* triple bottom line
technology. *See also* information, communication, and technology
access to, 23–24, 47, 70, 102–4
adoption of, 28, 36–37, 49, 62–63
advances in, 2, 29, 58, 145
clean, 48, 171, 183
as core competency, 168
education for, 32
expertise in, 106–7
hydrocarbon, 138, 156, 160
irrigation, 112–13
patents, 29
as resource, 17, 100, 105, 119, 167
revolution, 34, 99
Text2Teach, 199–200, 212, 214
Timberland, 138, 158
City Year and, 111, 135, 152, 156, 232–33
City Year housed by, 129, 160
SOS and, 153
timeframe
differing, 165, 178–79, 186, 189, 212, 250
extension, 252
importance of, 178
limited, 125
long, 121, 200
negotiation, 120, 181, 241
realistic, 119
short, 16, 110, 115, 209
tipping point, 1–2
TNC. *See* The Nature Conservancy
trade liberalization, 24–25. *See also* freedom, economic
transactional services, 17, 116, 120, 130, 230
transnational corporations. *See* multi-national corporations
transparency. *See* accountability
trend, business
accountability as, 91–93, 94
consumer expectation change as, 79–80, 94
CSR as, 75, 80–91, 94
investor priority change as, 76–77, 93–94
private sector growth as, 75–76, 93
trend, global, 23, 48–50, 58
trend, NGO
business methods in NGOs as, 60
changing revenue sources as, 62–65, 69–70
conflicts of interest as, 60–61, 71
ICT advances as, 61–62, 70
NGO, 69–72
sector growth as, 58–60, 69
technical expertise as, 60, 69
tri-party partnerships. *See also* Partnership Lifecycle
definition of, 18
overview of, 165–68
summary of, 188–89

triple bottom line (TBL), 5, 80
trust
of business by public, 48–49, 79, 91, 94, 105
confidentiality and, 114
Edelman Trust Barometer, 85
between NGOs and business, 108–11, 114, 133
of NGOs by public, 48–49, 65, 111–12
by stakeholders, 84, 93

UBTI. *See* unrelated business taxable income
UN. *See* United Nations
UNDP. *See* United Nations Development Program
unemployment, 25, 26, 33–34, 48
UN Global Compact
CEO involvement in, 210
against corruption, 8–9, 13, 204, 213
CSR and, 94
ESG issues and, 37, 92, 194, 203, 211, 214
governance structure of, 206, 212–13, 216
history of, 13, 92, 218
member companies of, 86, 235
as MSI, 193, 203
principles of, 204
sanctions by, 211, 214
Who Cares Wins, 9, 13, 81
United Nations (UN)
Charter of, 14
Commonwealth Foundation and, 12, 67
environment and, 11, 12, 79–80, 106
GAIN and, 207
globalization and, 65–66
grants through, 63
KPCS and, 197
MNCs and, 75, 92
NGOs and, 36, 60
road safety and, 13, 195
Text2Teach and, 199
WCED and, 5
at World Summit, 7
United Nations Development Program (UNDP), 199, 225
United Parcel Service (UPS), 68–69
United States Agency for International Development (USAID). *See also* specific partnerships
development assistance through, 36–37, 63
Global Development Alliance (USAID/GDA), 13, 47, 168
New Partnerships Initiative of, 47, 168
United Way, 62, 65, 68–69
unrelated business taxable income (UBTI), 125
UPS. *See* United Parcel Service
Uruguay Round, 11, 25–26, 27
USAID. *See* United States Agency for International Development

value chains, pro-poor, 91, 121, 128, 171
value creation, 130, 181, 216
assessment of, 110, 114, 227, 250
continuous, 19, 226
Creating Shared Value, 10
by CRM, 243
ensuring, 133
by entrepreneurs, 15
increasing, 231
joint, 82
as key, 16, 121, 246
ongoing, 3, 159–60, 161, 252
potential, 243
visibility
as business benefit, 110, 112, 230, 239, 240
as mutual benefit, 100–101, 126, 156, 159, 161, 231
as NGO benefit, 102, 104, 122, 130
voluntary organization. *See* non-profit organization (NPO)

waste, solid, 106–7, 137, 150–51, 159
water, 169, 184, 186, 188
purification, 103, 107–8, 137, 143
WBCSD. *See* World Business Council for Sustainable Development
WCED. *See* World Commission on Environment and Development
WHO. *See* World Health Organization

Who Cares Wins (UN Global Compact), 9, 13, 81
wisdom-added features, 79
women
  Aparajitas, 128, 173, 183
  businesses owned by, 75, 121, 140–41
  communicating with, 154, 181, 182
  economic opportunities for, 128, 138, 139, 173, 238
  education for, 153
  empowering, 47, 137, 146–47, 186, 250
  farmers, 171, 172
  globalization and, 29–30, 32, 48
  nutrition for, 200, 239
  philanthropy by, 40, 45, 49
  professional, 120
  self-help for, 107–8
  unemployment of, 34
World Bank, 25, 63
World Business Council for Sustainable Development (WBCSD), 6–7, 8, 11
WorldCom, 81, 92–93
World Commission on Environment and Development (WCED), 5, 6, 11
  Our Common Future, 5
World Health Organization (WHO), 13, 199, 201
The World is Flat (Friedman, Thomas), 30
World Summit, 7–8, 13, 94
World Trade Organization (WTO), 12, 25–26
world view, 55, 109
World War II, 24–25
World Wildlife Fund (WWF), 193
  funding of, 228
  history of, 11–12
  MSC and, 201–4
  review by, 205, 216, 217, 219–20
WTO. *See* World Trade Organization
WWF. *See* World Wildlife Fund

youth. *See* children

Also available from Kumarian Press

Rethinking Corporate Social Engagement: Lessons From Latin America
Lester M. Salamon

"A fascinating and richly documented portrait of the distinctive features that have characterized the growth of corporate social responsibility in Latin America. This book adds significantly to our understanding of the cultural and social factors that shape how and why corporations chose to engage with social issues, and in doing so, makes an important contribution to the literature on the global spread of corporate social responsibility." ***—David Vogel**, Haas School of Business, University of California, Berkeley*

In this new book, Lester M. Salamon, one of the foremost experts on civil society, assesses the reality behind the "corporate social engagement (CSE)" hype in Latin America. Rejecting the "MBA approach" that has dominated much of the thinking about CSE globally as inadequate for a region like Latin America, Salamon posits what he terms the "corporate social engagement pyramid" and finds that many advanced Latin American companies have moved fairly far up this pyramid in ways that hold lessons for corporations everywhere. Brief and highly readable, the book offers a constructive critique of received wisdom about CSE and a roadmap that companies and civil society organizations in other regions can follow.

Advancing Nonprofit Stewardship Through Self-Regulation: Translating Principles Into Practice
Christopher Corbett

"This small book is destined to become the 'bible' of nonprofit managers, boards, and students. Corbett makes the case for nonprofit self-regulation feasible and accessible. Using 33 principles of self regulation proposed by the Independent Sector, Corbett elicits them, demonstrates how to apply them, and shows their interconnections. This is a major contribution to the fields of ethics and nonprofit management." ***—Ram A. Cnaan**, Former President, ARNOVA; and Professor and Senior Associate Dean, School of Social Policy & Practice, University of Pennsylvania*

Advancing Nonprofit Stewardship Through Self-Regulation points the way forward for nonprofits by identifying specific strategies for implementing Independent Sector's principles. It also urges other researchers and practitioners to create competing strategies of implementation to give nonprofits choice. This lucid and brief guidebook shows how organizations can navigate demands for increased accountability and transparency through constructing and executing improved bylaws while creating a setting of integrity and trust. It is essential reading not only for all US nonprofits but for NGOs facing similar challenges around the world.

Development and the Private Sector: Consuming Interests
Deborah Eade and John Sayer

Corporations clearly have the potential to contribute to sustainable economic growth in developing countries. However, their business can also undermine people's livelihoods. Contributors to this volume examine the impact of the private sector on development, whether through core business practices, corporate responsibility endeavors, or philanthropic activities. Bringing together both analytical chapters and case studies ranging from El Salvador, to Kenya, to Timor-Leste, this book focuses on how the private sector can do less harm, and even do considerable good by fostering equitable development.

22883 Quicksilver Drive
Sterling, VA 20166-2102

Subscribe to our e-mail alerts: www.kpbooks.com

Kumarian Press, located in Sterling, Virginia, is a forward-looking, scholarly press that promotes active international engagement and an awareness of global connectedness.

DISCARDED BY
FREEPORT
MEMORIAL LIBRARY